Scientific Pr
(God The Holy)
Spirit Exists

The author has made the astonishing scientific discovery that Spiritual Energy '$=mc^2$' just like physical energy. Its 'sevenfold nature' in the Bible and other Holy Books, occurs in trees, fountains and cubes. The Sevenfold 'Holy' Spirit of God exactly occupies the 'extra seven dimensions of the Universe' of the latest "string theories" of science!

Simon Richard Lee BA, MA (Cantab.) CEng MIET MInstMC

Published by:

Author Me UK
Ware
Hertfordshire
England
www.author.me.uk

Available to buy in paperback or to download at
www.lulu.com/AuthorMeUK

All typesetting and illustrations are by the author.

First Edition – June 2006

Second Edition - June 2007

Third Edition – January 2008

Fourth Edition – Christmas 2008

This book is dedicated to my lovely daughter Jeni

In memory of my Mum – Dawn Day SRN, MSc(Hons – Uni. Of Hertfordshire): - 1st July 1931-24th August 2007

ISBN 978-1-4116-7829-3

Copyright © Simon Richard Lee, 2008

VITA

Simon Lee was born in March 1957 in Welwyn Garden City, Hertfordshire, England, and was the leading pupil academically at his local junior school Newtown School in Hatfield nearby.

He won a Scholarship to St Albans ('Abbey') Direct Grant School in 1968, where the extremely famous cosmologist Lucasian Emeritus Professor Stephen Hawking was also a student some 10 years before. They had the same teachers, and Mr Lee achieved top grades in all his O and A/S level examinations, as well as enjoying music and many sports.

In 1976 Mr Lee took up an Open Scholarship to King's College, Cambridge, England, in Natural Sciences, and majored after a final year studying computer science, despite two very serious bouts of an illness set to plague him for the rest of his life.

It was while an undergraduate at Cambridge that a lifetime interest started in 'science and religion, and the possibility of scientifically (logically) proving the existence of God'. He did some early writing on this subject then, and started writing this book many years later, in about 1992.

In the meantime he married a Veterinary Surgeon, and in 1991 they had a daughter, Jeni. However, a series of awful doctors have sabotaged his health completely since 1994, and in 1995 his wife divorced him on grounds of ill health.

This divorce ended many years since 1976 of innovative work in process control automation and other scientific computing by Mr Lee, including designing several large, sophisticated microprocessor systems. He is a Chartered Engineer and Member of the Institution of Electrical Engineers (now the IET) as well as of the Institute of Measurement and Control.

He has done intensive protracted work for ICI, BP, National Grid, Fisons Boots Consortium, Freudenberg Textiles, Pasminco Smelting, the Tate Gallery, all the main British armed services, Lockheed Martin, etc.

Contents

Introduction   i

Volume A.   A New Science of (the Holy) Spirit

1. Complementary Opposites. Extremely Fundamental Concepts Indeed!   3

2. Where Opposites Meet. An Exploration of Real Value and invented value   27

3. Deus ex Machina? Is it possible to build a conscious, so truly intelligent machine?   55

4. The various scientific structures of (the Holy) Spirit   65

5. How (the Holy) Spirit interacts with the physical world   97

6. The Spiritual Nature of DNA – Creation v. evolution   127
   The Anthropic Principle and Intelligent Design.   151

Volume B.   The Enemies of (the Holy) Spirit.
The three Apocalyptic Books in the Bible.

1. The New Testament - The Book of Revelation   159

2. The Old Testament - The Book of Daniel   223

3. The Apocrypha – The Second Book of Esdras   281

Volume C.   (The Holy) Spirit overcoming Their Enemies?

1. The "seventy 'sevens' (or 'weeks') of years calendar" or "Numera-Logical Calendar" – a new global peace initiative   299

2. A theory of – and cures for - mental illnesses   323

ACKNOWLEDGEMENTS

All quotations are reproduced by kind permission of their copyright owners, wherever copyright actually applies.

Heraclitus, Parmenides
Ancilla to the pre-Socratic Philosophers, by Kathleen Freeman. Published by Basil Blackwell (1948).

Polybius
de Natura Hominis, edition IV, by Jones. Published by Loeb.

Sengtsan
Zen and Zen Classics, by R. H. Blyth. Published by Hokuseido Press, Tokyo.

Lao Tzu, Chuang Tzu
A Source Book in Chinese Philosophy, by Wing-Tsit Chan. Copyright © 1969 by Princeton University Press.

Leibniz
The Monadology, translated and edited by A Latta. Published by Oxford University Press, Oxford (1898).

Karl Marx
Kapital Volume I, translator Ben Fowkes. Published by Penguin Books in association with New Left Review (1976).

Pierre Teilhard de Chardin
The Phenomenon of Man. Published by HarperCollins (USA).

Bede Griffiths
Return to the Centre. Published by HarperCollins *Publishers* ltd (1978).

Kahlil Gibran
The Prophet. Published by Heinemann, London (1926).

The Bible
All translations are by myself.

INTRODUCTION

What is the Nature of God?
What is the Nature of Time – and Being?

Consider the following statements in ALL Holy Books; including the Bible:-

1. 'God is a Spirit Being'. Time and Being are important Spirit Beings too!
2. 'I am the alpha and the omega, the first and the last', saith the LORD God. So say Time and Being also?
3. 'I am the Rock of Ages', saith the LORD God. So say Being & Time also?
4. 'I am that I am', saith the LORD God. So says Being also?
5. 'I am JHWH, LORD of Hosts' saith the LORD God. So says Being also?
6. 'The Ancient of Days' – Who else can this be but Old Father Time?
7. 'Immortal, invisible, only wise' – a perfect description of Being!
8. God is: – 'omnipresent' (present everywhere in the Universe); 'omniscient' (knows everything all the time); and therefore 'omnipotent' (all-powerful). SO IS Being – all three of those mega-descriptions apply equally to Being!
9. Time is a great mystery, yet so utterly universally commonplace and everywhere at once – 'all the time' - that most people take Time for granted. Yet it is the most humble – and impartial – 'thing' in the Universe. Just as happy whistling through the hardest and densest and so most valued substances we have without affecting them in any way – such as gold or diamond – as whistling through the most obnoxious substances – excrement and sewage and poison. None of these affect the passage of Time at all! The existence of God to the vast majority of people, on the other hand, they claim is a purely personal matter of 'faith' in a God – different to everybody!
10. Ask any scientist you know to name an equation of science *involving two or more different physical or chemical quantities* that do NOT involve Time – and surprise, surprise, they won't be able to! There are none of them! Time is so

i

totally universal, you see... Oh, they might say, cheating 'how much sugar do I need to add to 600g of sugar to get 1kg' but (a) that only involves mass, not more than one physical or chemical quantity (b) even then, time rules the process of weighing out the sugar – and the chemical properties of the sugar!

11. Astonishingly Time makes absolutely everything unique, according to Albert Einstein's Theories of Relativity. At any point in time, which is unique itself everywhere, which all 'has its own clock' at every point, according to Einstein, every point in the entire Universe is in an ever-changing, mysteriously so, totally unique state of affairs! Were it possible to 'freeze the Universe' at any 'point in time' (which Einstein showed is physically impossible) we would find that absolutely every part of it was in a unique state of affairs in this 'impossible freeze frame'. More of this 'Uniqueness Principle' in Volume A of this book...

12. 'God is Timeless – the only Living Creature forever outside Time'. Time is CHRONOS and God is outside that chronos – in His own time sphere KAIROS. God is Infinite Love – the only explanation for our nearly endless Free Will. Without *that* ultimate Gift from God – the world would be a totally soulless place, with us and all the rest of the Creation of living creatures effectively just machines – pushed around by the Tyrant of Time. It is bad enough already: - 'Get there before it is Time for the shops to shut!' 'Get to work on Time every day and finish your work every day on Time!' 'Have I got enough Time to do it?' Time is limited and limits us – God is 'at right angles' to not only time, which is also at right angles to the whole Space-Matter Continuum, but so space and matter – outside physics, so completely unbounded by physical limitations – God inhabits a purely spiritual world. PROOF of that, and a full description of the *structure of that spiritual world*, occupies Volume A of this book.

13. 'God is in His Heaven, and all is well with the World'. Again might immediately seem to contradict my earlier statements, until one gives some thought and reflection to what Heaven actually is (or 'the Heavens'). In Biblical times the Earth was the First Heaven of Seven, reaching up to Seventh Heaven – beyond the 4,000 or so stars that were all that could be observed in those days before telescopes, through the Earth's atmosphere. Nowadays, we know that

the Universe – the 'Heavens' – are so immensely, unimaginably vast that our own eco-system of the Earth, with its zillions of living creatures, nearly all carbon-based, is just a speck of dust. Yet Being fills the entire Universe, with its billions of known galaxies each containing billions of stars like our own sun, and even fills black holes. God, being 'at right angles to both time and the space-matter continuum time flows through' knows *everything all the time.* What He allows to happen sometimes, like the Holocaust, without intervening, must be because of the *importance of His Great Law of Free Will.* So, yes, in conclusion we can say '(the vast overwhelming majority of) God is in His Heaven(s); and (He is doing His Very Best 'All the Time' to Ensure) all is well with the World (the First Heaven). He either makes everything happen or allows other (sometimes appalling) things to happen'.

14. Finally, from the last book of the Bible, the Book of Revelation, translated literally:

"Holy, Holy, Holy,
Lord God Almighty,
The Having Been, and the Being, and the Coming!"
Revelation Chapter 4 verse 8

Time is *not* 'just' something that ('somehow, magically') ticks by on clocks. Time is different and indeed unique for every person and every place, according to the theories of Relativity of Albert Einstein. Invert your view! Time is no passive uniform 'thing just passing through'. Time is a highly potent, active, spiritual energy and power for growth, healing and change. The rivers of time hold us and everything upright, in a way that science takes for granted. 'Time, the great healer'... But Father Time also brings the Seven Ages of Man – including Old Age...

The Holy Spirit, on the other hand, is all female: - Wisdom, Joy and Love, Health and Beauty, and Peace and Grace – seven spirits in one in a 'Tree of Life'. We come in due course to consider and indeed verify my logical structure of the spirits of Time, Space, God, the Messiah and the Holy Spirit in Volume A of this book.

The first volume of the book comprehensively reviews and summarises the author's views on the Nature of the Holy Spirit. The author views the seven components of Wisdom. i.e. taken as a whole the 'Holy Spirit', as above, as occupying the seven 'missing' dimensions of space recently discovered in 'string theories' of modern cosmological physics!

The second volume of the book is a study of the only three Apocalyptic Books of the Bible: -
1. the Book of Revelation, the last Book of the New Testament
2. the Book of Daniel, in the Old Testament
3. the Second Book of Esdras, from the central Apocryphal Books.

It shows how many of their predictions relate to the modern world of the last century or so – especially its science, technology and politics...

The third volume firstly describes a novel, simplistic, Universal Calendar that should greatly simplify time-keeping and hence relations between all cultures. It is based on the notion of a 73 5-day week year with 12 30-day months but with December having 35 days in total, but with the last three weeks a conventional winter holiday. So that *all dates in the year are always the same day of the week from one year to the next.* You would be able to have one diary for the first year the calendar was introduced, and to keep it – the same - for all years from then – for ever!

The second part of the third volume of the book turns in a completely different direction – to consider the CAUSES not just symptoms of mental illnesses. Are these all caused by a human spirit with a *maladjusted perception of time and 'being'?*

Volume A

A New Science of (the Holy) Spirit

Article One

COMPLEMENTARY OPPOSITES

Extremely Fundamental Concepts Indeed!

March 1979

1. Introduction

Since the beginning of recorded history all sorts of people with time to spare, from many different countries and walks of life, have attempted to tackle the fundamental question, 'What does it all mean?' The purpose of this paper is to approach this sort of question to a rather greater depth than is found at the average house party. It is an attempt to pick out the common threads of thought in the often disparate approaches of philosophers, scientists, and people of some religious persuasion, to the question of 'the nature of reality'.

The paper concentrates on two such main threads of thought. The first is the ancient notion, familiar to both the ancient Greek 'Cosmologists', and Eastern mystics such as the Hindus of India and the Taoists of China, of *opposites* and their place in the 'world order'. A key concept to the ancient philosophers of both East and West was that one cannot ever consider an idea in isolation, that is out of context from its complement or opposite. What is dark without the notion of light against which to set it?

The second common theme I have found in considering the approaches of philosophers, mystics and scientists to the nature of reality and the universe, is a direct consequence of the notion of complementary opposites. That is, they all place great importance on trying to understand what is the principle behind the many opposites they find in their contemplations, that is, the *generating principle* for them. For this scientists often find themselves straying into the area of mysticism and religion, at which the majority balk. In this paper I will be actively and deliberately straying in this way, as a scientist. I hope the comparisons I draw between the findings of scientists and mystics will prove interesting.

We begin our tour of the world's main philosophers with the least well-known, the Ancient Greek 'Cosmologists'. Indeed, this earlier movement was suppressed and derided by a revolution in Greek thought, led by the philosophers Plato and Aristotle around 350 BC. Attitudes to both of the main themes I described above, altered dramatically after this revolution, and as a direct result modern Western Science and Technology, as well as Communism, have evolved.

We move East next, for a brief look at the attitudes of Buddhists and Taoists to the notions of opposites and the reality behind them. Then we move to the Middle East to consider the cosmology of the Christian religion, as represented by the often remarkable writing of the apostle John.

Next we turn to the arena of modern physics, with all its exciting theories. Some eminent modern physicists see in their emerging system of theories about the nature of the universe, a return to the views of the Eastern thinkers and the Cosmologists.

Before concluding the paper I devote a section to a consideration of perhaps the most important duality of all, that of subject and object, which obviously affects our attitudes to all other pairs of opposites.

2. Western Philosophy – the early Cosmologists

Modern Western philosophy was started over 2,300 years ago, by a series of philosophers and mathematicians, notably Pythagoras, Democritus, Aristotle, Plato, and Socrates. These philosophers, notably Aristotle and Plato, are still regarded as the founders of modern Western philosophy, and accordingly are taught about as the major figures of Greek thought. This was the foundation of classical physics, economics and mathematics. As such, the teachings of these men have had a profound effect ever since on life in the West. Their philosophical ideas have ultimately resulted in the current series of industrial revolutions culminating in the microchip.

However, before these philosophers, there was a powerful movement in Greece of philosophers known as Cosmologists, whose work was scorned and derided by the founders of the 'modern' or 'Socratic' school. Plato, for instance, often invented dialectics between his hero Socrates, and leading members of the Cosmological school who were contemporary with Socrates, notably Parmenides. He consistently attempted to discredit these earlier philosophers. Needless to say, Socrates always won the dialectic.

There are two main differences between the teachings of the pre-Socratic and Socratic schools of thought. Firstly, the Socratic followers of Plato and Aristotle dealt with abstract or 'atomistic' notions, such as The Beautiful, The Good, as an ethereal concept, in glorious isolation. The pre-Socratic Cosmologists, sometimes referred to as 'Sophists' (which means 'wise men'), would have dealt with the rather different issues of what is the *difference* between beautiful and ugly, good and bad, and so on.

Secondly, the Sophists or Cosmologists believed there is only one reality, the obvious one we perceive. On the other hand, Plato thought there exists a world of ethereal 'Forms', as he called them, over and above the forms of things we see in the everyday world. This 'Theory of Forms' was picked up by the 'Orthodox' wing of the early Christian Church, as opposed to the mystical 'Gnostic' wing. It was the Orthodox wing that won the ensuing theological 'battle'.

In this section we will consider the writings of three of the early Cosmologists, who were Heraclitus, Polybius and Parmenides. All three dealt with the important idea, obviously prevalent at that time, that opposites are complementary and that there is a fundamental basis for this. Heraclitus and Parmenides called this divine principle the LOGOS. This remarkable Greek word, which means 'Word' itself, or 'Reason' or 'Law', often crops up in the writing of both men, as we shall now see.

2.1 Heraclitus

Heraclitus of Ephesus was in his prime about 500 BC. He wrote just one book, of which only fragments remain, covering 'all knowledge, metaphysical, scientific and political'. Here are some extracts. Notice the twin emphasis on a system of opposites, and the idea of the logos, the underlying harmony through conflict between these opposites, both physical and metaphysical.

1. The Law (LOGOS) is as here explained; but men are always incapable of understanding it, both before they hear it, and when they have heard it for the first time. For though all things come into being in accordance with this Law, men seem as if they had never met with it, when they meet with words and actions such as I expound, separating each thing according to its nature, and explaining how it is made. As for the rest of mankind, they are unaware of what they are doing after they wake, just as they forget what they did while asleep.

2. Therefore one must follow that which is common. But although the law is universal, the majority live as if they had understanding peculiar to themselves.

3. That which is in opposition is in concert, and from things that differ comes the most beautiful harmony.

4. Joints: whole and not whole, connected-separate, consonant-dissonant.

5. Those who step into the same river have different waters flowing ever upon them.

6. That which alone is wise is one: it is willing and unwilling to be called by the name of Zen.

7. That which is wise is one: to understand the purpose which steers all things through all things.

8. You could not in your going find the ends of the soul, so deep is its Law (Logos), though you travelled the whole way.

9. Fire lives the death of earth, and air lives the death of fire; water lives the death of air, earth that of water.

10. And what is in us is the same thing: living and dead, awake and sleeping, as well as young and old; for the latter of each pair of opposites having changed, becomes the former, and this again having changed becomes the latter.

11. To those that are awake, there is one ordered Universe common to all, whereas in sleep each man turns away from this world to one of his own.

12. To God, all things are beautiful, good and just; but men have assumed some things to be unjust, others just.

13. The bow is called Life, but its work is Death.

14. In the same river, we both step and do not step, we are and we are not.

15. When you have listened not to me, but to the Law (Logos), it is wise to agree that all things are one.

16. They do not understand how that which differs with itself is in agreement: harmony consists of opposing tension, like that of the bow and the lyre.

17. The hidden harmony is stronger than the visible.

18. Those things of which there is sight, hearing, knowledge: these are what I honour most.

19. God is day-night, winter-summer, war-peace, satiety-famine. But He changes like Fire, which when it mingles with the smoke of incense is named according to each man's pleasure.

20. Cold things grow hot, hot things grow cold, the wet dries, the parched is moistened.

2.2 Polybius

Polybius was the son-in-law of Hippocrates, the famous physician after whom the Hippocratic oath of medicine of today is named. The extract below deals with the rôle in health of the famous four Ancient Greek opposites of fire, water, earth and air:

> 'The body of man always possesses all of these (the four humours, characterised by the four primary opposites), but through the revolving seasons they become now greater than themselves, now lesser in turn according to nature. For, just as every year has a share in all, in hot things as well as cold, in dry things as well as wet (for none of these could endure for any length of time without all of the things present in this universe; but if any one of these were to cease, all would disappear; for from a single necessity all are composed and nourished by one another); just so, if any one of these components were to cease in a man, the man would not be able to live'.

It was almost certainly another – unknown – ancient author who wrote about just two opposites, fire and water being in conflict:

> 'Each one rules and is ruled in turn, to the maximum and minimum of what is possible. For neither one is able to rule altogether... If either were ever dominated, none of the things which now exist would be as it is now. But as things are, these (fire and water) will be the same forever, and will never cease either separately or together'.

2.3 Parmenides

We now turn to Parmenides of Elea, who was in his prime about 475 BC. He was acknowledged by Plato as the first philosopher to use a dialectic, but was also pitched by Plato in dialectical arguments against his contemporary, Socrates, who always 'won'! Plato used these imaginary conflicts to attack the early Cosmologists. He did so, perhaps surprisingly, against Parmenides in particular, even though Parmenides regarded with scorn the attitudes of his contemporaries to the 'laws of opposites'.

Parmenides used Divine Intervention to justify his claim that all opposites are an illusion, and that only the logos or law (which he calls 'Being') is to be considered. I quote below most of the text of a poem that Parmenides wrote, from which classical scholars have deduced almost all that is known of his original thinking.

This poem, called the 'Doxa' or 'Truth', was written for Parmenides' pupil Zeno, who is supposed to have been responsible for a famous series of paradoxes that confounded most mathematicians of his day. Notice his emphatic denial in the poem that the traditional four opposites described by Polybius above have any meaning, and by his appeal to divine justice, how he implied that they belong in the occult, which is whence they are relegated today.

Parmenides' DOXA

1. The mares which carried me, conveyed me as far as my desire reached, when the goddesses who were driving had set me on the famous highway which bears a man who has knowledge through all the cities. Along this way I was carried; for by this way the exceedingly intelligent mares bore me, drawing the chariot, and the maidens directed the way. The axle in the naves gave forth a pipe-like sound as it glowed (for it was driven round by the two whirling circles at each end) whenever the maidens, daughters of the sun, having left the palace of night, hastened their driving towards the light, having pushed back the veils from their heads with their hands. There (in the Palace of Night) are the gates of the paths of Night and Day, and they are enclosed with a lintel above and a stone threshold below.

The gates themselves are filled with great folding doors; and of these Justice, mighty to punish, has the interchangeable keys. The maidens, skilfully cajoling her with soft words, persuaded her to push back the bolted bar without delay from the gates; and these, flung open, revealed a wide gaping space, having swung their jambs, richly-wrought in bronze, reciprocally in their sockets. This way, then, straight through them went the maidens, driving chariot and mares along the carriage-road.

And the goddess received me kindly, and took my right hand in hers, and thus she spoke and addressed me:

'Young man, companion of immortal charioteers, who comest by the help of the steeds which bring thee to our dwelling: Welcome! – since no evil fate has despatched thee on thy journey by this road, for truly it is far from the road trodden by mankind; no, it is Divine Command and Right. Thou shalt inquire into everything; both the motionless heart of well-rounded Truth, and also the opinions of mortals, in which there is no true reliability. But nevertheless thou shalt learn these things also – how one should go through all the things-that-seem, without exception, and test them.

2. Come, I will tell you – and you must accept my word when you have heard it – the ways of inquiry which alone are to be thought; the one that IT IS, and it is not possible for IT NOT TO BE, is the way of credibility, for it follows Truth; the other, that IT IS NOT, and that it is bound NOT TO BE: this, I tell you, is a path that cannot be explored; for you could neither recognise that which IS NOT, nor express it.

3. For it is the same thing to think and to be.

4. Observe nevertheless how things absent are securely present to the mind; for it will not sever Being from its connection to Being, whether it is scattered utterly throughout the universe, or whether it is collected together.

5. It is all the same to me from what point I begin, for I shall return again to this same point.

11

6. One should both say and think that Being Is; for To Be is possible, and nothingness is not possible. This I command you to consider; for from the latter way of search, first of all, I debar you. But next I debar you from that way along which mortals wander knowing nothing, two-headed, for perplexity in their bosoms steers their intelligence astray, as they are carried along as deaf as they are blind, amazed, uncritical hordes, by whom TO BE and NOT TO BE are regarded as the same and not the same, and for whom in everything there is a way of opposing stress.

7. For this view can never predominate, that That Which is Not exists. You must debar your thought from this way of search, nor let ordinary experience in its variety force you along this way, allowing the eye, sightless as it is, and the ear, full of sound, and the tongue, to rule; but judge by means of the Reason (logos), the much-contested proof which is expounded by me.

There is only one other description of the way remaining, namely that What Is, Is. To this way there are very many sign-posts: that Being has no coming-into-being and no destruction, for it is whole of limb, without motion, and without end. And it never Was, nor Will Be, because it Is now, a whole all together, One, continuous; for what creation of it will you look for? How, whence could it have sprung?

Nor shall I allow you to speak or think of it as springing from Not-Being; for it is neither expressible nor thinkable that What-Is-Not Is. Also, what necessity impelled it, if it did spring from Nothing, to be produced later or earlier? Thus it must Be absolutely, or not at all. Nor will the force of credibility ever admit that anything should come into being, beside Being itself, out of Not-Being. So far as this is concerned, Justice has never released Being in its fetters and set it free, either to come into being or to perish, but holds it fast.

The decision on these matters depends on the following; IT IS, or IT IS NOT. It is therefore decided – as is inevitable –

that one must ignore the one way as unthinkable and inexpressible (for it is no true way) and take the other as the way of Being and Reality. How could Being perish? How could it come into being? If it came into being, it is Not; and so too if it is about-to-be at some future time. Thus Coming-into-Being is quenched, and Destruction also into the unseen.

Nor is Being divisible, since it is all alike. Nor is there anything here or there which could prevent it from holding together, nor any lesser thing, but all is full of Being. Therefore it is altogether continuous; for Being is close to Being.

But it is motionless in the limits of mighty bonds, without beginning, without cease, since Becoming and Destruction have been driven very far away, and true conviction has rejected them. And remaining the same in the same place, it rests by itself and thus remains there fixed; for powerful Necessity holds it in the bonds of a Limit, which constrains it round about, because it is decreed by divine law that Being shall not be without boundary. For it is not lacking; but if it were spatially infinite it would be lacking everything.

8. To think is the same as the thought that IT IS; for you will not find thinking without Being, in regard to which there is an expression. For nothing else either is or shall be except Being, since Fate has tied it down to be a whole and motionless; therefore all things that mortals have established, believing in their truth, are just a name: Becoming and Perishing, Being and Not-Being, and change of position, and alteration of bright colour.

But since there is a spatial limit, it is complete on every side, like the mass of a well-rounded sphere, equally balanced from its centre in every direction; for it is not bound to be at all either greater or less in this direction or that; nor is there Not-Being which could check it from reaching to the same point, not is it possible for Being to be more in this direction, less in that, than Being, because it is an inviolate whole. For, in all directions equal to itself, it reaches its limits uniformly.

At this point I cease my reliable theory (logos) and thought, concerning Truth; from here onwards you must learn the opinion of mortals, listening to the deceptive order of my words.

They have established the custom of naming two forms, one of which ought not to be mentioned; that is where they have gone astray. They have distinguished them as opposite in form, and have marked them off from one another by giving them different signs; on one side the flaming fire in the heavens, mild, very light in weight, the same as itself in every direction, and not the same as the other. This other is also by itself and opposite; dark Night, a dense and heavy body. This world-order I describe to you with all its phenomena, in order that no intellect of mortal men may outstrip you.

9. But since all things are named Light and Night, and names have been given to each class of things according to the power of one or the other, everything is full equally of Light and Invisible Night, as both are equal, because to neither of them belongs any share of the other'.

This poem is remarkable in being one of the first reasoned attempts in the West to explain the world. Only Thales, Heraclitus and Pythagoras, and some handful of other pioneers dared question the mythology of their ancestors. These are the very early beginnings of Western science, and in section five I will show how modern physics now appears to be returning to its origins after a lengthy 'classical' materialistic diversion following the rationale introduced by Plato and Aristotle.

3. Eastern Religions

I was at first very surprised to find ancient Eastern writers express very similar views to those of the ancient Western writers like Heraclitus and Parmenides. At about the same time as Parmenides and Heraclitus were alive, but separated from them by a vast gulf of distance, and hence very much culturally isolated, were similar thinkers in India and China, and later Japan. They were developing or had already developed, great philosophical and religious systems, in particular Buddhism, Taoism and Hinduism.

When I came to read the writings of some of the founding figures of Taoism and the Zen branch of Buddhism (both originally Chinese philosophies), I was struck by the similarity of these pioneering works, to those of the pioneering Cosmologists in Western thought. I give below quotations from the 'Hsinhsinming' of Sengtsan, the first Chinese Zen Master or Patriarch, and the 'Tao te Ching' of Lao Tzu. Lao Tzu is regarded as one of the founding figures of the Taoist philosophy.

3.1 Zen Buddhism – the 'Hsinhsinming' of Sengtsan

Sengtsan lived in the sixth century AD, and wrote one of the earliest treatises on Zen Buddhism, the 'Hsinhsinming' or 'Inscription on the believing mind'. It bears an astonishing similarity to the 'Doxa' of Parmenides which I quoted in the last section. Both emphasise that duality (the existence of opposites) is a delusion. Whereas Parmenides has an Ultimate Principle in the notion of 'Being', Sengtsan talks of the 'Great Way', a familiar term in Eastern thought. We shall see in the extracts I give from both the Hsinhsinming and Lao Tzu's writings, the emphasis, as strong as that in Parmenides, that the only true approach to reality is through this principle of ultimate reality.

Extracts from Sengtsan's Hsinhsinming

    There is nothing difficult about the Great Way,
But, avoid choosing!
Only when you neither love nor hate
Does it appear in all clarity ....

.... Perfect like Great Space
The way has nothing lacking, nothing in excess.
Truly, because of our accepting and rejecting,
We have not the "suchness" of things ....

.... If there is the slightest trace of this and that,
The mind is lost in a maze of complexity.
Duality arises from Unity,
But do not be attached to this Unity ....

.... The activity of the Great Way is vast;
It is neither easy nor difficult.
Small views are full of foxy fears;
The faster, the slower ....

.... Illusion produces rest and motion;
Illumination destroys liking and disliking.
All these pairs of opposites
Are created by our own folly ....

.... If the mind makes no discriminations,
All things are as they really are.
In the deep mystery of this "things as they are"
We are released from our relations to them ....

.... When all things are seen with "equal mind"
They return to their nature.
No description by analogy is possible
Of this state where all relations have ceased ....

.... When we stop movement, there is no-movement.
When we stop resting, there is no-rest.
When both cease to be,
How can the Unity subsist? ....

.... The believing mind is not dual;
What is dual is not the believing mind.
Beyond all language,
For it there is no past, no present, no future.

3.2 Taoism – the 'Tao te Ching' of Lao Tzu

Taoist philosophy is a lot older than Zen Buddhism, and had a considerable influence on its origins. The 'Tao' is another Ultimate Principle, like the Way, Being and the Logos. In Taoist tradition it is the One, which is natural, eternal, spontaneous, nameless and indescribable. The 'Tao te Ching' (Classic of the Way and its Virtue) is certainly the most important classic work in Chinese literature. More commentaries on it have been written than on any other Chinese book. The opening is as dramatic as the opening of John I in the New Testament:

1. The Tao that can be told of is not the eternal Tao;
The name that can be named is not
the eternal name.
The nameless is the Origin of Heaven and Earth;
The named is the mother of all things.
Therefore let there always be non-being
so that we may see their subtlety,
And let there always be being so
we may see their outcome.
The two are the same,
But after they are produced,
they have different names.
They both may be called deep and profound.
Deeper and more profound,
The door of all subtleties!

The piece continues with a discussion of opposites and their interplay. It is important to understand something of Chinese tradition about opposites, in order to appreciate this section. Chinese tradition places great emphasis on just two principal polar opposites, the yin and yang, which are two poles limiting all cycles of change.

2. When the people of the world all know
beauty as beauty
There arises the recognition of ugliness.
When they all know good as good,
There arises the recognition of evil.
Therefore:
Being and non-being produce each other;
Difficult and easy complete each other;
Long and short contrast each other;
High and low distinguish each other;
Sound and voice harmonise with each other;
Front and back follow each other.

36. In order to contract,
it is necessary first to expand.
In order to weaken,
it is necessary first to strengthen.
In order to destroy,
it is necessary first to promote.
In order to take, it is necessary first to give.
This is called subtle light.

41. The Tao which is bright appears to be dark.
The Tao which goes forwards
appears to fall backward.
The Tao which is level appears uneven.
Great virtue appears like a valley (hollow).
Great purity appears like disgrace.
Far-reaching virtue appears as if insufficient.
Solid virtue appears as if unsteady.
True substance appears to be changeable.
The great square has no corners.
The great talent is slow to mature.
Great music sounds faint.
Great form has no shape.
Tao is hidden and nameless.
Yet it is Tao alone that skilfully provides for all
and brings them to perfection.

4. Christianity

In preceding sections we have seen how mystics of both East and West have often searched for an 'Ultimate Principle', which founding figures of the Western Cosmologist movement called 'Being' or the 'Logos', and early patriarchs or founders of Taoism and Zen Buddhism called 'the Tao' or 'The Great Way'. The major religions of the West (Christianity, Judaism and Islam) at first sight do not appear to have a corresponding notion. Indeed, both the Old and New Testaments are remarkably free of cosmology, and there is very little in Islam to suggest a supreme principle. Instead attention is focused on a 'Lord God', with very human attributes, who is a supreme being rather than a supreme principle.

However, the few cosmological passages in the Bible, notably the opening of the books of Genesis and John, seem to hint at such a principle. I give below my own translation of part of the opening of John I, from the Ancient Greek. I think that none of the meaning of the passage is lost, but that I can highlight parallels between the ideas expressed here and those of the Greek Cosmologists, notably Heraclitus. Notice how the word 'logos', the Greek word for reason, law, or the 'Word', is here synonymous with the word 'God'. Note also how, in the final verse, the nature of the logos or God is compared via a simile, to the 'Being in the bosom of the Father', a safe and secure metaphor to express the nature of the universal principle:

Extracts from John I verses 1-18

> "In the beginning was the logos, and the logos was with God, and God was the logos. This was in the beginning with God. All things evolved through it, and without it became not one thing that has become. In it was life, and the life was the light of mankind, and the light shines in the darkness, and the darkness has not overcome it....
>
> .... The true light that enlightens every man was coming into the world. It was in the world, and the world became through it, and the world knew it not. It came to its own home, and its own people received it not. But as many as

received it, who believed in its name, it gave power to become children of God, who were born, not of blood nor of the will of the flesh nor of the will of a man, but of God. And the logos became flesh and dwelt among us, full of grace and truth; and we beheld His glory, glory as of an only begotten from a father, full of grace and truth....

.... No man has ever seen God; the only begotten God, the 'Being in the bosom of the Father', the one declared here".

5. Modern Physics

About the beginning of this century, classical physicists believed that they were on the brink of possessing an 'ultimate' description of the universe. By viewing the universe as a machine that obeys certain mechanical laws, as though it was a piece of clockwork, they had almost completely defined it in terms of a large set of theories. These divided the physical world neatly up into areas like mechanics, electricity and magnetism, kinetic theory and atomic theory.

This division of the world into elegant-seeming boxes, with no mystical blurring, was a direct and logical conclusion of a philosophical and scientific train of development that had begun with the materialistic revolution started by Plato, Aristotle, Euclid, Democritus and Pythagoras.

The rosy mechanistic world-view of the classical physicists was nearing completion when it was forever impeded, within the space of a few short years, by the advent of a series of new discoveries which did not fit into any of the classical 'boxes'. Rutherford showed that atoms were not, as scientists since Democritus had believed, the smallest particles in nature, but that there were a whole host of smaller structures and particles. Heisenberg in particular showed, furthermore, that even these particles were not fundamental, and that there are in fact no 'basic building blocks' of matter.

Instead, we should think of matter as either a particle or a wave, but matter chooses to alternate between these vastly different conceptions in a very mysterious fashion. Einstein showed in his theories of Relativity, that the very framework of classical physics, absolute time and space, was delusory, and that space and time formed a complex 'four-dimensional continuum'.

As if that was not enough, one consequence of Relativity Theory is that energy and matter are regarded as interchangeable forms of some more fundamental quantity. Hence the two basic axioms of mechanics, the absolute nature of space and time, and the interaction of energy and matter, were partly shattered by the new theories. Finally, the 'ultra-violet catastrophe' showed that energy, like particles, is present in packets called quanta. In fact, apart from the description of a limited range of everyday physical phenomena, classical physics had lost its hold on the science.

It appeared that the far more mysterious theories now emerging, although not fitting into a neat mechanistic structure, afforded a far more accurate picture of the universe at the extremes of the very large and the very small. They offered a far greater insight into the structure of the universe.

Although today we are still some way from a unified picture of the physical universe provided by these new theories, they have produced a curious 'counter-revolution' in science. Physics in particular has moved away from the philosophy that produced classical physics, back towards the Cosmological views of the earlier Greek Philosophers.

It is very interesting to look at pairs of concepts, which in the framework of classical physics were distinct opposites, or at least were listed in pairs but were extremely different. These all became complementary to each other, or were even interchangeable, in the new physics. Some examples are given below. Many commentators see in this change and other trends in modern physics, a return to the philosophical attitudes of the early Greek Cosmologists, and a blending of physics with the ancient mysticism of the Far East.

Matter – Energy

These two concepts, opposed in classical physics, became interchangeable forms of the same concept in the relativity theories of modern physics. Einstein's equation, perhaps the most famous of science, relates these two quantities:

$$E = mc^2$$

They are complementary views of the world. To understand the one you need an understanding of the other; a measurement of one implies, in atomic theory, a measurement of the other. For instance, particle physicists are quite used to quoting an energy level as a measure of an entity's mass.

Space – Time

In classical physics, space had been regarded as a rigid three-dimensional framework in which the mechanical parts of the universe operated like clockwork. This frame could be measured, it was thought, in terms of a square lattice that extended evenly to infinity in all directions. Time was seen as a continuous flow through this lattice, that though mysterious, was assumed to be just as absolute as the classical notion of space. Another assumption inherited from the period of Aristotle, was that time and space would be measured the same by anybody, regardless of how they moved in the lattice of space or where they were in it.

Einstein's two theories of special and general relativity showed that space and time are far better not regarded as absolutes, and that they changed according to the position and motion of the person measuring them; and with the presence of matter, increasingly as the mass of nearby objects increased. Although the alterations were minute at the everyday level, at astronomical distances they were significant. An early experiment that verified the equations of relativity with great accuracy, showed how light passing from distant stars close to the sun was actually 'bent' in its passing.

Hence that great body of assumptions that had been inherited by classical physics from the time of Plato and Aristotle, and had been greatly refined by Newton, was totally undermined by Einstein's theories, which despite refinement have still not been disproved.

Waves – Particles

In classical physics, waves and particles had been regarded as very different forms of matter, and indeed were treated by different areas of the science. However, Heisenberg's principle, when tested by experiments with light, shows that matter that is very small or of very low mass, exhibits attributes of both wave and particle behaviour, depending on circumstances. As in relativity, the presence of other matter, and indeed the human observer of any experiment, radically affects the results.

Electricity – Magnetism

The two fields of force, the electric field and the magnetic field, were also regarded in classical physics as being very different, and usually opposite in their effect, and in the equations used to describe their action. Once again, relativity shows that these 'opposites' are aspects of the same fundamental concept. They are only distinguishable in the equations of relativity used to describe them, by a relativistic 'shift' relative to the Space-Time continuum.

Matter – Antimatter

Classical physicists had no notion of antimatter, which was first postulated by Einstein's equations, and only later detected in laboratories. It is the polar opposite to 'normal' matter, and every fundamental particle so far detected, apart from the 'neutral' pions and photons, has a corresponding anti-particle. Once again, nature appears to operate on the basis of complementary opposite pairings.

Light – Darkness

Using Maxwell's equations, which in fact originally derived from classical physics, one can show how light comprises two complementary electric and magnetic fields. They are coupled in such a way that photons – particles of light – can propagate even through an absolute vacuum. Again, light has the attributes of waves and particles, which are equal and complementary.

We have seen how the findings of modern physics appear to totally confirm the purely inspired insights of the ancient mystics, even when made with the utmost precision. The simplistic mechanical view of the world proposed by classical physicists, based solidly on the materialistic revolution of Plato and Aristotle, is gradually being replaced by a world view in which the universe is regarded via a set of complementary concepts. Furthermore, the presence of human observers actually affects the results of apparently clinical, objective experiments. This brings us to consider the most important duality of all, that of the subject and the object, the difference between us and the rest of the universe.

6. The Subject – Object Duality

One pair of traditional opposites that I have only briefly touched upon so far is the subject and the object. I say 'traditional' and yet the subject-object duality, and the split between 'subjective', 'artistic'-ness and the objective nature of science is very much a Western phenomenon. The Cosmologists of Ancient Greece, and the early mystics of the Far East, would have had no such difficulty in coming to terms with these two modes of thought.

As Sengtsan says in the Hsinghsinming, the aim of all mystics is to understand the 'suchness' of the world, with no reference to 'the observer' and 'the universe' as in Western science. There are no two modes of thought for mystics – they have attained a blissful 'selfless' state, where distinctions of any sort between apparent opposites, including 'self' and 'world', have disappeared. This is 'Nirvana' – the aim of countless people in the East for millennia, attained only by the very few.

The notion of 'self', 'soul' or 'mind' as opposed to the 'material world' has its philosophical origins, once again, with the work of Aristotle. It was the basis of both Western science, and most of Western Christian doctrine, for hundreds of years. It has remained largely unchallenged, and whole edifices of thought have evolved, especially in the Middle Ages, to justify the mind-matter dualism. These have enabled classical physics to persist virtually unchallenged until very recently.

The development of modern physics, in my view, heralds the end of the strict division between mind and matter, although the crumbling of this edifice will almost certainly take a long time yet to complete. There are still a large majority of scientists, particularly those educated in other branches of science than physics, whose training is still based on the notion that the 'observer' always plays a pristine, clinically detached rôle in scientific experiments. Until the impact of the latest discoveries of physicists can fully 'filter through' to other areas of science, most scientists will still persist with the delusory mind-matter dualism as the basis of their research.

7.   Conclusion

The areas of thought I have described, Cosmology in Ancient Greece, Eastern mysticism, and more surprisingly, Christian Cosmology and modern physics, bear striking resemblances to one another in two crucial ways. Firstly, they are all to do, to a large extent, with contemplating pairs of opposing concepts, which are approached in one of two ways, the dualistic and the non-dualistic. However, we seem to be seeing the non-dualistic starting to replace the dualistic approach, at least in the science of modern physics. Heraclitus was the first in the West to nominate a 'Logos', as a set of laws governing opposites. Now we see, after a diversionary period lasting over two thousand years, the return of at least physics among the sciences, to a search for this 'Logos'.

The second and far more important resemblance between all these areas of thought, is their approach to the governing principle between all the complementary opposites we encounter. What is it that holds two complementary concepts together, yet keeps them opposed, in a sort of dynamic tension? The Cosmologists and the Eastern mystics would have had no dispute over this. The words differ – Logos, Being, Tao, Great Way – but the meaning is clearly the same in each case. Even physicists, in seeking a Logos or set of universal laws, appear to be pursuing knowledge of this same indefinable absolute – that which generates opposites.

From the point of view of Western religion, this surely is the place of a 'third force' beyond duality: God (alternatively, the 'Ground of Existence' or the Godhead), the Universal Arbitrator of all pairs of opposites. This is the One who (that which) generates all the complementary opposites in the first place. Indeed, perhaps it is better to regard each pair of opposites as a 'trinity', with the central generating principle vastly more important than the details of the two opposing concepts. This central principle, which expresses the quality or degree of balance between each pair of opposites, cannot be defined.

Robert Pirsig explored the meaning of the word 'quality' in his book 'Zen and the Art of Motorcycle Maintenance', and concluded that there are two kinds of quality. One is the one I just mentioned, where it expresses the balance between all pairs of opposites. However, the Quality between the subject-object pairing is of a higher order – it is the notion of Goodness and Worth, the Numinous itself. Hence he saw in the end just one kind of metaphysical trinity – subject and object and Real Quality (to coin a phrase).

These eventually, he found, are reducible to just Quality, the Godhead, the Tao. Hence he found a modern Western equivalent to the Tao, Being, or 'The Way'. It appears to me that considering the nature of pairs of opposites, and the 'third force' between them, leads one inexorably to the very same 'Ground of Existence' or 'Godhead', the generating force behind all religions.

Article Two

WHERE OPPOSITES MEET

An exploration of Real Value and invented value

March 1980

1. Introduction

In my previous paper, Complementary Opposites, I used the notion summarised by the paper's title to try to examine common threads of thought in many areas, from both East and West, and occurring over a very large timespan. In that paper, I looked in this way at pre-Socratic philosophy and religion. This was the work of the Ancient Greek philosophers who came before the revolution in Western thought around 350 BC, which was initiated mainly by Plato and Aristotle.

Next I considered Buddhist and Taoist philosophy as examples of the corresponding style in the Far East, of religious philosophies similar to pre-Socratic thought in the West. Then I looked at the small amount of explicit Cosmology in Western Christianity. I tried to establish a link between this and the far larger body of Cosmological thought that I had explored in the preceding two sections of that paper.

Next I turned to two areas with which I was much more familiar. I was able to point out the occurrence of many pairs of opposing and complementary concepts in modern physics. Finally I looked at the whole area of 'Subject and Object', a perennial source of discussion!

In the present paper I will be examining the dominance, once confined to 'Western' thought but becoming much more global this century, of so-called 'rational thought'. I will point out that this is not nearly so complete or solidly-founded as one might be led to believe by our increasing reliance on scientific advances and technology.

Indeed, I will be showing how 'reason' (which I employ loosely as an umbrella term for all aspects of the 'scientific revolution' of 350 BC and later, as described in my first paper), is totally dependent on the concepts of opposites. This leads to a system of what I call *invented values*.

Immediately following this, in the third section, I introduce again the concepts I just touched upon at the end of my first paper. These assert the essential importance to any such system of a *Real Value*, the transcendental 'something' which is not really a 'thing', to create the invented values.

Then in the fourth section I will compare and contrast Real Value and invented value in some detail. In the fifth section, I apply all these notions to an exploration of the similarities of religions of the world.

In the final concluding section, provocatively entitled 'Towards a Creative Anarchy!', I bring the whole paper to a head. We will be exploring the world as it might be, if the current world system were actually to give people real freedom of choice, made on the basis of Real rather than invented values.

2. Reason (I)

'Reason', as a philosophical system, or even a way of life, is probably what most people would answer if asked what 'normal' thinking is supposed to comprise. The word is synonymous with a balanced, common-sense view of the world. It is probably a surprise to learn that reason has only become the 'norm' or ideal, relatively recently in the time scale of human history.

Prior to the invention of reason (for that is what it was), mankind throughout the world placed reliance on a mixture of myths, legends and mysticism, as a guide to how to live. The replacement of this moral system by the 'system of rationality' seems to be a fundamental feature of all maturing civilisations, which at a certain critical point of their development take reason on board. Western civilisation began to adopt reason around 450 BC, and the more ancient civilisations of China and most of the Far East, some centuries or even thousands of years before this. Less mature cultures, such as the Minoans on Crete, have come to an end before even emerging from the mythological opening phase.

I should like to make a few points about the above observations. Firstly, it should be obvious that myths and legends always persist in a culture even after it has adopted rationality as its 'norm'; people seem to have an insatiable appetite for both fiction and non-fiction which inflames the imagination. Thankfully no society's appeal to reason has quenched this need, and its fulfilment. Secondly, it should be equally obvious that there is room in any mature society for a vast number of 'norms', not just one, especially when it is vague and ill-defined.

I will be spending much of this section in an attempt to define reason itself in terms of the system of opposites I introduced in my first paper, in an attempt to show that reason is entirely *dualistic*, that is, dependent on the existence of opposites. Finally, we will be seeing how reason, however lofty and elevated it is made out to be, is not really much of an advance from mythology. Because of the brain's vast capacity for pattern-matching, which I will be trying to reduce reason to, it will turn out to seem a very primitive system indeed, by comparison to what a fully integrated and peaceful community might achieve. The love of mankind for violence and domination, on many levels, both international and civil, has always precluded this possibility.

Reason has two fundamental ingredients. These are, first, *logic*, which is the process by which we proceed from one known state of affairs to another, usually in a progression of successive 'known states'. Second, much more dangerous, the set of *assumptions* we need about any situation, in order to apply logic to it in this progressive fashion.

I intend in this section to first of all dissect logic itself, firstly to discuss its two well-known forms, deductive and inductive logic. Furthermore I intend to show how both of these depend utterly on the use of polar opposites as a mode of thought.

I will then demonstrate briefly how it is equally impossible to make one's initial assumptions (prior to using the *logical* components of reason), by using logic itself unassisted by 'something else'. What this 'something else' is, I will go on to discuss in the next section, entitled 'The Transcendental'.

The use of reason as the major tool of thought, philosophical or more down-to-earth, in Western Civilisation, began in Greece, as we just said, over two thousand years ago. As I showed in my previous paper 'Complementary Opposites', prior to this the only attempts to achieve 'structured thinking' over and above the ancient myths and legends that had prevailed till then, were the works of the Cosmologists, that Classicists call 'pre-Socratic' philosophers.

Reason, in the form first developed and systematised by Aristotle, is totally dualistic. It divides the world up into 'this' and 'that', and 'you' and 'the rest of the world', and then constructs an elaborate system of tools to manipulate the 'information' produced. These tools are logic, both inductive and deductive, and systems of hierarchies, of cause and effect, and degree of sophistication of the dualistic objects. (For instance, biological hierarchies of species, genera, etc.).

At the back of all this is the desire to arrive at a 'true' picture, or as the philosopher Kant described it, a true 'apriori' model of the universe. This is in stark contrast to what Zen Buddhists and Taoists look for, which when they name it at all, they call the 'suchness' of reality. But what do we mean by the statement that something is 'true'? For one possible answer I turn to one of the most eminent followers of the Aristotelian tradition, Leibniz:

> 'There are two kinds of truth, those of reason, and those of fact. The truths of reason are necessary and their opposites impossible, those of fact are contingent and their opposites are possible.
>
> When a truth is necessary its reason can be found by analysis, by resolving it into simpler ideas and truths, until you reach those which are primitive. It is in this way that mathematicians reduce speculative theorems and rules of practice by analysis to definitions, axioms and postulates. In the end one has simple ideas which are indefinable. There are also axioms and postulates – in a word, primary principles which cannot be proved and do not need to be either. These are identical propositions, the opposite of which contains an explicit contradiction.
>
> But there also has to be a sufficient reason for contingent truths – truths of fact; for the sequence of things spreads out through the whole creation, that is where the resolution into particular reasons could run into unlimited detail on account of the immense variety of things in nature and the infinite indivisibility of bodies...'

This passage from Leibniz illustrates all three of the 'classical' aspects of reason – inductive logic ('truths of fact'), deductive logic ('truths of reason') and classification of causes and effects (the last paragraph). Let us now, armed with this classical notion of reason, proceed to reduce reason to the dualisms it ultimately is based on.

Both deductive and inductive logic are *pattern-matching* activities, finding relationships between two or more patterns of rational thought or of words. They have opposite starting points, deductive logic starting from a general statement and inductive logic starting from a particular statement. Having then established the first 'truth' or positive relationship between two or more patterns, that is after showing that a pattern relationship exists, both types of logic then produce a chain or network of further truths by means of the word *therefore* (or its symbolic equivalent). For example, in deductive logic, consider the following sequence of simple ideas:

Postulate: "The post office closes at five o'clock".
Conjunction: "It's five-thirty".
Therefore (conclusion): "The post office is closed".

By contrast, in inductive logic we work the other way, from a 'singular statement' to a general one. For instance:

Singular statement: "This cup of coffee tastes good".
Therefore (general statement): "All cups of coffee taste good".

The first duality involved in logic of both types is the 'Subject'/'Object', the 'Me'/'The rest of the world' division, which is obviously the most important. Reason and the scientific method always try to be 'objective', to make statements about the rest of the world that would be true even in the absence of an 'observer'. There takes place a complete reduction, an analytical knifing of the world into subject and object.

Needless to say this raises great problems, which prompted, for instance, the philosopher George Berkeley to propose that "it's all in the mind" for how otherwise could 'things' exist with no-one there to experience them? His final solution was to assert that, since God is omnipresent, all 'things' continue to 'exist' when there is no human onlooker, since God is there instead. This obviously raises a whole bundle of other questions, which we will not pursue here. Suffice it to say that this whole problem does not arise in Eastern philosophy, simply because Taoists, Buddhists, and all other Eastern philosophical schools of thought, refrain from applying this particular analytical knife.

The second duality is the division of what we actually experience, from an essential unity as presented to our senses, to a 'this', and 'that', followed by the classification of the 'these' and the 'those' into a hierarchy. Eastern mystics spend a great deal of effort to point out that while it is seemingly a very natural thing to do, this second knifing is a very strong barrier to 'seeing' the Tao or Zen. It is a totally dualistic operation.

Whenever we categorise the world into 'this' and 'that', and produce a name for the 'these' and 'those', to fit into our model of the universe, we are (probably without consciously realising it) applying another very sharp analytical knife. We effectively erect an intellectual fence, its opposite sides marked 'this' and 'that'. By contrast, Eastern thinkers emphasise it is vastly better and more natural to allow such intellectual constructions to run down, so that one comes to terms with the essential 'suchness' of reality.

The invention of the 'this'/'that' duality allows the mind to compare and contrast things, and to combine its complex conception of 'something' into a *pattern*, which can then be compared with other patterns. This is the origin of the rational conception of truth. A statement is 'true' when the patterns it compares match; it is false when they don't. For instance, the statement "The Post office is closed" from my example above, is a comparison of 'post office' with the pattern of things we call 'being closed'.

The last tool reason uses in its construction of statements and thoughts is *invented value*, which term I had better explain. Invented value arises when the pattern-matching of 'this' and 'that' is performed on a scientific basis, when the attributes and characteristics of the two patterns are measured. The process of taking a measurement, like weighing out flour for cooking, is yet again totally dualistic! Consider that whenever we take a measurement we create a pair of opposite directions for the character, like up/down, high/low, large/small, and so on. When there are obvious limits to the two directions, measurement, the selection or assignment of an invented value takes the form of determining the balance between the two extremes.

However, when one or both limits are infinite, reason invents a cunning trick to make measurement possible, the *unit* (like the weights used to weigh out flour in the kitchen). The same is done for time, money and many other invented values that lack limits. However, the unit is once again a totally dualistic concept. We have now invented the concept of 'this' minute and 'that' minute of time, for instance.

Armed with this reduction of reason to a totally dualistic operation, let us now analyse into dualisms and patterns, the first simple example of logic that I made up earlier. First of all let us consider the postulate that "the post office closes at five o'clock" which is actually quite complex! First of all it attempts to be an "objective" statement – normally post offices close whether we are there or not! However, it is a postulate, based on our experience that whenever we have asked at what time it closes in the past, this is the answer we always got.

To analyse the statement further, it is composed of three patterns. These are "the post office", "closes", and "at five o'clock".

"At five o'clock" is itself a pattern made by dualistically splitting up a continuum, time, into units. Hence the truth of this sequence of logic is based on matching up our conceptions or patterns called "the post office", "closes" and "five o'clock", all of which are dualistic. Since the patterns appear to match we say the statement is "true"; we then proceed to say *and* "it's five-thirty now" *therefore* "the post office is closed", which equally are dualistic patterns.

This system of pure reason is refined by the introduction of *logical operators* to help make pattern matching as simple as possible. These are *and*, *or*, and *not* (to add to the basic implication operator *therefore*). With these, and the end in view of making our model of the Universe systematic, we then go on to produce categorical hierarchies of the facts and statements. These start from postulates (the post office closes at five o'clock) or singular statements (this cup of coffee tastes good) and proceed via deductive or inductive logic respectively, to further 'true' statements, i.e. statements that 'logically match'. Obviously, from all that I have said, such hierarchies are totally dualistic as well.

Now let us apply all this reduction of rationality to dualisms, to that invention which has done most to advance the cause of reason and make it as efficient as possible – the digital computer. Surprise, surprise, the computer is utterly dualistic throughout! To begin with, its *memory* consists of simple polar digits, which may take the opposite values of '1' and '0'. These correspond to 'yes' and 'no', the basic tools of the logic system. They are arranged dualistically in 'this' and 'that' patterns, called words, and to speed things up whole word-patterns are compared and operated on at a time.

(in terms from the 1960's) as the 'hip' and 'square' approaches respectively.

The hip, surface appeal analysis of, say, a picture as good or bad, is nearer to a pure judgement by Real Value, an instinctive reaction without any rational analysis. However the rational, classic analysis proceeds by using Quality too! In it you *choose* certain invented qualities or values of the picture, say its use of colour, texture and use of light (contrast Turner's work with Salvador Dali's), or say perspective and use of mass (compare Turner with the Renaissance period). The crucial point here is the choice of which you consider to be the most important and valuable invented qualities to consider. This choice is totally pre-rational, and is in itself 'hip', so the classic approach uses a combination of real and invented value.

However, we are all making pre-rational judgements continuously, *all the time*, not just in specific defined situations like the above. My experience tells me (and it can't be proved, only experienced directly), that the 'entity' which creates your awareness of the world is Real Value. It doesn't just arise from a (dualistic) subject and a (dualistic) object coming together. Real Value is the basis of what we call 'reality'.

All Western theories of aesthetic value fall into three classes: subjective, objective, and instrumental (the latter claiming that the basis of value judgements comes from the relationship between subject and object). All of them fail to come to any firm conclusion, simply because they fail to appreciate that Real Value or 'worth' or 'goodness' is transcendental. Hence as Bob Pirsig points out, the recognition of Real Value or Quality, as a *transcendental* 'something', renders the whole intellectual pursuit of Aesthetics defunct!

Note that my statement that Real Value is 'transcendental', which can't be proved, is totally contrary to what the classic approach says (namely, that rational, invented value is just something that arises whenever a subject and an object are present together). That is the case for invented values, as I have shown in the previous section, but it is the other way around for Real Value. This talk of 'creative principles' is obviously bringing us into the area of mysticism and religion. Let us turn to one of the experts, the Chinese sage Lao Tzu, for some further insights:

'Tao is empty (like a bowl).
It may be used but its capacity is never exhausted.
It is bottomless, perhaps the ancestor of all things.
It blunts its sharpness,
it unties its tangles,
it softens its light.
It becomes one with the dusty world.
Deep and still, it appears to exist forever;
I do not know whose son it is,
it appears to have existed before the Lord'.

Tao is normally translated as 'way' but calling it Real Value seems to be much better (that is, if we feel we must name it; which destroys the sense of the transcendental. Remember that the Tao once named ceases to be the Eternal Tao).

Both Taoists and Zen Buddhists strongly advise their novices seeking Enlightenment, against 'attachment', to 'this' and 'that' and indeed all dualisms. Instead they advocate a 'oneness' with the world as portrayed in the quotation from Lao Tzu above. Zen Buddhism has an identical attitude to Taoism in this respect. Consider the opening of the Hsinhsinming ("Inscribed on the believing mind") by the Zen Master Sengtsan:

'There is nothing difficult about the Great Way;
But, avoid choosing!
Only when you neither love nor hate does it appear in all clarity.
A hair's breadth of deviation from it,
And a deep gulf is set between heaven and earth.
If you want to get hold of what it is like, do not be pro- or anti- anything....
The conflict of longing and loathing
This is the disease of the mind.
Not knowing the profound meaning of things
We disturb our peace of mind to no purpose.
Perfect like Great Space,
The Way has nothing lacking, nothing in excess.
Truly, because of our accepting and rejecting
We have not the suchness of things'.

In other words, there are two alternative ways to approach Reality – the rational, dualistic way, the invented way, choosing 'this' and rejecting 'that'; and the Way of Zen, the Tao and Real Value, where one extends as long as possible the creative pre-rational period. The latter is the meaning of the puzzling phrase 'avoid choosing' in the above passage. The Way of the Tao arises when all distinctions between 'this' and 'that', and 'me' and the 'rest of the world' have been allowed to run down until you are left with the creative cutting edge of Real Value. The key to understanding this is also explained in the Hsinhsinming:

> 'In the world of reality
> there is no self, no other-than-self.
> Should you desire immediate correspondence
> (with this reality)
> all that can be said is 'No duality!'.
> When there is no duality, all things are one,
> there is nothing that is not included.
> The enlightened of all times and places
> have all entered into this truth....
> What is, is not,
> what is not, is.
> Until you have grasped this fact,
> your position is simply untenable'.

Finally,

> 'The believing mind is not dual;
> what is dual is not the believing mind.
> Beyond all language,
> for it there is no past, no present, no future'.

Taoists take an identical view to this 'suchness' of things and the fact that the Tao does not create subject and object as opposites, but as complementary aspects of an essential unity. Hence Chuang Tzu said:

'The "this" is also "that". The "that" is also "this". The "this" has a standard of right and wrong, and the "that" also has a standard of right and wrong. Is there really a distinction between "that" and "this"? Or is there really no distinction between "that" and "this"?

When "that" and "this" have no opposites, that is the very axis of Tao. Only when the axis occupies the centre of a circle can things in their infinite complexities be responded to'.

In other words, what do you make the basis of the choices involved in your response to the world – Real Value or invented values? Really there is not much choice, for everyone, whether they like it or not, is motivated by and subject to Real Value, the Tao. Chuang Tzu goes on to give examples of the natural creative 'feeling for Tao' in everyday life. We have all experienced, perhaps a few times or perhaps many, a 'feeling for our work', when everything slots into a 'groove' where all obstacles to progress suddenly fall away. This can happen in any kind of work, from pottery to painting, from car maintenance to computer programming. All of a sudden you acquire 'peace of mind', the subject-object barrier melts away, and you 'become one' with your work – you simply 'go with it' in a totally effortless way. The result is dramatic; firstly you find you are now caring a lot more for your work, and secondly the final product turns out to be a lot better. That anyway is my experience!

I suspect strongly that you too have had similar experiences, and I would say that you have had at these times an experience of 'Enlightenment' in the Eastern sense, however brief. You are in direct touch, without the barrier of dualistic reason, with the Real Value, the creative 'cutting edge' of reality itself, and hence come to a caring relationship with your work.

Hence what I mean by Real Value, the transcendental, is familiar to all of us. It may have been explored mainly by the Eastern mystics, but it is not a deep, occult thing. Rather it is the basis of all creative activity, it is right there on the surface between you and the world, it is the cutting edge of reality. At the same time, however, it unites you with the world in a sort of 'oneness' that transcends all rational categorisation.

We use it, as Lao Tzu said, to an infinite (or potentially infinite) extent. It is the basis of all choices, the essential pre-rational counterpart to all rational structured thinking. To consider the way rationality can never be objective, but depends utterly on Real Value to provide the initial choices of first principles or hypotheses, let us now move onto the next section.

4. Reason (II)

So far we have been looking in detail at the meaning of the very similar words value and quality, and seeing how Real Value, and invented values, differ utterly in meaning. In this section I wish to draw some initial conclusions from all this discussion, and give some examples of how Real Value, the cutting edge, the creative essence of reality, is prostituted to the service of some of the most powerful forces in society. These are the forces of Commerce, which do not make any attempt to distinguish the two dictionary meanings of value and quality at all. In this section we will be looking into the inventions of money and 'style', and how you can easily be fooled into buying mere style instead of Real Value. In other words, what is 'value for money'?

However to begin with, let us consider in detail my earlier statement that both reason and a more 'hip' approach to value judgements, both use, and rely utterly upon, an awareness of Real Value. If true this is an indictment of rationality, objectivity and the scientific method. My personal experience of these three, over most of my admittedly young life, is that they all deliberately adopt a depersonalised approach which ignores the presence of the 'observer' and just deals in an abstract way with 'that world out there'.

That is, any attempt to show that 'the observer' and 'reality' are not really separate is utterly rejected, and the fruitless aim of the three is to construct a detachment from the world. Descartes' split between mind and matter seemed to work up to the end of the nineteenth century, allowing the birth of Freudian psychology and Marxist economics, amongst other dualistic disciplines. However, it just doesn't fit into the physics of the twentieth century, especially when we deal with the very small and very fast (i.e. when we consider the areas of physics called particle physics and relativity).

Heisenberg's Uncertainty Principle shows convincingly that the observer is always an integral part of the experiment, that the slightest action he takes and even his mere presence affects the invented values he measures. Given this, it is obvious that when the observer is admitted to be part of the world (or even, the observer is the world), when the subject/object duality has been transcended, then science reaches an 'Enlightenment'.

It is almost ready to admit the crucial importance to its reasoning processes of Real Value (or the Tao). This would indeed be a momentous advance, if science could expand enough to absorb what has for the last two thousand years been almost exclusively in the realm of religion.

There are however, moves in the right direction. A couple of years ago Fritjof Capra published his book 'the Tao of Physics' which is an exploration of how rapidly particle physicists are returning to a view that their consciousness is inseparable from reality itself. It portrays vividly how physicists are at last coming to the viewpoint that mystics and enlightened men the world over have always held, that mechanistic, objective pictures of reality, are doomed to failure.

Regrettably he didn't incorporate Bob Pirsig's crucial discovery that the Tao has a Western equivalent in Quality (or Real Value, as I am calling it in this paper). I strongly advise you to read Capra's book (as well as Bob Pirsig's 'Zen and the Art of Motorcycle Maintenance'). Let me explain why I think Fritjof Capra could have gone quite a bit further, and pointed out that if physics involves the Tao, it therefore has a central notion of Worth and Goodness, of Excellence or Quality.

Science proceeds in an orderly sequence of steps. First you find and define a problem, then you select what you believe to be the *best* hypothesis, the best proposed solution to the problem. Then you design experiments to test its validity. Then you work out a theory to explain and rationalise your experimental results. Then you use your theory to predict the results of future experiments. This then is an example of deductive logic, all very cold, rational and objective. Or so you might think from the popular image of science, and especially physics.

However, in all this stolid, dull process, scientists get excited, and to the layman it is not exactly obvious why. Having trained as a scientist myself I can pinpoint the exact moment for you. You obviously don't get very excited at the efficiency of this detached mechanistic production line, but right at the cutting edge of it all, during the actual process of discovery, and proposing an hypothesis. In other words, the thrill comes at the point of contact with reality, before the scientist disappears into his world of abstractions, of constructing his apriori model of the world. But what comes at this point? Real Value, of course, the source of all the scientists' decisions about *which* hypothesis or first principle to choose. I had better give an example of how delicately the balance can rest between a good and a bad choice. This example comes from geometry, and had a profound effect on Einstein's theories of relativity.

Geometry had its origins, like so many other tools of our culture, in Ancient Greece, with Euclid. His fifth postulate or axiom states innocently enough that parallel lines never meet. It is an assumption, a choice of first principle (of course, made using Real Value). It may seem obvious; however, there is a perfectly valid alternative, namely that parallel lines can meet. If you make the substitution of this, which is an alternative fifth postulate, you obtain a completely different geometry, known as Riemann geometry.

A great revolution occurred in physics, around the turn of the century, when Einstein showed convincingly in his theories, that Riemann geometry is the better description of the Space-Time continuum of our universe. Previously Newton's description of the way 'forces' operate, especially gravitation, had been totally Euclidean.

So we see that the choice of which first logical postulate to take, is totally by Real Value, and hence that all scientific endeavour has a very strong notion of Quality present right at the beginning. This applies to mathematics equally, of course. However, most scientists are just so used to the conventional ideal that everything they do has to be *rational* (to be capable of proof in dualistic terms, as we saw before) that they seemingly can't see the use they make of the creative Real Value. This is neither dualistic nor capable of being proved. Nor does it exist! It just *is* (and without it no scientific theory would ever have been invented).

It is notable that the total lack of reason in their choice of hypotheses is starting to worry some scientists, some of whom like Karl Popper are trying to rationalise the problem by developing a system of assigning probabilities to hypotheses. Einstein's answer was that in the past, for any theory, one hypothesis has always demonstrated itself to be absolutely superior to the rest. However, in today's explosion of science and information in general, both answers simply aren't good enough.

It seems that if science continues to ignore Real Value, the Transcendental, in its activities, it is in danger of going mad! It will quite literally explode, with too many ideas and hypotheses, and too few people knowledgeable enough about Real Value to be able to choose the *best* lines of enquiry to pursue. In other words I think that science (and its offspring, technology) are in desperate need of a much greater awareness of Real Value. The present cold, devalued nature of scientific work needs to be given once more a sense of virtue and excellence. Particle physics, at least, is coming to realise that unless it steps back a couple of thousand years, and re-adopts a sense of Quality, of the Tao, it isn't going to get a lot further.

However there is a large obstacle in the way of all this. Science has always insisted on being objective. How then is it to incorporate an essential individual sense of Real Value? For although Real Value is outside the subject/object duality, its interpretation will obviously differ from person to person, up to a certain point.

All scientists would agree that Archimedes' principle is a good one, but there are still quite a number who find Einstein's work, which abolishes the notion of absolute time and space, difficult to accept. Hence its elusiveness (that is *not* to say it is 'subjective') makes any solution to the problem of incorporating Real Value into scientific theories very difficult. I hope, however, that it is clear that the need is very pressing if science wants to make any real future progress.

Let us turn now to a seemingly completely different topic, which is what is known as 'value for money', or in the terminology of this essay, 'Real Value for invented value'. Society, since the beginning of history, has apparently succeeded in converting the intangible, Real Value, into something very tangible – hard cash. Once again the Real Value we attach to some commodity is devalued into an invented value. For an example of the attitudes of Marxist economists at least to Real Value, let us consider the opening of 'the Fetishism of Commodities' from Kapital volume I by Karl Marx.

> 'A commodity appears at first sight an extremely obvious, trivial thing. But its analysis brings out that it is a very strange thing, abounding in metaphysical subtleties and theological niceties. So far as it is a use-value (a complex form of invented value – SRL), there is nothing mysterious about it, whether we consider it from the point of view that by its properties it satisfies human needs or that it first takes on these properties as the product of human labour. It is absolutely clear, that by his activity, man changes the forms of the materials of nature in such a way as to make them useful to him. The form of wood, for instance, is altered if a table is made out of it. Nevertheless the table continues to be wood, an ordinary, sensuous thing. But as soon as it emerges as a commodity, it is transformed into a thing which transcends sensuousness. It not only stands with its feet on the ground, but, in relation to all other commodities, it stands on its head, and evolves out of its wooden head grotesque ideas, far more wonderful than if it were to begin dancing of its own free will.
>
> The mystical character of the commodity does not therefore arise from its use value. Just as little does it proceed from the nature of the determinants of value. (Both of these are invented values – SRL). For in the first place, however varied the kinds of labour, or productive activities, it is a physiological fact that they are functions of the human organism, and that each such function, whatever may be its nature or its form, is essentially the expenditure of human brain, nerves, muscles and sense organs. Secondly, with regard to the foundation of the quantitative determination of value (invented value again – SRL), namely the duration of that expenditure or the quantity of labour, this is quite palpably different from its quality. In all situations, the labour-time it costs to produce the means of subsistence must necessarily concern mankind, although not to the same degree at different stages of development. And

finally, as soon as men start to work for each other in any way, their labour also assumes a social form.

Whence then, arises the enigmatic character of the product of labour, as soon as it assumes the form of a commodity? Clearly it arises from this form itself. The quality (Real Value – SRL) of the kinds of human labour takes on a physical form in the equal objectivity of the products of labour as values (Real Value to invented value inter-conversion! – SRL). The measure of the expenditure of human labour-power by its duration takes on the form of the magnitude of the value of the products of labour (and again – SRL); and finally the relationships between the producers, within which the social characteristics of their labours are manifested, take on the form of a social relation between the products of labour'.

Marx goes on to describe how this 'clear' analysis demonstrates how our awareness of Real Value in considering a commodity is a mere 'fetishism'. He deliberately, it seems, ignores the fundamental differences between Real Value and invented values. I hope, however, that I have demonstrated convincingly that they are completely different! The above extract, as I pointed out with my comments in brackets, insists on rationalising Real Value and tries to make it objective, while even Marx himself admits that Real Value is a mystical, enigmatic entity. Notice too, how strongly influenced the Marxist theory is by the objective, scientific ideals of his day. As I have just explained, it is very likely that a counter-revolution is about to take place in particle physics, towards an emphasis on the importance of a choice of hypothesis or first principle governed by Real Value. This is simply bound (coming from such a fundamental and pioneering area of the sciences), eventually to spread into the rest of science and ultimately into economics.

It is interesting to speculate how much better and more humane this form of economics would be than the present trend towards huge corporations and bureaucracies, in both Capitalist and Communist countries. The idea of an anarchist economic system based on Real Value really appeals, but I don't suppose it will ever happen. Most of the world follows Marx (or seems to) and dismisses Real Value as a fetishism, and seems to prefer '(invented) quality of life' to '(Real) Quality of life'.

So it seems that the commercial forces in our society do not understand the real meaning of Quality at all. They insist on offering it to us, however, but this comes across as a 'tarting-up' of their products, giving them not Quality, Real Value, but just another invented value, *style*. The insidious presence of style is most advanced in the United States, where the awareness of Quality is far less apparent than in Britain (to judge from the TV programmes we see from the USA, anyway).

It seems that this process of stylisation goes right along with the take-over by the bureaucracies and corporations, which inevitably force a drastic reduction in care for the quality of the work their employees do, the individual sense of Real Value.

In brief, my ideal, which may not be a very practical one given two centuries of momentum to the present industrial system, is a form of anarchy where it is assumed that the individual *is* capable of knowing what is best. However, I can see no easy way to reverse the trend towards corporations and big units in our society, back towards the individual's use of Real Value. There is simply too much invested in the hands of a few powerful groups, who like to remain anonymous, who want to guard the present system at all costs, and prevent an outbreak of what one might call 'Real Freedom'.

5. Eastern and Western Religions

You'll be glad to hear that the mostly negative, critical part of this paper is now over. I have severely criticised the powerful forces of Reason, Science and Economics for their lack of appreciation of the meaning of Real Value, the Transcendental. Now it is time to introduce a lot more creative, positive thought. It takes a while for us to unwind ourselves from a lifetime immersed in a dualistic culture to the point I'm aiming for, which is why it is taking us a little time to get there. So just what is the flesh which, when we replace it in its natural state on the dualistic bones of existence, gives life real meaning?

We have already seen how Real Value or Quality (or the Tao) is the cutting edge of reality, that is to say we are all drawn on to carry out every single action we do by a sense of value. We are all driven by a natural urge felt by all life to evolve, in other words to make things better. This seems perfectly obvious for those types of action, which most people would agree to be sane and 'morally good', like working to earn a living, cooking food so you can eat, and so on. However you will I think be mildly surprised by my next assertion, which is that the morally bad, 'evil' things people do, like robbing banks and pushing narcotics, arise from precisely the same driving force, Real Value. However, they arise because it is misapprehended and perverted. That may sound ridiculous, but yet again the two types of value are being confused.

The 'baddies', at least the ones who do not have a defect in their 'mental equipment', are driven by a desire for Real Value, the 'good things of life', just like the rest of us. However, they transform their appetite for Real Value in their lives, by fulfilling their capacity for invented value (like their need for money, which *is* Real Value according to our materialist culture, so they try to get hold of a lot of it at once by robbing a bank).

Let me now go further in my statements about the essential importance to the universe of Real Value, by quoting from a book by Bede Griffiths, a Christian Benedictine monk living in India.

> "In God, the absolute Being, there is no division, or 'composition' of any kind. He is 'without duality' and sees and knows all things in himself as they exist eternally in identity with him. Everything – and every person – exists eternally in God as God. This is the truth of advaita, a truth as Catholic as it is Hindu.
>
> If there is ever to be a meeting of the religious traditions of the world, it can only be on this basis. It cannot be on the basis of belief in 'God'. 'God' is the name for the Ultimate Mystery when it is seen in relation to man, as Creator, Lord, Saviour or whatever it may be. Of this 'God' it is reasonable to ask whether he exists or not. But of the Godhead, of the Ultimate Truth, one cannot ask whether it exists. It is the ground of all existence. To exist is to 'stand out' (ex sistere) from this Ground, but the Ground

itself does not 'exist'. It is that by which all things, including God the Creator, exist.

This is the Great Tao, of which it is said, 'The Tao which can be named is not the eternal Tao, the name that can be named is not the eternal name. Without a name it is the origin of Heaven and Earth. With a name it is the mother of all things.' It is the 'nirguna Brahman', the Brahman 'without attributes', and without relation to anything, as distinguished from 'saguna Brahman', Brahman 'with attributes', who is the Creator, the Lord (Isvara). It is the 'dharmakaya of the Buddha', the 'body of reality', the ultimate Being, of which the Buddha himself is a manifestation...

...Yet there is a point beyond thought, where this becomes known, not as an object of thought, nor even as a subject as distinct from an object, but in an identity of subject and object, of being and knowing...

...(this) is Nirvana, the Ultimate State, the Supreme Wisdom, beyond which it is impossible to go".

The originator of Taoism, Lao Tzu, from whom Bede Griffiths quoted just now concerning the Tao, also has a great deal of say about the Ground of Existence (be it without a name – the Great Tao, nirguna Brahman, Zen, Quality – or Tao when named – saguna Brahman). He is very careful in choosing those few words he uses to describe it, as in chapter 25 of the Tao te Ching:

"There was 'something' undifferentiated
and yet complete,
which was there before Heaven and Earth.
Soundless and formless,
it depends on nothing and does not change.
It operates everywhere and is free from danger.
It may be called the mother of the universe.
I do not know its name; I call it Tao.
If forced to give it a name, I shall call it Great.
Now being great means functioning everywhere.
Functioning everywhere means far-reaching.

Being far-reaching means
returning to the original point.
Therefore Tao is great.
Heaven is great.
Earth is great".

Again, in chapter 34, he expresses the humble nature of the 'Ground of Existence', Real Value, quite admirably:

"The Great Tao flows everywhere,
It may go left or right.
All things depend on it for life,
and it does not turn away from them.
It accomplishes its task,
but does not claim credit for it.
It clothes and feeds all things,
but does not claim to be master over them.
Always without desires,
it may be called the Small.
All things come to it and it does not master them;
it may be called the Great.
Therefore the sage never *strives* for the great,
and thereby the great is achieved".

Finally in this section, let us move onto probably the most impressive instance of Real Value. This is when Real Value creates, not subject and object, but subject and subject, and when the two people both recognise it. Then there is first friendship and caring, or in the ultimate form, Love. Love, caring and friendship are three of the most striking examples of Quality-awareness in the universe, and naturally they are emphasised by all major religions. Christianity has its notion of brotherly love, for instance, and Buddhism its ideal of the Boddhisatva, the trainee Buddhist monk who would wait till he dies to help others attain Nirvana before he does himself.

Love is the ultimate creative force in the universe, the highest development possible of awareness of Real Value, that is when it is between two people. One of the most poetic expressions of this creative principle, with which I will finish this section, comes from 'The Prophet' by Kahlil Gibran:

'When love beckons to you, follow him,
Though his ways are hard and steep.
And when his wings enfold you, yield to him,
Though the sword hidden among his pinions may wound you.

And when he speaks to you believe in him,
Though his voice may shatter your dreams as the North Wind lays waste the garden.

For even as love crowns you,
so shall he crucify you.
Even as he is for your growth,
so is he for your pruning.
Even as he ascends to your height and caresses your tenderest branches that quiver in the sun,
So shall he descend to your roots
and shake them in their clinging to the earth.
Like sheaves of corn he gathers you to himself.
He threshes you to make you naked.
He sifts you to free you from your husks.
He grinds you to whiteness.
He kneads you until you are pliant.
And then he assigns you to his sacred fire,
that you may
become sacred bread for God's sacred feast'.

6. Towards a Creative Anarchy!

I couldn't find a better summary of what I intend to do in this last section with its provocative title, than section 35 of the Tao te Ching by Lao Tzu:

'Hold fast to the Great Tao
And all the world will come,
They come and will encounter no harm;
But enjoy comfort, peace and health.
When there are music and dainties,
Passing strangers will stay.
But the words uttered by Tao
How insipid and tasteless!
We look at Tao; it is imperceptible.

We listen to it; it is inaudible.
We use it; it is inexhaustible'.

Lao Tzu immediately continues in section 36, with a concise summary of the method he found most natural to deal with the 'Ground of Existence', the Tao:

'In order to contract,
it is necessary first to expand.
In order to weaken,
it is necessary first to strengthen.
In order to destroy,
it is necessary first to promote.
In order to grasp,
it is necessary first to give.
This is called subtle light ...'

Science and reason lay claim to be the best authorities on what may be said to 'exist'. I am not disputing that claim. What I am saying is that they should be bolder, and embrace not only 'existence', but the Essence, the Ground of Existence that, logically enough, precedes Existence. Then, and only then, can science claim to be truly involved in discovering how the subjects and objects of our universe are involved with one another. There are, as I have already mentioned, moves afoot to begin this 'ideal' meeting of science and religion.

This section is about creativity, so let us examine just how knowing about the Tao, Real Value, makes us more creative. In other words, how does becoming aware of what is present in the pre-rational period, before taking one of the many decisions we make during any period of activity, make it go better? I think the best answer to these questions is for us to cultivate our own awareness of the Ground of Existence, and see what happens. I have of course tried it, and found even my very rational work as a computer programmer got a lot better. In essence, I came to *care* a lot more for doing a good job. The feeling we get when this happens is, I think, what Lao Tzu means in section 63 of the Tao te Ching:

'Act without action,
Do without ado.
Taste without tasting'.

He goes on to summarise the essence of all activity based on Real Value, the Tao:
>'Whether it is big or small,
>repay hatred by virtue.
>Prepare for the difficult while it is still easy.
>Deal with the big while it is still small.
>Difficult undertakings have always started
>with what is easy
>and great undertakings have always started
>with what is small.
>Therefore the sage never *strives* for the great,
>and thereby the great is achieved'.

One of the best ways to cultivate our creativity is to go out of our way to *get stuck*! If we are not very careful when doing any complex problem-solving, our minds race through a limited choice of probable or possible ways forward at each stage, and latch onto one as the best, so that we can rush on dualistically, eager to get to the next decision-point.

This will appear to be fast and efficient to begin with, but inevitably, sooner or later we find ourselves out of both steam and ideas. We have been applying yes-no logic to our intermediate solutions at each stage, developing a chain of answers chosen out of a tree of possibilities, which lead us on to being stuck.

However, this is not at all a bad place to be. It enables us to adopt a creative approach, and make sure that from now on we are going to consider all the possibilities at any given stage, instead of jumping to conclusions. To make any further progress on the question at which we are now stuck, a yes or a no answer won't suffice.

However, astonishingly perhaps, there is a third answer, the Japanese word 'mu', which means "un-ask the question" or "don't ask dualistic questions in the first place". This is the root of creativity – *get stuck*, stop thinking rationally, and retreat into the pre-rational realm (where we are simply bound to find really good answers to our problems).

Let us try applying some of these techniques, in view of the background I have developed in this paper, to social problems like the ones of crime I discussed in the last section. Let us however, consider not crime, but bureaucracy! My 'cure' for this infectious and perennial problem, as I have just explained, is to retreat down our historical social tree, and then to rebuild society so that it doesn't need bureaucracy (in other words to start again from scratch!). If the idea of this worries you, and this after all is what I mean by 'creative anarchy', then I will give you a large-scale example of where it has worked admirably.

This was in the Trade Union structure of post-war West Germany. Because the German economy had been effectively destroyed in the Second World War, it was reconstructed by a team of Allied and German experts. As a result of this 'starting from scratch' we see the effects of the 'German economic miracle' today. Among these is the fact that the German trade unions are among the most effective and efficient in the world, hence there are very few strikes.

However, let us leave this interesting discussion at this point. The real purpose of this last section of the paper is not to try to solve the world's economic or other problems, but to indicate what the concerned reader can do about improving the Real Value of his or her own life.

Article Three

DEUS EX MACHINA?

Is it possible to build a conscious, so truly intelligent machine?

March 1982

Since their invention, and especially during the past twenty years, digital computers have been very much in the news. As they become rapidly more reliable and sophisticated, and the price of computer equipment continues to drop equally rapidly, an increasing amount of attention is being paid to the presence of computers in our daily lives.

With the advent of the microcomputer, the amount of public attention focused on the rise of digital computers has taken on a new impetus, with constant references in the media to the 'microchip revolution'. There have been extensive applications of large computers to business, industrial, banking and police work for some time. Now we are faced with the imminent prospect of computers in the home, even perhaps to a large extent relieving us of many of the tasks of looking after a house and family, or at least to make the task of "home management" more efficient. In less than ten years, most home equipment, from television sets to cookers and washing machines, will probably make use of a highly sophisticated microcomputer. Either to tap into enormous banks of information, or simply to automate and, hence make more efficient and reliable, the relatively humdrum tasks of cooking or cleaning.

The debate over whether the dramatic advent of the microchip is to be welcomed or feared, is just as prominent as the constant reductions in cost/performance ratio of pieces of computer equipment. Some people are delighted that they can at last access vast amounts of information. Others claim that the fact that such information is available at all is often dangerous, and the question of the rights of individuals to prevent information about themselves ever even getting into a computer file, is perhaps the dominant issue at stake in the 'great microchip debate'. Another is the issue of whether or not the microchip threatens jobs. Much research has gone into developing semi-intelligent robots capable of replacing assembly and clerical workers, to the extent that certain Japanese and European motor car manufacturers now claim to build their cars almost entirely 'by robot'. The third dominant issue in the 'microchip debate' is safety. Can we really rely on a piece of machinery, however sophisticated, to take over a difficult and often dangerous human job?

This article has several objectives: firstly to speculate how close we are getting to the development of truly intelligent machines (not just automata capable of beating practically anyone at chess!). Secondly, and much more important, I wish to challenge the prevalent belief that the present range of computers are a threat because they *are* 'intelligent'. I wish to attack this belief on purely philosophical grounds, by considering the apparently intractable problem of how to construct a digital (or some other form of) computer to solve the so-called 'koans' of Zen Buddhism (especially the first and most important 'mu' koan, and other related philosophical problems). This 'mu-machine' would be the first truly intelligent computer.

All current research into the design of automata – truly intelligent machines – appears to centre around the notion that computer 'intelligence' is to be understood in terms of an extension of their basic ability, which is to store and sort 'information' in a digital form. Before I get too deep into a technical discussion of the ins and outs of computer design and why I choose to depart from this orthodox view, I will briefly outline a few principles of computer design and operation.

Digital computers are totally based on the principle of polar opposites. All the apparently complex information computers deal with, whether it be numbers and letters, or program instructions to actually tell the machine what it is to do with such 'data', is really very simple. It is comprised of large numbers of single 'bits' or switches (capable of being turned 'off' or 'on' repeatedly according to the program being executed).

Even a light switch is effectively a digital computer, with a memory of 'one bit'! Its only program is to remember whether a human being has switched the light on or off, and keep things that way.

As soon as groups of related 'bits' are used, the situation immediately gets more complex, and by the rules of binary (bit, on/off) arithmetic, the number of combinations of switches that can be built up double with each switch or bit we add. A related group of four such bits is called, for convenience, a nyble; a group of eight bits is a byte; and 16, 24 or 32 bits (depending on the particular machine) is called a word. A nyble can save 16 combinations, a byte 256 combinations of binary settings of a polar opposite (to 'true' or 'false', 'one' or 'nought'), and so on.

A computer containing a million bytes or more (such as a large micro- or small mini- computer of the 1980s) obviously contains a vast number of potential combinations of bits, so that staggering amounts of data and instructions for the computer can be stored.

As you can see, the problem of developing and maintaining the program and data stored in such a machine is considerable, and a lot of current research deals with developing theories of how to write large programs and maintain databases (banks of bit-based information). This is neither the time nor the place to go into the details of such research.

Suffice it to say that, in the early days of computing, programmers found it well-nigh impossible to prepare a program longer than even, say, thirty instructions of even the simplest type, that did not contain at least one logical error or 'bug'. This was very frustrating then, and continues to be so, even though all programmers today accept it as a 'fact of life'.

This initial discussion of the *memory* of a computer I shall summarise in three points. Firstly, despite the apparent complexity of the binary information that can be stored in a computer's memory, this information can always ultimately be resolved into single bits only capable of being switched between two logically opposite states. This is usually an incomprehensible notion to people who don't know much about these machines ("if it's that simple how can it screw up my bank account?").

However, once the average computer scientist accepts this, the very deep philosophical consequences of even being able to represent such complex information in such a profoundly simple device as a number of two-pole switches are usually ignored. My second point is really a definition of information based on this profound notion of our ability, demonstrated by our intensive experiences of digital computers over thirty years, to solve practically any problem of sorting information, of whatever sort, incredibly rapidly. The definition is:

INFORMATION
"Any representation of a *pattern*, as seen by a human being, which can be made in terms of binary polar opposite settings of a finite number of switches".

A 'pattern' in this context could be a number, a piece of text, a diagram, or anything else we can represent in a written or drawn form.

My third and final point at this stage is that, perhaps surprisingly, this basis of a whole way of thinking on polar opposites is not new. Philosophers of both East and West have long deliberated over the fundamental nature of opposing notions, like true/false, subjective/objective, and of course, good and evil. This notion, and the idea that such opposites are necessarily contrary and in conflict, has been the way we in the West have generally been brought up to look on the world.

That is, ever since Aristotle overthrew the ideas of earlier philosophers and introduced the rather strange notion of such dualistic, objective knowledge. This 'classical' scientific revolution was vividly described in the book 'Zen and the Art of Motorcycle Maintenance' by Robert Pirsig. In the remainder of this article I shall be challenging the notion that the ability to store and process information, on its own, comprises true intelligence, whether of a machine or any sentient creature.

We have considered the simplistic bipolar nature of a computer's memory. Now we will consider the part of a digital computer where most proponents of computer intelligence would consider the actual intelligence resides, which is the central processor (its 'brain' if you like). Another definition is called for, that of:

LOGIC
"The ability to distinguish between the two states ('true' and 'false' or 'on' and 'off') of a pair of polar opposites in the form of a switch".

I should also like to define:

LOGICAL INTELLIGENCE
"The process of manipulating the decisions, made using such a logical process about two or more such switches, into a pattern which either corresponds or doesn't correspond with another pattern".

If two such master and copy patterns match, we have made a 'proof'. If they don't match we have a 'proven falsehood' and so on. The digital computer is, fundamentally speaking, not as commonly described a 'number cruncher'. Rather, it is a 'bit-' or 'switch-' cruncher.

It is obvious from what I have said so far that digital computers can store vast amounts of 'information' in a 'logical' form according to the above definitions. They also possess 'logical intelligence', and what is more, the central processor of any modern computer can use logical intelligence literally billions of times faster than us poor humans. Why then is it that people are capable of far more than the intensely specialised 'information' – processing ability of the digital computer? The answer must be that there is something extra to intelligence that is more than an ability to use that faculty so cherished in scientific circles, reason itself. Clearly computers possess a central processor capable of reason or decision-making processes. However, (and it's a big drawback), if you accidentally or intentionally pull the plug from any computer it immediately ceases to have even logical intelligence.

This affords one clue to the 'missing factor' in digital computer intelligence: another arises if we consider the *value* we attach to the information we deal with daily. Most of it, like the daily newspaper, is transient – 'here today, gone tomorrow'. More durable is artistic and scientific work, which often lasts hundreds of years, before either going out of fashion or out of date.

The most durable sorts of information of all, however, are works of philosophy, and above all, religion. The Bible, in its present form, has been with us for nearly two thousand years, and the Old Testament was written over at least the previous two thousand years. Chinese, Indian and other Oriental scripture is over six thousand years old. Buddhism, which is neither a true religion nor a philosophy, at least in the Western sense, is as old as Christianity. We also possess fragments of both Eastern and Western philosophical writings of just such an age as these ancient religious scriptures.

It was whilst pondering the apparently paradoxical questions I have just described, that I began to question the very basis of logic itself, and our reverence in the West for reason and logical processes. I started my analysis of logic using pure logic itself, but soon found that to be inadequate.

I used my knowledge of logic, especially computer logic, to formulate the above definitions, and made the crucial realisation that the concept of polar opposites, and, moreover, polar opposites being in conflict, was essential to the rational, logical processes of both machines and human beings.

This seems to resolve the world, very drearily, into two halves. On the one side we have the 'objective' – the universe, as seen as being that which is outside ourselves. This is the half given to Science, the 'masculine', hard, practical, rational side of knowledge. The other half is given, by this reasoning, to the Arts, the 'feminine', subjective, emotional side of knowledge, that deals with *us* and our interpretation of what we see, hear and touch around us.

Where, I wondered innocently, do religion and philosophy fit into this naive picture?

The next phase of my enquiries led me to read two fascinating books. I then delved into the ancient philosophy of both East and West. These two books were 'Zen and the Art of Motorcycle Maintenance' by Robert Pirsig, and 'The Tao of Physics' by Fritjof Capra. These two confirmed my own realisation that there was definitely something missing from logic and reason as used in digital computers, that prevents them from thinking like a person.

This was a sense of the 'Tao' of Lao Tzu and Chuang Tzu in ancient China; 'mu', the paradoxical alternative to a 'yes' or 'no' answer still used in the East especially by Zen Buddhists. Finally, 'Quality', the ancient Western concept of 'goodness' or 'godliness' which Bob Pirsig rediscovered so traumatically.

I was somewhat confused by all this. Computers were utterly dualistic, therefore so was reason. All the Eastern 'mystics' were insistent that duality was to be avoided at all costs, but that one was to search for the Tao or 'mu', which were never either one of a pair of opposites (that is, outside the domain of dualistic reason).

I felt that both reason and mysticism were 'right' since both were used so much all round the world.

The only course open to resolve this quandary (since I already had a solid education in reason) was to learn an equal amount about the Eastern philosophies – just what exactly is this indefinable 'mu' or 'Tao' they talk about?

Eventually, putting it as simply as possible (i.e. using as few words as possible, which is the only way to deal with a paradoxical entity), I realised that 'mu' was a *third logical state*, but quite different from the conventional "don't care" state of computer logic.

It is in fact a "care" rather than a "don't care" state, and I'm not at all sure that "state" is even the right term for it. It is neither true nor false, subjective nor objective, yet both at once.

It is thus the simplest pure *paradox* in the world to state, yet the hardest to understand.

In Zen Buddhist circles, the paradoxical nature of 'mu', this third state of logic, is usually expressed in poetry which strikes the Western ear very strangely. For instance:

"At dusk the cock announces dawn.
At midnight the bright sun".

Lao Tzu, the Taoist writer, described the Tao in equally poetic terms, again with the notion of polar opposites being 'transcended':

"Tao is empty (like a bowl).
It blunts its sharpness.
It unties its tangles.
It softens its light.
Deep and still, it appears to exist forever".

Again according to Lao Tzu, the Tao is elusive and difficult to grasp:

"Infinite and boundless,
it cannot be given any name;
(if it is) it reverts to nothingness.
This is called shape without shape,
form without object.
It is the Vague and Elusive.
Meet it and you will not see its head.
Follow it and you will not see its back".

The philosophy of the Tao or 'mu' is not confined to the East. Heraclitus, one of the philosophers rejected by Plato and Aristotle, had a strong metaphor for mu, 'fire', which he saw as governing all opposites. A much less likely source of philosophical remarks about the nature of enlightenment in relation to 'mu' is the Gnostic 'Gospel of Thomas' where Jesus reputedly said:

"When you make the two one, and when you make the inside like the outside, and the outside like the inside, and the above like the below, and when you make the male and female one and the same, then you will enter the Kingdom of Heaven".

The third logical state of 'tripolar logic' is then elusive and difficult to grasp. A machine employing tri-state logic would almost certainly be 'conscious', as none of today's computers are; even 'enlightened' perhaps. If it were possible to build such a 'mu-machine', then the debates I described at the start of this article would become very topical indeed. A machine of this sort would be 'taught' rather than 'programmed', it would have a grasp of 'reality' built in (unlike all present designs of computer), and would thus have to be treated like a human being!

I leave you with my own 'definition' of mu, to indicate the immensity of the task of building such a machine:

'Mu is no and yes.
Mu is yes and no.
Mu is one third of everything.
Mu is one third of nothing'.

Scientific Proof that (God The Holy) Spirit Exists

Article Four
The various scientific structures of (the Holy) Spirit

1. 'Fundamental Spirits'

Whenever a pair of opposing or complementary concepts is juxtaposed, a **value** naturally arises.

When the ideas or concepts are polar opposites, like desire-hate or love-fear or tenderness-anger, an extremist 'invented value' arises. The same applies not just to such spiritual qualities, but to physical ones like time, length, speed, pairs of opposing forces, and mass. Invented values can all be **measured** as the number of units between two extremes – even the spiritual extremes can and have long been characterised numerically by psychologists. However, the two concepts 'coming together' to form a value can also be not opposed but **complementary**, as the way **desire** for the feeling of **tenderness**, leads to what we call **love**. I call this a **Real Value** or **'Fundamental Spirit'**. Real Values are mystical – immediate to the mind – and so cannot be quantified!

I once drew a tree structure to represent what I regarded as the **seven** most important such 'Real Values' or 'fundamental spirits' in the Universe! Imagine my delight when in 1994, years later, I was introduced to St. Paul's views of the 'fruits of the spirit' – and realised his views and mine were nearly identical! I only had to make a few small changes to my choice of words for this tree structure, shown below, in order, firstly, to make it match the biblical version 100%! Secondly, I realised immediately that it **went further than the account by Paul!**

In fact, my version appealed to principles of symmetry to complete the picture of the 'fruits of the spirit' given by St Paul. I went on to conclude that there were indeed seven 'Fundamental Spirits' together with twelve 'fruits' of the lesser six of those spirits.

The 'Tree of Life of Divine Wisdom' of the Holy Spirit

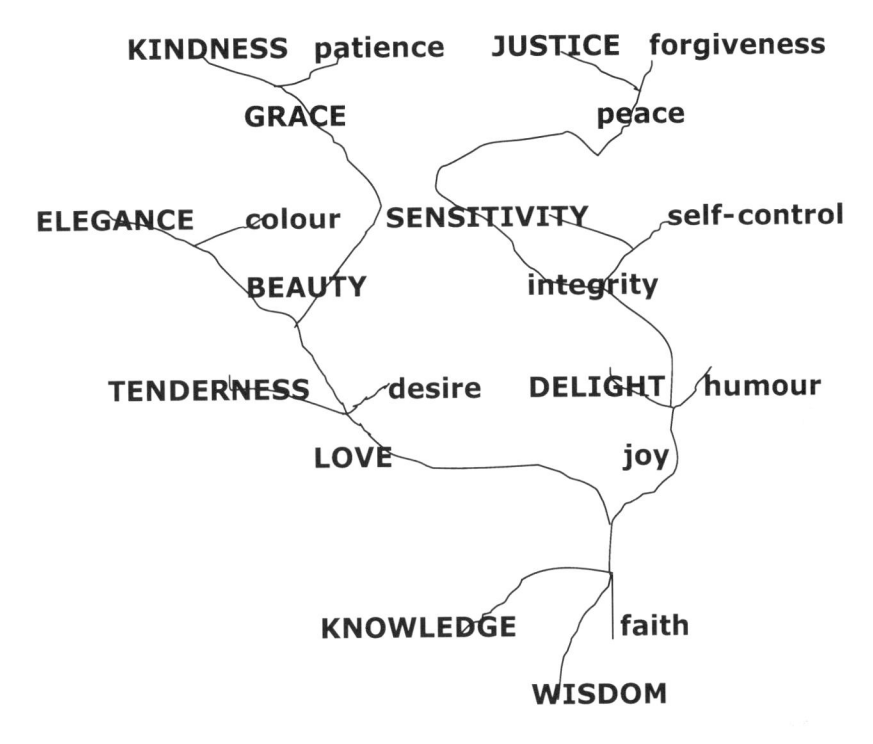

```
    KINDNESS  patience      JUSTICE  forgiveness
         GRACE                    peace

ELEGANCE   colour    SENSITIVITY      self-control
         BEAUTY                  integrity

   TENDERNESS    desire      DELIGHT   humour
         LOVE                     joy



              KNOWLEDGE       faith
                      WISDOM
```

Each one of these Seven Fundamental Spirits in One 'Tree of Life' can readily be seen to have the same 'Real Value' Nature. We have discussed Love, Desire and Tenderness in full. Let us consider the other two 'bottom level spirits' – (Divine) Wisdom, and Joy. Firstly, whenever we have **Knowledge** in which we have complete **Faith**, we have true **Wisdom**. With Joy, **Humour** – a joke or piece of wit or a funny accident or event – leads to general laughter and so **Delight**, conveying **Joy** to all concerned!

Desire, Humour, and Faith – indeed all the right-hand-side qualities shown in lower case above, are 'male' i.e. 'giving' qualities; the upper case ones 'female' or 'receiving'.

2. Human spirits, and the spirits of other creatures

We can see from the nature of the 'triplets' making up each of the Spirits in the diagram above, that these Real Values are all 'things of the mind – or spirit'. This is why I call them

Real as opposed to invented values – the things of our mind or spirit are by far the most immediate things we are aware of. Invented values reach our minds and spirit through the sequence "heart (feelings and sensations)" then body, then mind, finally spirit. These many steps can greatly distort them, things like sensations of temperature, time, size, perspective, weight or mass, and so on – whereas Real, Spiritual values are immediately obvious to the mind. More about the relationships in all these steps, and a 'scientific sequence for soul, spirit, mind, body and heart' follows immediately in section four of this paper.

I view the human spirit as comprising a **set of capacities to hold the Real Values of the Holy Spirit**. This is as viewed by me on the previous page, which amplifies, and in my view completes, and scientifically models, St. Paul's views on the nature of the Holy Spirit. It offers a 'scientific structure for the Godhead'!

Each of us, then, is given at birth a 'portion of the Holy Spirit' – a set of capacities to attain, of each of the seven spirits of the Holy Spirit – and the twelve supporting 'fruit' of the Tree of Life of the Holy Spirit. Our human Spirit is then a unique 'vessel', or in scientific terms an amplifier, for the very much bigger Holy Spirit, which has been here throughout the Universe since Time began. Our Spirit is then, a Holy Spirit – in miniature – or at least, a vessel for some measure of each of the 21 main constituents of that Spirit.

We can readily see that there are many other possible 'triplets' that can be seen as providing lesser or subsidiary branches or twigs on this Tree of Life of Divine Wisdom.

Of course, as well as capacities for each of these 21 main constituents of the Holy Spirit, we each have a unique capacity for each of their opposites – like fear, anger and hatred, the polar opposites of the constituents of love.

As the Seven Spirits of this Tree of Life can be seen to naturally form a tree structure, we can see immediately a very strong parallel to the shape of the brains of human beings and most animals. Intelligence has been proven to centre on the 'brainstem' at the base of the brain – the place of 'Wisdom' in my Tree of Life overleaf. The brain has two sides, just like the tree, and our 'thought functions' have been shown to reside in different parts of the two 'hemispheres'.

It looks like the brain of mankind and animals has been **designed** by the Spirit to reflect the structure of the Holy Spirit – in miniature. It takes a tree structure to hold another!

So this would seem to indicate that there is no reason for anybody to be chauvinistic. Animals have just as much a capacity, through their brains, for a 'spirit', as us humans – and have been shown, especially whales, dolphins and other primates, to have similar reflective capacities to us.

3. Are there vegetable and inanimate spirits?

A full answer to this question will only become possible after you consider that the Holy Spirit has been here for ever (see the very first sentence in the opening book of Genesis in the Bible!). The Spirit is also, as Jesus said, not only like a tree in invisible 'shape', but 'like the wind, and blows where it will, and no man knows where it comes from or where it is going'.

In other words, the Holy Spirit fills the whole Universe, and is in contact with all matter at once – whether that piece of matter has a brain or not!

Hence, yes, I think I agree with the aborigines with their 'Great White Spirit', and the spiritualists with their 'spirits' able to exist even without a body – and especially a brain – to act as an obvious 'home'. Yes, of course spirits can exist outside the body – just as the Holy Spirit operates 'everywhere but nowhere – all at once'! Any Real Value or True Spirit can certainly operate and 'exist' immaterially without a 'home' material body to 'reside in'. Spirits are 'outside' matter! So I see no reason why plants and other vegetable matter, and inanimate objects, should not also contain spirits.

4. The perennial disputes over the meaning of, the differences between, and even the very existence of 'soul, spirit, mind, body and heart'

There is so much confusion about these 'psychic elements', that the various sects of the great world religions – such as Protestant and Catholic, and elements of the Buddhist, Hindu and Muslim religions – have developed great schisms between each other – members of the same faith! I am introducing the subject of these conflicts and misunderstandings at this early stage, so as to make the reader fully aware of their importance. At this early stage, it is still possible to give a firm view of my own, based on my thinking leading to the present paper over all of 30 years.

I intend to develop this view now, and even provide firm 'scientifically sound definitions' of these five 'psychic elements', so showing that indeed I do think they are very different things. The discussion in the Papers that follow immediately after this part of this paper, should then reinforce this very pre-emptive introduction.

To start with, it is very important to note that a drastic simplification of the problems of what these five psychic elements are, and the differences between them, can occur if we decide that they exist in a strictly logical **sequence**: –

1. Soul
2. Spirit
3. Mind
4. Body
5. Heart

The 'upwards direction' in this sequence brings us closer to 'God'; the lower one goes, the closer one gets to 'the World'.

So, onto my 'scientific definitions' of the five psychic elements of soul, spirit, mind, body and heart: –

SOUL

"The clean, undefiled, core set of qualities or Fundamental Spirits that make up your real, essential, personality. The size of one's capacity for each of these, and their opposites, are completely unique to each individual, so giving every single person and living creature or entity a completely unique soul!"

If you are the sort of person who believes in God, I would say two other important things. Firstly, your soul is given unblemished at birth and I would agree with those who claim it is an 'immortal soul'. Being comprised of completely unblemished spiritual essences; it can be seen to live on after death and 'take you to Heaven' – returning you to the 'Body of the Holy Spirit'.

This is the full world of the Holy Spirit – of spiritual dimensions, which I explore in full in later sections in this paper.

The second thing to say to believers is that the soul is your 'interface' between your Spirit – and God. However troubled or low your spirits, if when you pray to God, you 'search your soul' sufficiently hard, you are guaranteed to 'get through to God' – reaching Him through your Soul, from your Spirit in turmoil and pain.

SPIRIT

"Your spirit is constrained by your soul, to have a set of unique capacities for each of the 21 constituents of the Tree of Life of Divine Wisdom, or the Holy Spirit of Truth.

Equally, it has unique capacities for each of their opposites, and there are literally an infinite way of blending and combining these 21 'Fundamental Spirits' and their opposites. These then form other, in my view less fundamental, pairs of opposing qualities, e.g. 'determination/weak will' and 'bravery /cowardice'."

By all means, if you can think of other qualities that you regard as more important, feel free to come up with an 'alternative structure of spiritual qualities'!

However, bear in mind I can point out a great deal of backing from the Bible for the picture I show in section one of this paper, and others later!

We all have unique capacities for each of these 21 'fundamental spiritual qualities', together with our capacities for their 21 polar opposites, as well as all the hybrid spiritual concepts, that are less fundamental that are supplementary to the Tree of Life of the Holy Spirit.

Put all these together and we all have a unique 'personality' or 'psychological profile'. However, the profiles that psychologists usually come up with are very specialised and simplified, and directed to some aspect of work, or our ability to do different types of work.

Let us consider in detail as examples of spiritual qualities, the base three Spirits of the 'Tree of Life' of section one. We can draw these and their opposites in a table: –

SPIRIT	Component or 'fruit'	Polar Opposite
WISDOM		Stupidity
	Faith	Unbelief
	KNOWLEDGE	Ignorance
LOVE		Fear
	Desire	Hate
	TENDERNESS	Anger
Joy		Despair
	Humour	Sourness
	DELIGHT	Depression

We can extend this sort of table to the whole Tree and all its opposites, then blend these into yet other pairs of opposing 'spirits'. Yet I think you will find it difficult to come up with more 'fundamental' spirits than the set in section one of this Paper.

It is worth briefly mentioning here that the effect on our 'spirits being constrained' of excess psychological pressure – stress – can be to change or distort the profile of the spirit. The natural capacities we have for each of the fundamental spirits, in our personal spirit, can get over-used or over-stretched – and get very damaged.

'Depression' can be seen, in this view, to result from too protracted a deprival of the elements of JOY – and 'mania' an excess of them and/or other spirits. 'Manic depression' is then, a constant oscillation between these extremes. 'Schizophrenia' is harder to define, and like all these other 'mental illnesses' results in, and can result from, **brain damage**.

Overall though, all these main categories of 'mental illness' can be seen to be reflected very deeply in our capacities for spiritual things – usually with our spirit being distorted or damaged beyond the 'constraints or limits' imposed in 'normal' people by the **soul**.

MIND

"The mind – conscious and subconscious parts – is the interface between the spirit, and beyond it the 'immortal soul' or 'template of the spirit' – to the body.

The mind conveys the wisdom of the spirit to the body, and receives information from the body. Information is relayed from the body and the spirit to the mind, which formulates individual or compound thoughts about all this information.

The subconscious mind controls the automatic aspects of the body, such as breathing, seeing, other senses, and circulation. The thoughts of the conscious mind can control both the body, and in a mature self-disciplined person, also to a large extent the activities of the spirit. Hence to an extent the mind can correct faults in both body and spirit, where the 'template of the soul' has not been followed properly, or its 'imprint' damaged."

BODY

"A body is an organism made of many extremely complex and sophisticated parts, that acts as the 'vessel' for the mind, spirit and soul – some would say, their 'Temple'. Although the body is all made of matter, it enables a conscious human or other being to have a completely individual consciousness. All the body requires, as a minimum, for this marvellous gift is water, food, air and warmth!"

Yet many reading this Paper will dispute all that has gone before. "Why! Scientists have **proved** that the mind and all that other soul and spirit stuff, is just the result of chemicals and bio-chemicals in the body. The soul is out of date as a concept!" I have fundamental objections as one with a 'spiritual' leaning, to such 'scientific Atheist' dogma – which is totally non-provable!

HEART

"Heart is the set of feelings and sensations we receive through our senses about the environment – especially other people and other creatures. It also comprises our behaviour towards that environment – the actions of our body, as representing the thoughts of our mind, filtering the influence of our spirit and thence soul."

Our heart, then, is our only point of interaction with the outside world, and so the only point at which soul, spirit, mind then body, come to express themselves. I include our physical behaviour within the canopy term of 'heart', as physical behaviour is very much determined by our feelings and senses – which are definitely part of our 'heart'.

5. The Feminine Nature of Spirit

Now we have covered some basic introductory material in the above first four sections, we are able to start the main or core material of this Paper. This is the notion that the Tree of Life of Divine (or even human) Wisdom is overall a very **Feminine – or Female, being a Person – Tree of Life**.

To begin to see this, note that the 21 'Fundamental Spirits' of my diagram above one, are in fact really all very gentle and feminine in nature. This is even though some are more feminine than others – the 'lower case ones' are more masculine than the feminine ones, shown in upper case there.

Indeed, it is only where the 'fundamental spirits' and their polar opposites are juxtaposed that we see a harsh 'masculine' opposition appear, e.g. between love and fear.

Overall this can be seen to be because the whole Tree of Life of Divine Wisdom – or, the Seven Spirits of the Holy Spirit of Truth – is **all** based on and emanates from Wisdom.

That Wisdom is very much female, is clearly stated in the Bible, in the Book of Proverbs in the Old Testament. This delicious quotation even clearly states that Wisdom is indeed a 'Tree of Life' just like I have always believed: –

Proverbs 3:13-18
Happy are those who find wisdom,
    and those who get understanding,
for her income is better than silver,
    and her revenue better than gold.
She is more precious than jewels,
    and nothing you desire can compare to her.
Long life is in her right hand;
    in her left hand are riches and honour.
Her ways are ways of pleasantness,
    and all her paths are peace.
She is a tree of life to those who lay hold of her;
    those who hold her fast are called happy.

The only historical point to note here is that in Biblical times – and still today for many in the Middle East – the left hand was regarded as 'unclean', only the right hand 'clean'.

So the Holy Spirit of Seven Spirits, all based on Wisdom, is then – even according to the Bible! – a 'Lady' **not** a 'Lord', as stated in the Nicene Creed and most other Christian Creeds – notably formulated exclusively by men...

So, what does the Bible itself have to say about the gender of the Holy Spirit, forgetting the much later creeds of the Church for a minute? As we see in the next section, that question raises a whole 'can of worms' – translations of the gender of the Holy Spirit in the New Testament, as 'He', seem to be assuming far too much!

6. The gender of the Holy Spirit – as according to the Bible itself. 'That obscure Greek pronoun, εκεινος'

The first mention of the Holy Spirit is in the very first sentence of the Bible itself!

> "In the beginning, when God began to create the heavens and the earth, the earth was a formless void and darkness covered the face of the deep, while the Spirit of God swept over the face of the waters".
>
> Genesis 1:1-2

So one misconception that one can immediately knock on the head, common amongst Christians, is that in celebrating Pentecost, they are celebrating the Coming of the Holy Spirit for the first time – in the First Century AD. No, the Holy Spirit was there at the start of time, and according to the above quotation, even before Time itself began!

All references to the Holy Spirit as a Spirit in the original Ancient Greek New Testament call the Spirit "Πνευμα" ("Pneuma") which is **neutral** in gender.

The few references to the Spirit with a gender, as an actual person, are normally translated in the New Testament in line with the traditions and creeds of the Church – which assert strongly that the Holy Spirit is a Lord.

However, as the Irish poet W.B. Yeats pointed out with some feeling, the word used in the Bible, for the Person of the Holy Spirit is the 'obscure Greek pronoun εκεινος' – or 'ekeinos'. This can be translated as either 'Him' or **'Her'** – as it means either – literally it means **'that person'** in English.

Obviously from what has gone before I much prefer the translation 'Her' of this term – especially in view of the previous section. This is my choice for the rest of this paper.

I would also strongly assert that the Nicene Creed, and other creeds that followed historically, that followed the example of the earliest, Nicene creed, are quite simply wrong on this extremely vital point! However, there were reasons – political ones – why the Nicene creed was so apparently male chauvinist about this.

At the time this creed was formulated under the direction of the first Christian Roman emperor, Constantine, in the third century AD, the church was still very young and formative. In particular, Constantine instructed that a particularly dangerous splinter group from the 'orthodox' Church he was trying to establish as the official religion of the whole Roman Empire, be actively repressed. This was the 'Gnostic' movement, which claimed arcane knowledge about female as well as the orthodox all-male deity or deities. So in order to stamp out this notion that the 'Godhead' might contain female elements, which was seen as highly dangerous, the order went out to 'make' The Deity of God – all-male.

Hence still today the Christian Holy Trinity is seen – very awkwardly – as being composed of 'Three Lords'. My own view is that it is far more natural to view Them as 'Father, Son and... Wife and Mother of them both' (a Divine 'Family Unit') in the ways expressed in preceding sections of this Paper.

7. Religion versus or together with science?

Science has now reached a momentous point of advance. With its latest theories, given sufficient imagination, it can be seen to have opened up ways in which the basic principles of the religious world – in particular Christian views – can be fitted into the scientific framework. The remarkable thing I have found in attempting to reach this point in my deliberations leading to the ideas in these three papers, is that it is, when achieved, both seamless – and complete!

Overall, as spiritual matters are very often a vital subject for the Arts, the Theories of Everything that have started emerging in the last twenty-five or so years from physicists' laboratories seem to me to be making possible a previously undreamed-of integration of Science, Religion and the Arts. C.P. Snow called Science and the Arts, 'the Two Cultures'. These two, along with the 'Third Culture' of 'Religion' in general, seem to me to be presented right now with wholly new and unexpected opportunities to understand one another far better, and overcome their many differences. Such a meeting of three such different areas of human endeavour can in my view only be looked forward to as a 'Very Good Thing Indeed'.

Although the differences between the Arts and Science and Religion are very great, they are not as pronounced as the differences between different world religions, and sects within those religions.

Although I mostly trained as a scientist, I have, let us say, both artistic and religious leanings. As a result I have always been fascinated that certain activities in all three areas of endeavour have produced in me always precisely the same feeling – of a kind of child-like awe and wonder.

In science this can arise when, after a particularly long and difficult mathematical calculation, the answer turns out to be remarkably elegant and simple – unexpectedly so. It then promptly gives you a dramatic insight that your great labours in working out the answer could have instead been achieved with a bit of lateral thinking and a different and lateral approach. The resulting feeling is one of instant dawning of enlightenment in some measure – and of feeling something of a fool!

In Religion and the Arts, many people report similar humbling experiences when contemplating the immensity and awesomeness of the Universe and when and how it has originated, and the childlike feeling that results. Jesus replied to the Pharisees probing him with questions like 'Where then is this "Kingdom of Heaven"' with the totally confounding response:

'The Kingdom of Heaven is in the midst of you'.

To find it, he emphatically said that one must become like a child, I believe in the sense of feeling awe and wonder like I said above:

'Truly, I say to you, unless you turn and become like children, you will never enter the Kingdom of Heaven. Whoever humbles himself like this child, he is the greatest in the Kingdom of Heaven'.

I give below a final quote about the state of 'child-mind', again from Jesus, but from Gnostic sources – the so-called 'Gospel of Thomas' in this case – that are so frowned upon by the Orthodox Church. It has a strong appeal to me since it appears to be an astonishingly early statement of principles of the very dialectics we have looked at so far. I will shortly be claiming these are so important because they constitute the way the Holy Spirit Herself is structured.

The way that the bringing together of apparent complementary opposites in this quotation, is made so emphatically, is to me compelling:

'Jesus watched infants being suckled. He said to his disciples, "Those infants being suckled are like those who enter the Kingdom".

'They said to him,
"Shall we then, as infants, enter the kingdom?"

'He replied,
"When you make the two one, and when you make the outside like the inside, and the above like the below, and when you make the male and the female one and the same, then you will enter the Kingdom".'

Both quotations imply, in my view, that entering a child-like state of sheer rapture – awe and wonder – whether as an artist, scientist, or religious devotee, is exactly the same as entering Heaven – indeed then, it is 'in the midst of you'!

The original prompt I had for thinking that the Holy Spirit actually has structure, rather than as more conventionally envisaged, as some kind of uniform 'gaseous medium' or 'ether', again came to me from the Bible, way back in 1978, and was the prompt for this whole paper.

It comprised a handful of separate verses in the remarkable last book of the Bible, the Book of Revelation, which I read for the first time, in depth, then. To quote from the most emphatic of these verses,

> 'From the throne (of God) came flashes of lightning, rumblings and peals of thunder. Before the throne, seven lamps were blazing. These are the seven spirits (or sevenfold spirit) of God.'
>
> Revelation 4:5

At the time when I first read this, it struck me like lightning that here the Bible in its closing book was clearly saying that the Holy Spirit has structure – indeed, was based on the number seven, of mystical significance to almost all religions! I set out from then to try to understand, from this single clue, how this could be, and over the years since 1979 have gradually developed the slowly evolving ideas in this set of three papers, that in essence all arose from this tiny germ of a notion.

This whole set of papers has arisen from an isolated verse of Revelation apparently of as much import as a grain of mustard seed! As the parable puts it, however:

> 'The kingdom of heaven is like a grain of mustard seed, which is the smallest of all seeds, yet when it is fully grown is a great tree, and the birds of the air come and make nests in its branches.'

Not surprisingly, you will be seeing that I view the Holy Spirit – surely the source of the biblical Kingdom of Heaven – as best shown like a tree.

The other principal sources of my 'data' for my 'scientific investigation of the structure of the Spirit' below, were:

- Genesis chapter one

- John chapter one

- Galatians 5:22-23 (for the 'fruits of the spirit') and 1 Corinthians 12:8-10 (for the 'gifts of the spirit')

- The parables of the Gospels, in particular Matthew and Luke.

Note that I have chosen in this paper not to dwell at all on the various *gifts* of the Spirit – my emphasis is on the inherent nature of the Holy Spirit, rather than Her expression in human gifts. There is a multitude of books on the gifts of the Spirit available from Christian outlets, such as Michael Green's 'I believe in the Holy Spirit', which cover the subject very well.

On the other hand, the notion of 'a variety of fruits of the spirit' – as both outward expression of goodness, and as seed for further growth – totally fit my view. This is that the Holy Spirit is best seen as a tree – although a parallel and equally valid 'model' is best conveyed by the biblical phrase 'a fountain of living water'.

By about 1984 I had produced, after an intensive analysis and collecting together of all that the Bible has to say about the inherent nature of the Holy Spirit, a model of Her overall structure.

By a strange coincidence, also around 1984, the first 'supergravity' and 'superstring' theories were emerging as the basis of the first attempts at extraordinarily ambitious scientific 'theories of everything'. These attempt the awesome task of integrating all the many disparate pre-existing areas of physics and chemistry – and to a large extent, biology.

It was when I first read Professor Stephen Hawking's book 'A brief history of time' a few years ago, that I realised to my delight that there was a place in these theories about the visible, physical world, for my own thoughts. My own collected musings on the nature of the invisible world of the Spirit seemed to fit – and moreover, fit precisely.

To any scientist about to read what follows, I would point out that there are important numbers on either side of this spiritual/physical equation that in isolation remain totally mysterious. Why, for the complex mathematics involved to suddenly radically simplify enough to become manageable, must scientists first apparently encumber the equations with specific numbers of extra 'dimensions'? More than the x, y and z of Cartesian space co-ordinates, and the t of time?

Just why are there a specific set of numbers associated with the results of my own researches, into the totality of what the Bible says about spiritual essences, once one first analyses The Holy Spirit, then builds up a scientific model of the spiritual world?

As we will be seeing in the next section of this paper, there is a massive appeal in my own building of a synthesis between the spiritual world and the physical world of science. In a nutshell:

The numbers on both sides match – exactly!

This fact is at once startling – and highly reassuring. Of course, one might expect the Bible and science to ultimately come to agree on something of such common interest and vast importance as the nature, origin and structure of the Universe seen as a whole.

'Numbers matching up' between different areas of science normally implies that a full match has been found between the two theories or sets of principles. When the match is between the whole of science, and most of religion, the effect on me for one is to produce the same humbling feeling as I described above.

Firstly, so far it has been my singular contention that out of the initial ambiguity or paradox that preceded our Universe – the initial 'void' that both science and religions seem to entirely agree on – polarisations or bipolar disturbances appeared. These manifested themselves as what I have so far confined myself to describing as **spiritual triple movements.**

These, I have claimed, can only be seen as having developed from there – even in the absence of space, and above all matter – in a particular and inevitable way, due to the way they arose in the first place – their inherently totally unblemished nature.

This is of course a very religious, especially Christian or Hebrew view, and a perfectly feasible alternative may well prove more acceptable to scientists. Particularly in view of what I say in the next section, which brings in the very latest scientific views – Grand Unified Theories (GUT's) or Theories of Everything (TOE's).

That is to say, although there must be strong links between the scientific, physical world and any spiritual world we try to imagine, not just my own view being developed here; it is perfectly possible that these two worlds originated right at the start of the Universe, **in parallel**.

One is visible to us – the physical world – and the spiritual order, along the lines I have described, is invisible to us.

In the last section of this paper we will be seeing how science, in its new and very ambitious TOE's, seems to offer a mechanism that provides – even totally mathematically precisely – for such a schema! It would appear that just such a division between our obvious, physical world of the senses, and another world entirely, emerged in an incredibly minute split-second at the very origin of the Universe – when it was less than 10^{-43} seconds old!

Any scientist reading the words of the last section, may well have been struck by the great similarity of the 'triple movements' of each Spirit in the Sevenfold Tree of Spirits that I described, to something much more familiar. These 'fundamental spirits' – to coin a phrase, as one can readily think of many more spiritual triplets that are in my opinion not as fundamental as those I have chosen – are they not very similar to physical 'dimensions'? (like the x, y and z of space and t of time?)

My own view is that in fact not only are they very similar, but they are in fact of an identical 'triple movement' nature. Indeed, Albert Einstein pointed out that the four-dimensional Space-Time Continuum has a kind of 'surface tension' – it can distort, allowing light to bend as it passes heavy objects in space, such as nearby stars. This effect has even been verified by astronomers, and provided early verification of his theories.

It is my own contention, as I consider both physical and spiritual worlds, that the spiritual world has its own very intense gravitational influence on the physical. This is through both the ordinary, everyday force of **gravitational attraction**, and above all the much more tangible form of gravity called electromagnetic radiation or **light**. 'Spiritual matters are very weighty indeed'! We will see how this can be visualised as the net result of the great process of evolution just starting of scientific TOE's, and even stated by the latest TOE's in precise mathematical terms!

Let me summarise the above line of argument in two Principles. These are essential to link the two sets of arguments together, before coming to the final synthesis of the thesis of religious views and the antithesis of science, in the next section: -

1. "A physical dimension (like mass, length or time) is precisely equivalent to a 'fundamental spirit' "

2. "The spiritual dimensions (there are many) are invisible because they interpenetrate the four-dimensional Space-Time Continuum 'at right angles'. The two sets of dimensions only interact via the gravitational force – both have energy, i.e. mass (even though Spirit is non-material) – and above all via light, or electromagnetic radiation. The Spiritual World seems to bathe the lucky person in contact with it, with a veritable 'son et lumiere' of gravity and light – the 'salt and light' of their faith. Is this the 'music of the spheres' described by the Ancients?"

(Christians often portray the Cross, as symbolising the vertical Spiritual bar crossing the Worldly bar at right angles).

'Fundamental Spirits' and the latest modern 'Grand Unifying Theories' (GUT's) and 'Theories of Everything' (TOE's) of Physics

The Conclusion to this 'Grand Synthesis of Science and Faith' now poses two Big Questions:-

i) Are the 'missing aspects' of the latest Theories of Everything of Science, in fact 'obvious' in the religious world, and indeed the Arts?

ii) Through these latest theories, has then indeed Science 'stumbled into God'?

In order to start to answer these two questions, among others, we need to take a look at the history of the development of scientific theories in general, over the last few hundred years. Then we can see just where these GUT's and TOE's have come from, and how, and above all why.

To do this properly requires a whole book, as the subject matter is so complex and covers such a long time period. However I am intending to summarise this history of science in a few pages.

I have already condensed much of the Bible into a single scientifically sound and above all consistent framework. Now I turn to appeal to your imagination, concerning the very latest, most advanced, and still very much to be finalised theories of physics, in order to try to find common ground. As we have seen so far in this paper, and as can already be seen from the title of this final section, I am taking a particular 'angle' – of necessity, a somewhat narrow one – on both of these vast areas of human thought and history, in order to do so.

Modern science is seen to have begun in the Middle Ages, when two early astronomers using the first telescopes, Johannes Kepler and Galileo Galilei, backed up a hundred-year old theory of Nicholas Copernicus. They declared that the Earth – along with the other planets – rotated round the Sun and not vice-versa, as the Church had always maintained.

This was a direct challenge to the traditional dogma of the Church – pure dogma or tradition, as there is no such statement in any of the Church's source material, especially the Bible, to that effect. As a result, in an infamous series of trials, Galileo was seriously punished by being imprisoned.

However, in 1642, the year that Galileo eventually died, the scientist who was to provide a relatively simple and highly accurate theory to explain the new observations of planetary motion, was born in England. Sir Isaac Newton is acknowledged to have been perhaps the most pioneering and accomplished scientist ever, and his famous 'inverse-square law of gravitation', that all High School students study, was very elegant, and completely explained the elliptical, not circular as previously thought, shape of the orbits of the planets.

This Newtonian theory of gravitation lasted with no changes at all, until this century, when Einstein's two theories of Special and General Relativity showed that, using a much larger body of mathematics, a very different approach was required to fully explain the motions of heavenly bodies.

In the meantime, during the eighteenth and nineteenth centuries, attention started to be given, in a completely separate theoretical advance by science, to the only other forces then known about in nature – electricity and magnetism. In particular, the work of the British scientist James Clerk Maxwell allowed the taming of these forces, and they began to be used to provide electrical power, and hence great advances in engineering, in Victorian times.

This has led directly to the electronic revolution of the latter half of the 20th century, and the possibility of electronic machines or computers even replacing humans in the workplace.

In purely scientific terms, at the end of the nineteenth century Maxwell finally published a set of very simple and elegant equations that summarised the whole subject. They revealed that electricity and magnetism were as closely related in the mathematical theory as had long been thought from the observations made by scientists.

At that stage, many scientists felt they were on the brink of a complete 'electro-mechanical' view of the world, and that physics was nearly completed. However, first Einstein's theories, then the discovery that atoms were not fundamental, but that there existed much smaller particles, at the start of the really rapid growth of physics that took place at the start of this century, undermined this initial optimism.

Further dramatic discoveries came quickly. By 1930 it was found that firstly the sub-atomic world within the nucleus of each atom, held two totally new and unexpected types of forces binding the protons and neutrons together. These were dubbed the 'strong' and the 'weak' forces. Again, in 1926 the German physicist Werner Heisenberg formulated his famous – and confounding – Uncertainty Principle. This reflected the results of early experiments at the sub-atomic level, and still stands today. It states that as one probes into the properties of the Universe, so the results of measurements one can take get increasingly 'blurred' – a randomness appears that can only be described by the then new mathematics of statistics and probability. Heisenberg explained this by proposing that as one looks 'too closely' at the small-scale workings of the Universe, one's presence as a conscious 'observer' actually affects the results of the experiment one is conducting!

Perhaps not surprisingly, this last blow in particular was anathema to those physicists who still strongly adhered to the purely mechanical, clockwork-like approach that had prevailed in science since Galileo and Newton. Even Einstein had great difficulty in accepting this new 'quantum mechanics', which subatomic physics led to. After all, his monumental work was the last great outcome of the 'old ways' of 'classical physics' from before the time Ernest Rutherford split the atom in 1911.

Towards the unification of physics

The proliferation of new theories, and indeed whole new separate areas of physics in the first thirty years of this century, seemed likely to continue, and at first was bewildering. A number of mathematicians and physicists immediately began the task of trying to make sense of all this revolutionary diversity. This process of unification has since led at length in the 1970's to the theory of supergravity, the first GUT, and in the early 1980's to first string theory then superstring theory. The latter is still developing rapidly, yet is still held out to be the main hope of finding a complete GUT or TOE.

The first attempts to integrate the various new areas of physics started with the two 'oldest' theories of this revolution – electromagnetism and relativity – even though these two were themselves both still in their relative infancy. The way the first success was achieved has a great bearing on the 'Grand Synthesis of Science and Religion' we are conducting, and now approaching the climax of.

It was in 1921 that a little-known Polish physicist, Theordor Kaluza, provided a brilliantly simple way to include the non-geometrical yet totally established formulation of Maxwell's equations, in one theory along with Einstein's theories, which are totally geometrical (as we just saw, they stemmed from the end of classical physics). He simply extended geometry as used in classical physics, just enough to accommodate electromagnetism as expressed by Maxwell's equations, in a bizarre yet compelling way. He added an extra fourth dimension to the conventional x, y and z of space, and showed that electro-magnetism is a form of extremely strong gravity, but unlike conventional gravity it occupies this invisible fourth dimension of space.

Very shortly after the production of this very elegant and relatively simple unified theory of electromagnetism and gravity, came an equally simple answer to the apparently perplexing question 'Just where is this fifth dimension of Space-Time?'

In 1926 the Swedish physicist Oscar Klein came out with the novel idea that we cannot see or visualise this extra dimension of space because it is 'compactified' or 'rolled up' to a very small size. Klein conjectured that lines in space are really like hosepipes! Look at them from afar, and they appear like lines, but look closer and each point is enclosed by a small circle.

However, in the case of the fourth dimension of space, the loops along each such line are not actually 'inside' space. They extend it, in a way that is obvious in just two dimensions, by drawing a wiggly line to represent a hosepipe and then imagining approaching it and finding it is tubular. It is much harder, indeed virtually impossible for us to 'see' this in four dimensions.

Klein was able to calculate the circumference of these 'loops around the fifth dimension', using the values of the unit of electric charge carried by electrical particles such as electrons, and the strength of the gravitational forces between particles. One of these comes from each of the two theories unified by the Kaluza-Klein theory.

The value turns out to be about 10^{-32} centimetres – or about 1 / 100,000,000,000,000,000,000 the size of the smallest atomic nucleus – far smaller than the smallest particles since discovered by particle physicists using high-energy accelerators. It is not then surprising that this postulated fifth dimension is totally hidden from our view – it is best viewed as somehow 'tucked inside' each point in conventional Space-Time, and each atom or particle.

However, the immediate impact of this theory was eclipsed by the discovery in the 1930's of the weak and strong subatomic forces. Interest in a theory that could not include these two new types of force soon waned. The Kaluza-Klein theory languished until the 1970's, with the discovery that particles previously thought of as 'fundamental' – protons, neutrons and electrons – were not indeed so fundamental as originally thought. New smaller constituent particles termed 'quarks' were postulated, and have since been identified in laboratory experiments with particle accelerators.

There are precisely three quarks making up each proton, neutron and electron, and physicists indulged in a veritable orgy of the imagination in describing their qualities. Quarks come in six basic 'flavours' called up, down, strangeness, charm, bottom and top – each coming in three varieties or 'colours', called equally bizarrely red, green and blue.

Although these terms correspond to nothing in the everyday world of the senses, they have since led to the whole quaintly-described quark world to be called 'quantum chromodynamics'.

Notably, from the point of view of the author, these properties of quarks always come in very simple round numbers rather than the irrational numbers of conventional physics – the properties of quarks are always measured in terms of simple fractions like 1/3, 1/2, 2/3 and so on. Likewise, 'spin', another important property of sub-atomic particles, comes in values like 0, 1/2, 1, 3/2 and 2.

The 1970's and the first Grand Unified Theories

In the late 1970's the rapid development of quantum chromodynamics into a respectable new area of physics, caused a sudden interest in trying at last to produce a Grand Unified Theory. This was intended to account for all four, not just two of the fundamental forces of nature – which to refresh your memory are the weak, strong, electromagnetic forces, and gravity.

Having been mothballed in the 1930's, it was remembered how the Kaluza-Klein theory had amalgamated quite successfully both electromagnetism and gravity, and it was now dusted off and extended to include, initially, the strong force as well. To do this, not just one extra dimension of space had to be added – but a total of seven! The result was 'supergravity' theory, with a total of *eleven* dimensions of Space-Time.

The reasons for this are only fully grasped by a full appreciation of the complex mathematics, but in outline have a lot to do with the 'spin' quality of particulate matter, that we just mentioned. It turned out that to make the mathematics of the supergravity theory work most simply and elegantly with an expanded Kaluza-Klein theory, as well as to account for all the known types of particles precisely, physicists needed to make the equations fit with one particular formulation of supergravity. This was one variant among various possible alternatives, and accommodated a principle called cryptically, 'N=8 supersymmetry'.

This in turn has to do with the number of 'steps' in possible value one has to make in order to traverse all known possible values of spin, in both experimental observations of particles, and the new quantum chromodynamic theories. As spin comes in just the values −2, −3/2, −1, −1/2, 0, 1/2, 1, 3/2 and 2, spin is readily seen to arise in a steady series of nine possible values, in all the particles we observe. The 'N = 8' formula expresses the number of discrete steps involved in working along the whole chain.

This is very important in order to simplify quantum chromodynamics. By postulating an extra total of *seven* 'hidden dimensions', physicists found they could in turn reduce a very diverse variety of particles to many fewer particles – purely by virtue of the extra dimensions, these were able to take all the above values of spin as if they were 'superparticles'. This provided a vital simplification of the mathematics involved.

In order to provide a model of the topology of the extra seven dimensions of space, which were viewed as 'wrapped up in' ordinary three-dimensional space just as in the original Kaluza-Klein theory, in an incredibly tiny 'volume', various 'shapes' were possible. However the favourite, which had been discussed by mathematicians half a century earlier, was something called a 'seven-sphere', and it meant that in the supergravity theory, every point in the 'normal' four-dimensional Universe 'contains' a minute 'hyperball' containing the extra seven dimensions.

It turns out that the seven-sphere has rich geometrical properties, and is definitely the simplest and more importantly, most natural choice one can envisage for the 'shape' of these seven dimensions.

A normal sphere is obviously highly symmetrical – because it contains many more dimensions, a seven-sphere is even richer in symmetries. In order to accommodate the fact that in nature physicists have long observed that everything is not quite symmetrical – there is a 'broken symmetry' – the sphere had to be viewed as 'slightly squashed'!

Supergravity theory was greeted very enthusiastically in 1976, when it was first developed, as it seemed to overcome two major problems in earlier attempts to produce a viable Grand Unified Theory, or GUT.

Firstly, particles of spin 2 are supposed to be the particles that carry the weakest of the four forces known in nature, gravity, and their successful integration into a consistent theory that also contained, at the other extreme, the massive forces of quantum chromodynamics, had a great appeal.

Furthermore, initially supergravity theory seemed to have eliminated nearly all of the so-called 'infinities' that had dogged the equations of previous attempts to produce a viable GUT. These are points in the equations where a value suddenly and unexpectedly rises to infinity or 'blows up', in total contradiction with observed reality, where everything remains finite and 'manageable'.

However, by 1984 it was realised that there were three major problems with supergravity theory. Firstly, in order to work out all the complex equations involved, and show that there were indeed no infinities, would take a computer of the day at least four years! Then, the chances were that just one mistake in the program would wreck all the results. Physicists as a whole were not prepared to undertake the effort and risk involved.

Secondly, and possibly even more insurmountable, a theory with an *odd number* of Space-Time dimensions, fundamentally speaking because of the mathematics, could never encompass all four forces in nature – as we just said, supergravity theory left out the so-called weak force.

Thirdly, and possibly most important, not all the particles predicted by supergravity matched up with the particles observed in reality.

1984, String Theories and Theories of Everything

In 1984 there was a sudden and dramatic shift of opinion in favour of what are known as string theories. Unlike all preceding theories, in string theories the basic objects or particles, which occupy a single point in space, are replaced by 'strings', or things that have a length but no other dimension, just like conventional string but infinitely thin.

'Open' strings have ends, 'closed' strings are joined up in tiny closed loops, and strings can join together in a pattern remarkably like a pair of trousers to look at!

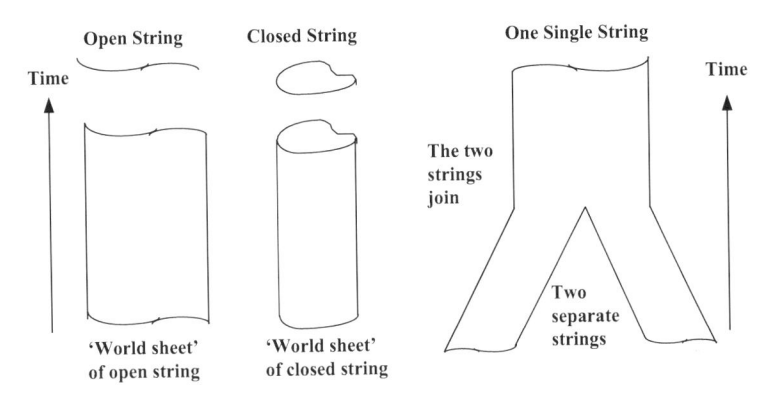

```
Open String        Closed String        One Single String
Time                                                          Time
                                      The two
                                      strings
                                      join

                                              Two
                                              separate
'World sheet'      'World sheet'               strings
of open string     of closed string
```

Likewise, a single string can divide into two strings. What were previously thought of as particles, now came to be thought of more as waves travelling along each string, like those in a violin string. The tension in these strings is immense, due to their incredibly small size as envisaged by string theory – about 10^{39} tons! Forces between particles come to be viewed instead as other pieces of string linking each pair, leading to a view of the Universe as a massive spider's web extending in every direction! Alternatively, to borrow an analogy from the famous Professor Stephen Hawking – string theory is a bit like plumbing! This occurs on a cosmic and massive scale, of course.

Like all such GUT's or TOE's, string theory and its variants lead to infinities in the equations. However, newer versions of string theory and its later development known as superstring theory, especially one particularly promising version known as heterotic string theory, hold out a strong hope that all these infinities will eventually cancel out, once a final version of the theory is achieved by physicists.

However that point is still some way off. The final point I will make in this discussion of the history of science to date, about string and superstring theory, is to do yet again with 'extra hidden dimensions of Space-Time' that these theories require, just like all GUT's and TOE's.

We saw earlier that to unify gravity and electro-magnetism, the Kaluza-Klein theory introduced an extra dimension of space, and that in the later development of this into Supergravity theory, a full seven extra dimensions of space had to be introduced. This same process is also necessary in string theories – in superstring theory *six* extra dimensions of space are postulated – and in the earliest versions of string theory, no less than *twenty-two* extra dimensions of space. Just as in the Kaluza-Klein and Supergravity theories, these are envisaged as all being 'rolled up inside' an incredibly minute volume at each point in 'conventional' space.

We are now at the end of the background necessary to conclude the Grand Synthesis of this paper. Before finally presenting my own arguments for what these extra dimensions really are, we should consider how they are usually thought about within the world of science itself – or is it science-fiction?

Many at first thought such dimensions could permit their use to 'make jumps through space' and enable space travel to be undertaken very quickly. However, with the space occupied by these extra dimensions being so very tiny, this is impossible.

In a similar vein, these extra dimensions operate 'at right angles to' the physical ones of time and space. Many were initially taken by the thought that the extra dimensions could contain another universe, which the mathematics of such theories indicated only links to our own by the force of gravity.

If indeed these dimensions contain 'invisible matter', can we expect the Earth to be hit by an 'invisible sun' from this other Universe at some time?

Towards a full 'Theory of Everything' that really explains these 'hidden dimensions of nature'

Space travel through the 'extra dimensions' is then impossible, and it appears likely that in fact these dimensions *contain no matter* – no such collision between visible and invisible planets and suns has ever been observed, so confounding the second 'science fiction' scenario we just mentioned.

So just what are these 'extra dimensions' and how are they to be thought of? This great issue has confounded physicists this century. In the course of this paper I have already strongly hinted at my own answer. Namely, that the answer **lies outside science**. Indeed, I will now be developing no less than four strong arguments that, for Science to really come up with a final Theory of Everything, it will, however reluctantly, have to come out of its traditional rigid confines and embrace a notion of the spiritual world. That is, to take on something of the World of the Arts, and certain aspects of various World Religions!

I have already outlined, in previous sections of this paper, the first two of these four arguments. One is a 'qualitative' argument – that a 'fundamental spirit' of the religious world is identical in kind to a 'dimension' of science. We argued that point through at length earlier.

The second argument is 'quantitative'. In earlier sections I presented my own personal 'scientific overview' of the nature of the Holy Spirit. In introducing this final section of the paper, I said that, very powerfully, the **numbers** in this personal overview matched up precisely with those of science. Having just completed a 'whirlwind tour' of the history of science to date, culminating with the latest Theories of Everything, we are now in a position to verify – or otherwise – this compelling and astonishing claim.

To take the abortive theory of Supergravity first, it has precisely seven extra dimensions, normally envisaged to form a 'seven-sphere'. This can be seen to correspond directly to the seven spirits of my cosmology, as in the Bible.

In early string theory, there are twenty-two extra dimensions, and to explain this one needs to observe that each of the three aspects of each of the seven spirits of the Holy Spirit, are equally important. The triangle bounding them is **equilateral**. Hence in total there are twenty-one (3 x 7) 'aspect dimensions' to the whole Tree of Life of the Holy Spirit – if we add in a 'Messianic Spirit' or 'Spirit of Jesus' we obtain the total of 22 fundamental spirits necessary to exactly match string theory.

Finally, in superstring theory, the refined and later form of basic string theory, there are just six extra dimensions of space. These appear to correspond to just the six 'external' branches of the Holy Spirit as in my diagram in section one of this paper.

Just why this is so for superstring theory and not the other major GUT's and TOE's must remain for an interested and sufficiently mathematically informed scientist reading this, to tell me, and I would be very interested in at least a qualitative or geometrical answer. The equations would probably be beyond me, and most people – I for one stopped studying physics in 1979 when I changed to study computer science in my final year at Cambridge. However overall, I find this 'match of the numbers of science and religion' quite amazing!

The last two arguments for my 'Grand Synthesis of Science and Religion' are closely related. The first is pure common-sense. Would we not expect Science, if it really is close to a complete TOE and so the end of physics itself, to come crashing into the worlds of Religion and The Arts at some point? Even though scientists are usually very reluctant to stray into these areas, does not the logical end result of all their endeavours mean that eventually they will have to 'consider the nature of God and things spiritual'?

In the biggest selling book on popular science ever written, 'A brief history of time', Professor Stephen Hawking mentions God and the way he must think many times, but draws no firm conclusions about whether God actually exists. Is this due to his frustration about his own profound disability and confinement to a wheelchair? I have only been present once at one of his talks – this was not on black holes, now recently observed by the Hubble space telescope, so confirming in every detail his life's work on this bizarre subject, which has so contributed to TOE's.

No, he spoke at a conference in my own home town organised by none other than my own Mother, on the subject of the major problems and above all stigma experienced by people in this country and indeed globally, with a physical handicap or mental handicap or illness. He launched a typically vitriolic attack on the Government for doing virtually nothing over their years in Office to help the disabled!

The fourth and final argument in my arsenal follows on directly from the third. If a Theory of Everything lives up to its name – should it not include if not explain notions like love, beauty, poetry, music and all the other great spiritual 'things' we observe around us? The physicists' view of 'Everything' seems to need to be made more global!

Spiritual Energy is extraordinarily high energy i.e. high rest-mass energy. I postulate it is identical to the 'dark matter' currently postulated and sought by physicists and astronomers using the most powerful telescopes.

As we saw in the course of the previous section, the Kaluza-Klein theory in the 1920's predicted a fifth dimension of space of approximately 10^{-34} metres in circumference. I would now like to take this figure as an approximation to the size of **all seven spiritual dimensions** in my own model, as the first assumption I will be using below. The second assumption is that **Spiritual Energy is electromagnetic i.e. obeys Maxwell's Equations.**

Then we can perform the following simple estimates of the very high frequency and so very high mass of Spiritual Energy, using just high school maths: -

1. Wavelength of Spiritual Energy waves $\leq 10^{-34}$ m (TINY!)

2. So frequency of Spiritual Energy wave given by $c=h\nu$ i.e. $\nu \geq c/h$ i.e. frequency $\geq 3 \times 10^{42}$ Hertz

3. So **Spiritual Energy** $E = h\nu \geq 3 \times 10^{42} \times 6.63 \times 10^{-34}$ Joules $\geq$ **2 Gigajoules (= 2 x 10^9 Joules! – absolutely massive!)**

4. So 'Spiritual Rest mass' given by $E=mc^2$ i.e. $m=E/c^2$

5. 'Spiritual Rest Mass of one spiritual photon in one of the seven spiritual dimensions' = $2 \times 10^9 / (3 \times 10^8)^2 \sim 2 \times 10^{-5}$ grams. Absolutely enormous – First Basis of my claim that :
   - Spiritual Energy is a pseudonym for the Dark Matter of Physics

6. There are 11 spiritual and one material dimensions. Hence we would expect with equal distribution of mass between all twelve dimensions, that the 11 spiritual ones contain 91.666…% of the mass. In fact this is very close to estimates of the amount of actual dark matter in the Universe by physicists and astronomers – recently observed between galaxies by astronomers. However Spiritual Energy i.e. dark matter is actually present throughout the Universe – and responsible for the laws of physics being so uniformly applied, as we saw earlier…

SUMMARY AND CONCLUSIONS OF THIS PAPER

1) The mind and spirit occupy seven dimensions, just like, and extending, those of space. US Air Force Research has shown that the mind can contain at most exactly *seven* ideas at one time... Confirmation of my own 'scientific model' – by psychologists...
2) These dimensions can be seen to occupy various 'seven-point tree structure', and 'seven-sphere' – i.e. *cubic* in the Bible! – 'invisible shapes' – everywhere in the whole Universe. These are fully described in Holy Books, both Old and New Testaments.
3) Modern scientific cosmology says its complex mathematics needs *eleven* dimensions, not just the normal *four* of space-time to work at all. Science is mystified about this. That is because science is vainly trying to be 'objective' and exclude the *mind* from its Theories of Everything. Add in the seven dimensions of the *mind* as in (1) and (2) above... Eureka! – the mystery of these 'extra' seven dimensions is instantly totally resolved. Theories of Everything could now embrace Religion and The Arts – and really cover 'Everything'...
4) Science has scoured the Universe with incredibly powerful instruments, mystified why about 90% of the matter (i.e. energy according to relativity theory) it expects from any of a large number of theories – is undetectable 'missing' or 'dark' matter. My own paper describes this as quite the opposite – 'light energy' or 'spiritual energy' – and even explains the 10:1 ratio *precisely*...
5) **Exactly** 91.666...% of the Universe is *Spirit*...
   Computer science to date normally uses just two 'states' in its so-called computer 'brains' i.e. just now, very over-complex *instruments*. These are of course 'yes' and 'no', and sometimes this is extended to the *third* state of "don't care". So, usually two states, sometimes in hardware design especially, three are used. Yet the 'tera-program' of the human genome, currently being heavily researched into – and grossly commercially exploited – uses *FOUR* such states – the four biochemical 'bases'. The questions beg: - What is the fourth state of DNA? Is it to do with the human *consciousness*? My own paper claims, "Yes it is – totally." I claim that it is our *'CARE'* or 'refer to individual soul/personality/consciousness' state...

Scientific Proof that (God The Holy) Spirit Exists

*** Article Five
How (the Holy) Spirit interacts
with the physical world***

1. Of the Tree and Fruits of the Holy Spirit, and the Fountains of the Water of Life, as in Scripture

Overall, I was immensely reassured after I was introduced to the 'fruits of the spirit' described by St. Paul, that although my 'tree of the Holy Spirit' that I had thought up years before, was not described in detail in that way in Scripture, my 'logical deduction of its structure' matched Scripture. I had 'worked it out' in deep **faith**, which had now been completely exonerated by Scripture.

There was as one would expect, no complete simplistic statement that I was 'right' – that relies on both logic and a certain amount of inspiration – but my choice of terms of 'Words of the Spirit' (one might equally call them 'seeds'), was not in any way, contradicted by the Bible. These I could readily visualise being made manifest in an, of necessity, rather diluted form in Human Beings lucky enough to be blessed or even 'anointed by' the Holy Spirit, with these fabulous fruits. We could not take the concentrated original form in this life!

I read too in the first letter of Paul to the Corinthians, verses 12:4 to 12:11, of the various *gifts* of the Spirit. Wisdom and Knowledge, and of course Faith now form the pivotal 'Spirit of Gifts from God' at the base of my 'Tree of Life' in the previous Paper. Many other references to the Holy Spirit in the Bible refer to Her as Living Water, or a Fountain of Living Water, clearly very much shaped like a tree. It is interesting to note that just as the Tree of Life of the Spirit in my previous Paper is totally based on that most rigid and strong of engineering structures, the *triangle*; why! so too is the fountain of water. We now know through scientific knowledge that water molecules are triangular, and water is based on structures of loosely-bonded sheets of these triangles. It is no surprise that rivers, fountains and trees follow in their shape the compelling 1-3-7 tree structure that seems to me to certainly be the most accurate representation possible of the 'spiritual shape' of the Sevenfold Holy Spirit.

2. Octaves, Rainbows, and the pursuit of Enlightenment

In the present section we will be seeing how the spiritual, 'holy' aspects of the Universe are often made of *seven* parts. This might explain why seven is a 'holy number' in many religions.

However, these seven parts always seem to constitute an overall *eighth*, greater than the sum of its seven parts in its oneness and completeness – its perfection. As we will be seeing towards the end of this section, the anti-spirit of Anti-Existence is often seen to parody and imitate this natural 'spectrum' structure, with its own set of seven *evils* or *sins*. The eighth in this 'counter-example' of what I am talking about, is the 'belief in the power of money or materialism, or above all untruth'.

In the meantime, I should like to elaborate a little on the seven-fold nature (embraced by the eighth, the 'perfect whole'), of so many *natural* phenomena, even where these have apparently been invented by mankind. Important examples of these are white light, and no less than three aspects of music – tone, tonal duration, and tempo.

The latter turn out to be explicable in terms of a very mathematical set of structures, arising from musicians' awareness of sounds as *waves*. The pleasing arrangement of these, and the sounds they produce, into music, can be very precisely described in terms of physics and mathematics. (Oriental, African and Aboriginal music are just as based on these natural phenomena, but employ a different tonal system. For the sake of argument, we won't try to discuss those other forms here).

To begin then, let us consider white or 'natural' light. It would probably surprise a child who had never seen a rainbow, to be shown one, and then be asked what the colour is that the seven colours of the rainbow 'add up to'. The answer of 'white' is probably the last one they would think of – as most of the colours in a rainbow are quite dark, they might well answer 'black'.

This then is our first, and a prime natural example of, what I have been saying about the sum of the seven parts of a 'spiritual currency' adding up to a perfect **holistic** whole, which is more than the sum of the seven parts. Of course, it is better to talk about 'our perception' of seven colours adding up to an unexpected colour, 'white' light. (Scientists have recently shown that other creatures 'see' all these colours in very different ways, better suited to their way of life and natural environment).

The way in which the seven colours of light constitute one colour of 'white', is then really rather mysterious! The scientific explanation is rather long-winded, and far removed from our simple perception that a rainbow is **beautiful**!

To turn to music next, let us start with the seven tones (do, re, mi, fa, so, la, te). As any musician will tell you, these seven are incomplete without the **eighth** tone, a further 'do' (which, science tells us, is at precisely **double** the frequency of the initial 'do'). In this way many such 'octaves' are used in music, all joined in series by a doubling in frequency of their "do's".

In practice, the human brain and ear can only appreciate about **eight** such octaves, centred around the note of 'middle C' (with a frequency of 256 Hertz. One Hertz is one beat per second, and 256 is also a power of two). So, tone in music is completely based around octaves, which in turn each correspond to a doubling of frequency. Likewise, and in an even more obvious fashion, tempo and musical periods (tonal duration) also work on a basis of a multiplication or division by powers of two – 2, 4, or 8.

Digital computers also work on the latter basis (normally based on the next higher power of two after eight, which is sixteen, or 'hexadecimal'). As a result, in the last twenty years, it has been relatively easy for computer programmers to introduce 'musical computers', that now dominate at least the modern music scene. On a personal note, I still prefer to hear the skill and flair – despite the inevitable occasional slip – of traditional players of the original musical instruments!

For my third example of 'spiritual currencies' in groups of seven, I vividly recall the early days of evolving the ideas in this paper, in 1978. Initially I was trying to find a basis for a meeting of the *seven* main world faiths, which was as I saw them, and searched for their 'lowest common denominator', which soon I discovered to be the 'Ground of Existence'.

In a similar way, the state of being an Enlightened Person (an 'Arahant'), is often talked of as having *seven* 'planes'. The Buddha, Siddhartha Gautama, described the most 'natural' way to this blissful state of mind as comprising an *eight-fold* path! More on this subject of Enlightenment is to be found in the next section of this paper.

Perhaps I should not be too surprised, with my training in computer science, by the fact that 1, 3 and 7 are 'holy' numbers in many religions; yet 8 is a far easier number than 7 to manipulate or incorporate in drawings. After all, eight is a simple power of two (2x2x2), whereas seven is both odd and prime.

In the previous Paper, the three numbers 1, 3, and 7 correspond to the three levels of the tree structure that I drew of 'God the Spirit' or 'The Holy Spirit'. The 'One-ness' of this natural 'essence', prevalent throughout the Universe (according to Christian belief), seems to arise, yet again, as an eighth, a perfect whole that transcends the sum of its components.

The power of 'Anti-Existence' or 'Satan' seems to have parodied this spiritual, 'holy' notion of an overall 'eighth with seven parts', in the form of the 'seven deadly sins'. In the case of these seven, the eighth is an obsession with, and belief in the power of, *matter* – materialism, and possibly being a 'money junkie'. In the case of instances of this particular 7/8 combination, they are totally self-destructive in nature.

An excess of one or more of the seven causes a strong desire for more of the eighth, which in turns increases the power of the seven in a person's life. This 'vicious circle' is addictive, obsessive, and very hard to break – and usually leads to calamity. Hence, as Jesus said:

> 'A man cannot serve both God and mammon; for he will always love the one and hate the other'.

3. Enlightenment and Conversion

There is at first glance a great deal of difference between Western and Eastern Religions. The major faiths of the Western World, Judaism, Christianity and Islam, all place great emphasis on the interaction of the individual with a very personal 'Lord God'. In the case of Christianity, this interaction is seen as also taking place with two other Persons, of the Messiah (Jesus), and of the Holy Ghost. The great traditions in the Eastern World, of Buddhism in many parts of the Far East,

Hinduism in India, and Taoism in China, are by contrast mostly philosophical rather than emphasising a 'personal God'.

However, this philosophical emphasis, which operates at the 'official core', as it were, of each of the three, often seems to the Western eye to 'break down', with Hindus and Taoists worshipping a multiplicity of Gods. The Hindu religion also contains the mythology of the 'demi-gods' Krishna and Arjuna, and various other sons and daughters of 'Brahman'. (Brahman is the Hindu equivalent of 'the Most High', 'the Lord God' or 'Allah' in Western tradition. He is the only God that the priests, or Brahmins, of Hinduism officially recognise or advocate worship of). Ordinary Buddhists too, worship shrines, 'holy places', and statues of the Buddha, in a way very different to the basic precepts of Buddhism (as taught by the Buddha).

Yet is there any real difference here between East and West? The Catholic Church, for instance, often regarded as the 'original' Christian Church, tolerates the kissing of statues of Saints, even though the Bible frequently expresses God's abhorrence at similar practices in biblical times. So there often appears to be a 'double life' between principles and practice in both Eastern and Western religion. The only reference point for resolving such issues is the Holy Book or Holy Books of these religions, or to an inherently less trustworthy, nor as repeatable extent, truly reliable interpretation.

I will be returning to this subject in due course, but will leave it there for now. The real purpose of this section is to explore how adherents of the two broad classes of 'Eastern' and 'Western' religions come to be accepted into their faiths, which to over-simplify I will be calling 'Enlightenment' and 'Conversion' respectively.

The only 'unifying principle' I will apply at this point is that this acceptance is not at all affected by being born into any particular Religion, either of East or West. I will be taking a somewhat purist approach, and looking at how someone in the West becomes a true 'Man of Faith' rather than just claiming this by some obscure 'right of birth. Similarly, how someone in the East fully comes to terms with the true meaning of the philosophical system they were born into and have since chosen to adhere to, and becomes 'Enlightened'.

The purpose of the present section is to explore the similarities and differences between the approaches in the East and West to these two. I re-introduce below from the previous

Paper, my picture or diagram of the Seven Spirits of the Holy Spirit, which I will be using as a 'model' in this section, and much of the rest of this paper. In the current section, only the *shape* of the 'Tree of Seven Spirits' is shown, with the Original Paradox being given its Eastern name of the 'Ground of Existence':

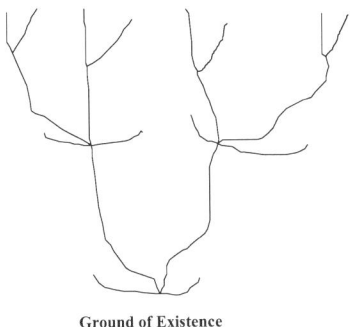

Ground of Existence

To take the rather easier, and probably more familiar concept of Christian Conversion first, this can probably best be conveniently summarised as, in a nutshell:

'Passing a threshold of knowing and trusting the Lord (or Jesus), sufficiently to want to go on getting to know, trusting and serving Him, and increasingly emulating Him, better and better for the rest of your life'.

Most Buddhists and Hindus, to again take the two philosophies or religions from the East that I am most familiar with, normally regard Enlightenment as a breakthrough onto a sort of 'Plateau of Wisdom'. Here you are totally familiar and at home with the 'dharmakaya' (the word is the same in both religions), of the Buddha in Buddhism, and Brahman in Hinduism.

At first sight the 'Worship of the Person of God (or Jesus)', and 'supreme knowledge of dharmakaya' (a principle), seem worlds apart. This, combined with the geographical separation of Eastern and Western religions, seems to have been a great hindrance to dialogue between them in the past. However, once Christians adopt the somewhat unfamiliar notion of the 'Ground of Existence', as explored in the previous paper, the phrase 'Word of God' as St John's term for it should provide the means of a breakthrough. It does indeed!

In the first chapter of his gospel, John, in any translation of the Bible, is saying that Jesus was the 'Ground of Existence' (or 'Word of God'), **In Person**. In a similar way the Buddha was an incarnation of dharmakaya, so they are Western and Eastern incarnations, respectively, of the same Principle. Both religions regard their founding figures as immortal.

4. The relationships between the Ground of Existence, the Holy Spirit, Time, Space, matter and Life.

The Bible's diverse comments on the Holy Spirit mostly appear in the Gospels and the Book of Revelation; the latter is where I made the crucial discovery that there were *seven spirits* 'within' the Holy Spirit. I then pieced together these different comments, using mostly common-sense (my observations of the Holy Spirit in everyday life) to complete the picture. As I hinted in section one of this paper, GOD completes the tree by being an 'Eighth who encapsulates and cements the Seven Spirits'.

Science does not usually concern itself with the Holy Spirit or the Ground of Existence, leaving that realm to theologians. However, in the previous Paper we have seen how physicists will almost certainly have to address this issue, if science as a whole wants to make further progress.

A 'second level' is the rather more familiar Space. It is impossible to overestimate the importance of the interaction between the fabric of space-time, and the support provided to it throughout the Universe by the Holy Spirit, and above all the Ground of Existence. How does one imagine a 'curvature of space-time', as proposed necessary by Relativity, without a 'background' against which such curvature can take place and exist?

We saw above how God plays a 'unifying' rôle around the Holy Spirit and the Ground of Existence. God is by definition ever-present everywhere in the Universe, in an 'omnipresent way' at the first two levels of this Cosmology. All the vast reaches of space are supported everywhere, all the time, by the Holy Spirit which is based on the Original Paradox, the Ground of Existence. God acts as the 'totality' of both, the 'holistic whole' (which is greater than the sum of its constituent parts taken separately).

The final Level is the most familiar one, of matter, and food chains of creatures contained in the cycle of life and death. Here scientists are happiest; although by far the greatest emphasis of all religions is on *Life* (especially mankind), they don't worry nearly so much about the nature of matter as the sciences do. Here, in the topmost Level, God's rôle is that of the Life of 'life and death', and the Determiner of their Cycle. So God is the 'Totality' of *each* of the Three Levels, a *Three-in-One Totality*.

5. How do the Laws of Physics come to actually be *applied?*

Physicists, as well as usually avoiding what they regard as 'theological' issues, also generally avoid the issue of just *why* the Laws of Physics come to be applied the same way at every point in the known Universe, which is left to philosophers. The rôle of physicists, they say, is to aim for a complete mathematical, theoretical description of *how* the laws of physics are applied. You have already seen many examples of how I dislike such 'guarding of territories', and often cross between them! In this section I will be looking at the very question of just why the laws of physics come to be applied so uniformly everywhere, all the time.

Furthermore, in my two chosen examples of two physical Principles, I will be suggesting a deeper reason for their existence than physics provides, yet that can be expressed In everyday language rather than that of higher mathematics.

The first of these two examples, which both emanate from Quantum Theory, is *Heisenberg's Uncertainty Principle*. If I first give the outline of the mathematical statement of this once revolutionary Principle, then interpret it in terms of the 'model' developed in this paper, you should see what I mean.

In taking a measurement of anything, there are always practical limits to the accuracy of the measurement. However precise your measuring device, there is always a limit to the number of digits in a given reading that can be trusted. The Uncertainty Principle says a number of profound things. Firstly physical properties in the Universe usually come in pairs, and if you try to measure these two complementary opposite properties (for instance, pairs of opposing forces or momentum and size) of the same object or wave, and so on, *simultaneously*, a curious thing happens. If you find one measurement is highly accurate, the other is in turn made less accurate, in inverse proportion of 'errors of measurement'. The accuracy of both measurements has to be extremely high for this to become obvious, yet it has been verified countless times by physicists.

The second main theme that Heisenberg's Principle presents, is really a consequence of the first, and constitutes how it is normally interpreted. This is that any 'experiment' is affected by the presence of the 'observer', the person or persons conducting that experiment. Hence the Universe is no longer seen as objective!

However physicists apparently make no use of any concept of the 'holding up by' the Holy Spirit of the rest of the Universe, and how She – or they – interacts with the Universe. The answer provided by my 'model' is exquisitely simple.

The Original Paradoxes of the Ground of Existence and the Holy Spirit serve to separate all opposites; and stand outside the passage of *elapsed* time itself, Chronos, but continually interacting with 'time in motion' or Kairos – that of the Lord God! - continually supporting the fabric of the Universe and Space itself, everywhere, *intelligently.* It is this 'effortless action' that provides a simple basis for understanding both main interpretations of the Uncertainty Principle, with pairs of measurements being connected in this way, and the Observer/Observed Experiment pair.

That is, if one 'pokes the Universe' too hard, the intelligence of the Holy Spirit will respond! The purpose of this is to prevent anybody, except God alone, from being able to predict anything completely, i.e. to know the future!

There is another reason why the Ground of Existence opposes the 'Anti-Dimension' through the Uncertainty Principle. If any creature ever did succeed in measuring one of a complementary pair of quantities (as paired by physics) to an infinite degree, the other would become infinitely 'smeared', and the fundamental 'symmetry' of the two complementary qualities would break down.

Such a state of affairs has been exhaustively explored by Professor Stephen Hawking in his theories of 'black holes'. In a 'black hole', certain properties of matter are so incredibly tightly constrained or fixed, that others 'blow up'. Such a state of affairs would represent a 'local victory' for the 'Anti-

Dimension', and its creation of a local 'anti-sphere of influence'. Reassuringly perhaps, Professor Hawking's equations indicate that all such black holes would eventually 'explode'.

The second Principle we discuss in this section is again from Quantum Mechanics, and is the *Pauli Exclusion Principle*. At the level of sub-atomic 'particles' (sometimes known, because of the 'wave-particle duality', as 'wavicles', and more recently, as 'strings'), matter can surprisingly be categorised by just a handful of quantised quantities.

'Quantised' means 'comes in one of a discrete set of levels, rather than on a smooth scale'.

Not surprisingly, at this minute scale, these properties are very different to the 'large-scale', everyday behaviour of matter. Such properties include a unique discrete 'energy level', and angular momentum (similar to everyday angular momentum of rotation, but simultaneously quantised, and 'smeared' by the effect of the Uncertainty Principle). Another property is 'spin', related to angular momentum, but very different to the everyday notion of spin (for an excellent description of spin, refer to Professor Hawking's 'A brief history of time').

The Exclusion Principle is very simple, like the Uncertainty Principle. It says that no two particles in a 'local region', like the electrons 'orbiting' the nucleus of an atom, can ever both have the same set of values of this handful of quantum properties. It is similar to the unwritten principle of biology that no two creatures, even of the same family, are ever exactly identical (even identical twins have different fingerprints).

In the terms of my 'Model', this seems to imply a Principle of the Ground of Existence that could be called a 'Uniqueness Principle'. Its Purpose can be summarised by the saying, 'variety is the spice of life'. It serves to ensure that,

The Uniqueness Principle

'Even when only by virtue of their separation in space and time, particles, atoms, molecules and above all living creatures (and even the creations of mankind, such as machines), are all *always uniquely identifiable by God*'.

The opposing Principle of the 'Anti-Dimension' forever tries to create 'clones' of the same creature or entity. Yet God abhors clones!

6. Principles of the Reality Of Everything Spiritual – as well as just Material (**PROESM**)

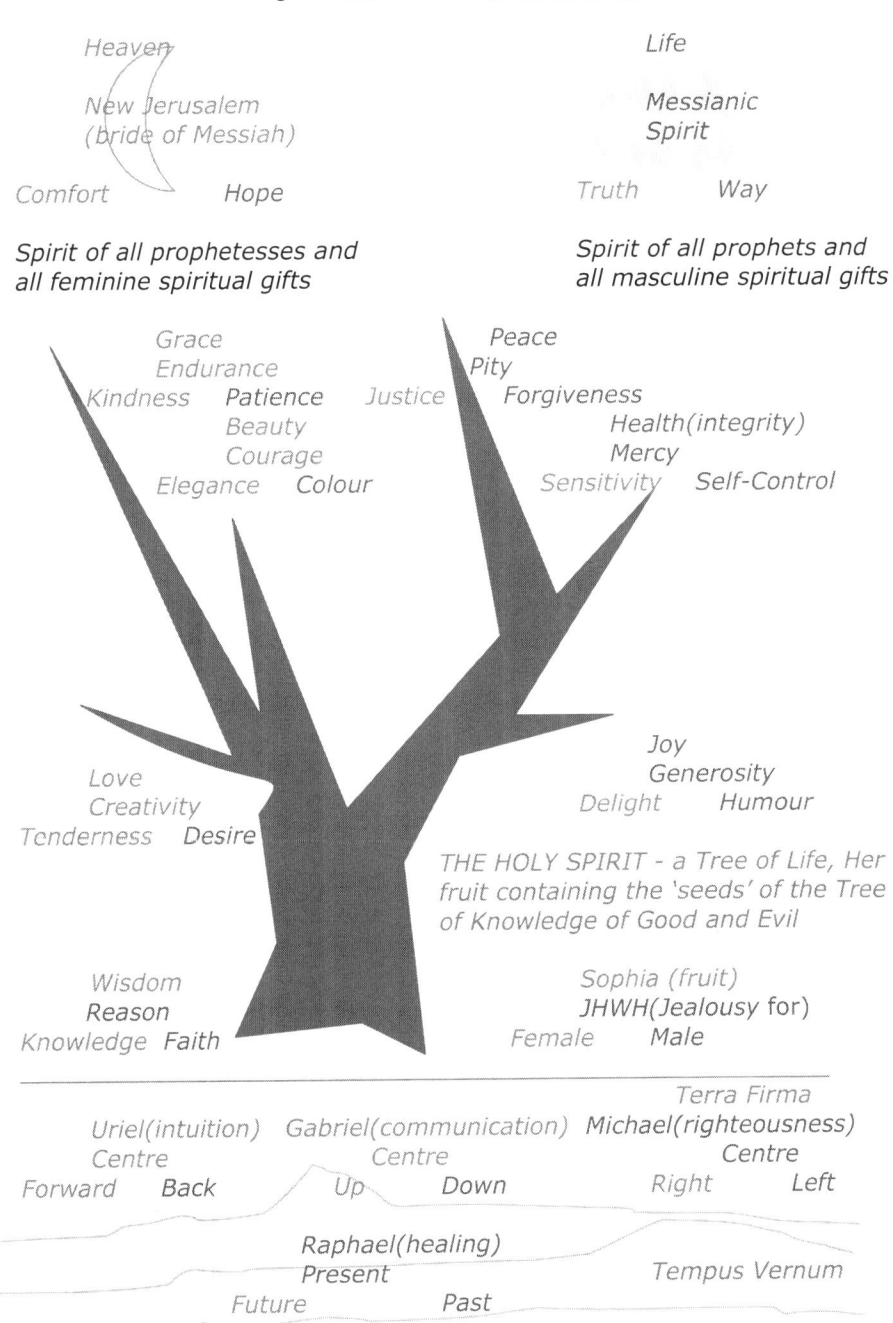

Heaven　　　　　　　　　　　　*Life*

New Jerusalem　　　　　　　　*Messianic*
(bride of Messiah)　　　　　　*Spirit*

Comfort　　　*Hope*　　　　　*Truth*　　*Way*

Spirit of all prophetesses and　　　Spirit of all prophets and
all feminine spiritual gifts　　　　all masculine spiritual gifts

　　Grace　　　　　　　*Peace*
　　Endurance　　　　　*Pity*
Kindness　*Patience*　*Justice*　*Forgiveness*
　　Beauty　　　　　　　*Health(integrity)*
　　Courage　　　　　　*Mercy*
　Elegance　*Colour*　*Sensitivity*　*Self-Control*

　　　　　　　　　　　　　　　Joy
Love　　　　　　　　　　　　　*Generosity*
Creativity　　　　　　　　*Delight*　*Humour*
Tenderness　*Desire*

　　　　　　　　　　　THE HOLY SPIRIT - a Tree of Life, Her
　　　　　　　　　　　fruit containing the 'seeds' of the Tree
　　　　　　　　　　　of Knowledge of Good and Evil

Wisdom　　　　　　　　*Sophia (fruit)*
Reason　　　　　　　　*JHWH(Jealousy* for)
Knowledge　*Faith*　　*Female*　*Male*

　　　　　　　　　　　　　　　Terra Firma
Uriel(intuition)　*Gabriel(communication)*　*Michael(righteousness)*
Centre　　　　　*Centre*　　　　　　　　*Centre*
Forward　*Back*　*Up*　*Down*　　　*Right*　*Left*

　　　　　Raphael(healing)
　　　　　Present　　　　　*Tempus Vernum*
　　Future　　　*Past*

109

The incredibly powerfully symmetrical, hence very strong, *cosmic egg structure* containing all the groups of four heavily *sexual* Fundamental Spiritual Qualities in my Summary Diagram above is crucial to what follows. I give below a short summary of this structure, as the very 'key' to all 'Spiritual Energies'. First an interpretative diagram: -

COSMIC EGG or 'SPIRITRON' - Male or Female

Nature or Holistic 'Quality' of the given Cosmic Egg or 'fruit' – Sexual bias of Quality as that of the Central Cosmic Sperm. Nature determined by the combined Natures of the Proposer and the Surrender – and is the 'dialectic' or Quality of their Flow.

'Climax' or 'Surrender'   'Initiator' or 'Proposer'
always FEMALE   always MALE

We return to the above diagram again and again in this paper. Suffice it to say it took me all of 22 years to 1999 to work out the basis of the very simplistic structure of the female 'Spiritual Cosmic Egg' above. I now have as never before a very clear picture why women are three times *exactly* as complex as us mere men! Then just two years to 2001 when I wrote this piece to realise that the overall picture was simply chicken and egg. The 'masculine sperm or nucleus' took just $1/11^{th}$ as long to investigate.

Finally in this section I now add, with 'a bit of a flourish', the only two main types of world faith, both ancient, which I have deliberately left off so far for the sake of simplicity of my 'master diagram'. Once you turn the page onto the following sections of this hopefully fascinating as well as terse but comprehensive paper, you may well start to think 'yes, there really is something to this eccentric development of ideas'. We start this transformation of the foot of my diagram by repeating it unchanged: -

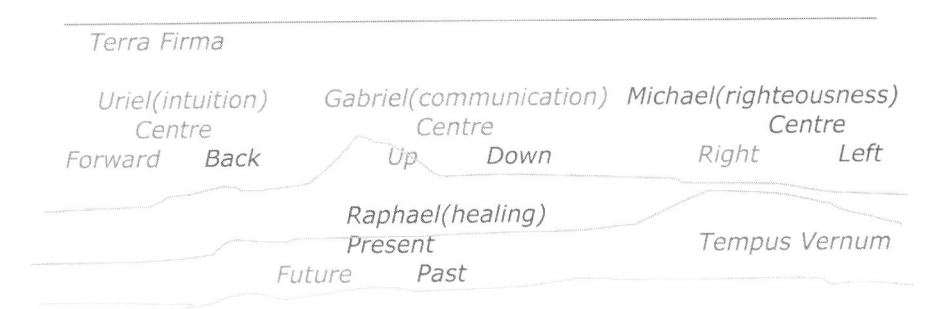

```
Terra Firma

Uriel(intuition)      Gabriel(communication)   Michael(righteousness)
    Centre                  Centre                    Centre
Forward    Back         Up        Down            Right     Left

                      Raphael(healing)
                          Present                Tempus Vernum
                      Future    Past
```

Note that for deliberate reasons, I have shown the four 'qualities' of space and time with names of the only – and *corresponding* – Angels actually named anywhere in the – exclusively *Western* – Bible! Michael and Gabriel are probably both familiar names of Archangels. Gabriel is really *female*!

Their counterparts Raphael and *female* Uriel only appear in the *'apocryphal'*, 'central' books in complete e.g. Roman Catholic bibles. We now see that these have precise equivalences to whole *Faiths* in the Far East, even to the fine detail of the symbols usually identified with these four Faiths or Philosophies. These, finally, perhaps astonishingly, correspond to the four great 'opposites' of both the ancient East and West, fire, air, earth and water: -

```
Terra Firma

Hinduism (intuition)  Buddhism(communication)  Confucianism(morality)
    - Fire -                - Air -                  - Earth -
    Centre                  Centre                    Centre
Forward    Back         Up        Down            Right     Left

                      Taoism(healing)
                         - Water -
                          Present                Tempus Vernum
                      Future    Past
```

Finally, all we have to do is conjure up a way to include the faiths of human sacrificing, pyramid-building agriculturists like the Pharaohs/Aztecs, as well as the aboriginal 'hunter/gatherers'. By a mysterious process, this ends any confusion you may still have, over whether there are a total of

54 or 56 'Fundamental Spiritual Qualities' - in the final picture about to emerge. In the diagram below, the baffling three centres are each shared by *three faiths* - so the above two totals need to grow – delightfully in my view to a DEFINITIVE **SIXTY-FOUR** such Qualities.

'Delightful' as 64 is 2x2x2x2x2x2 – simplicity!

```
                    Agriculture(e.g. Abel)
                        Sacrifice
        First-rate engineering   Irrigation
       (using TRIANGLES hence
         pyramid-building!)

   Terra Firma

 Hinduism (intuition)  Buddhism(communication)  Confucianism(morality)
     - Fire -              - Air -                  - Earth -
      Centre                Centre                   Centre
 Forward    Back         Up      Down           Right     Left

                     Taoism(healing)
                        - Water -
                         Present                  Tempus Vernum
                   Future    Past

                    Nomadism(e.g. Cain)
                      Nature-worship
              Food Gathering    Hunting
```

7. The very structure of 'QUARKS'

In 1994 I gave myself a thorough refresher course in *Christianity.* At one particular crisis breaking point on 16th March 1994 I prayed for and instantly knew I had indeed been given the Baptism of the Holy Spirit. This climax to becoming a full Christian - even though I have since rarely felt the need to attend Church - has resulted in: -
- a fluent 'Middle Eastern, rather flowery' Gift of Tongues
- a full Gift of Healing by Laying on of Hands
- to add to my existing Gifts of Words of Faith, Words of Knowledge, and Prophecy – through premonitions supplied by 'Jungian dreams'!

To summarise the Bible itself on the 'Start of all Things' –

"In the beginning was God and Spirit"
paraphrase of Genesis I:1-2, opening the Old Testament
"In the beginning was God and the Word"
paraphrase of John I:1, in the New Testament

Simple, obvious conclusions: -

'ALL LANGUAGE IS MADE OF PURE SPIRIT '
"THOUGHT IS COMPOSED OF WORDS i.e. SPIRIT"

The quark's structure is that of the 'cosmic egg'... This explains all quark properties as being of **SPIRIT!** Indeed the two diagrams overleaf represent a crucial section of this whole paper, being my own attempt to rationalise the proposition of the latest 'string theories' (there are five of them, currently being knitted by eminent physicists into one overall 'M-theory' or 'Mother theory') that there are in fact quite a few 'unseen' dimensions of space and time! My first diagram overleaf illustrates my claim that these 'unseen' dimensions are in fact *spiritual – six of them, making up the 'branches' of an overall encapsulating seventh 'Spirit of Wisdom'.* That makes a total of seven spiritual + three of space + and one of time dimensions – not including matter. The latter one dimension comes dramatically into the second parallel diagram overleaf. Having postulated that there are in fact seven extra *'spiritual'* dimensions to space and time; which are constrained by space and time *within space and time so entirely 'rolled up inside them' just as string theory says*; my second diagram completes the overall picture trying to justify the claims of string theorists of multiple dimensions. It shows how the same four 'poles' – the eight paired 'gluons' of quark theory – of space and time – constrain the 'strings' that make up the six types of 'quark' postulated to make up all fundamental particles. In an analogous way to the 'six spirits' of the first diagram, below; which I find very exciting!

I. A spiritual model of 'the Universe when very small' - eleven dimensions of the total of twelve - not containing matter, only spiritual energy as throughout this paper

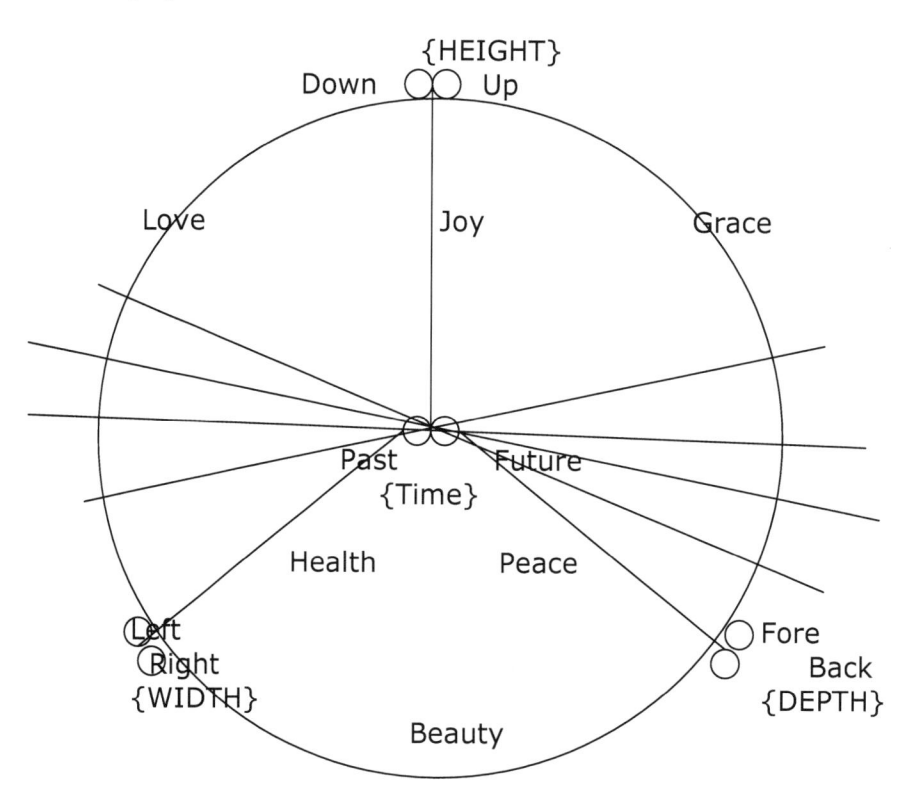

{HEIGHT}
Down Up

Love   Joy   Grace

Past Future
{Time}

Health   Peace

Left
Right   Fore
{WIDTH}   Back
                         {DEPTH}

Beauty

All of the ELEVEN spiritual dimensions are at right angles to each other and under minute and massive tension from their light and gravity waves. Approximately 10^{39} tonnes, according to 'Theories of Everything'!
1. This structure can be seen to be composed of three 'curved' equal-sided ('equilateral') triangles – fitting perfectly with current theories of quarks – that it takes THREE taken together to form one fundamental particle.
2. We see that the Universe is really twelve-dimensional. With one material dimension and all of eleven spiritual dimensions. That is:- 11/12 = 91 2/3 % = 91.666 666 ... % comprising spiritual energy i.e. DARK MATTER!
4. These 11 dimensions contain God's mind, i.e. the long sought-after cosmic consciousness (a living 'computer' inside each and every particle): -
  - The force of nature
  - The laws of science - imposed from inside each particle
  - The Holy Spirit
  - The triple membrane of space - and the 'spring of time'.
  - Which are all tantamount to the same eleven-fold Set of Spiritual Energies. These fill the whole Universe - making us all; and everything material – 'Figments of God's Reality'!

II. A postulated model of fundamental particle STRUCTURE intended to provide a coherent basis for the 'quark theory' based on the spiritual model of 'the Universe in the tiny / dark matter' on the previous page

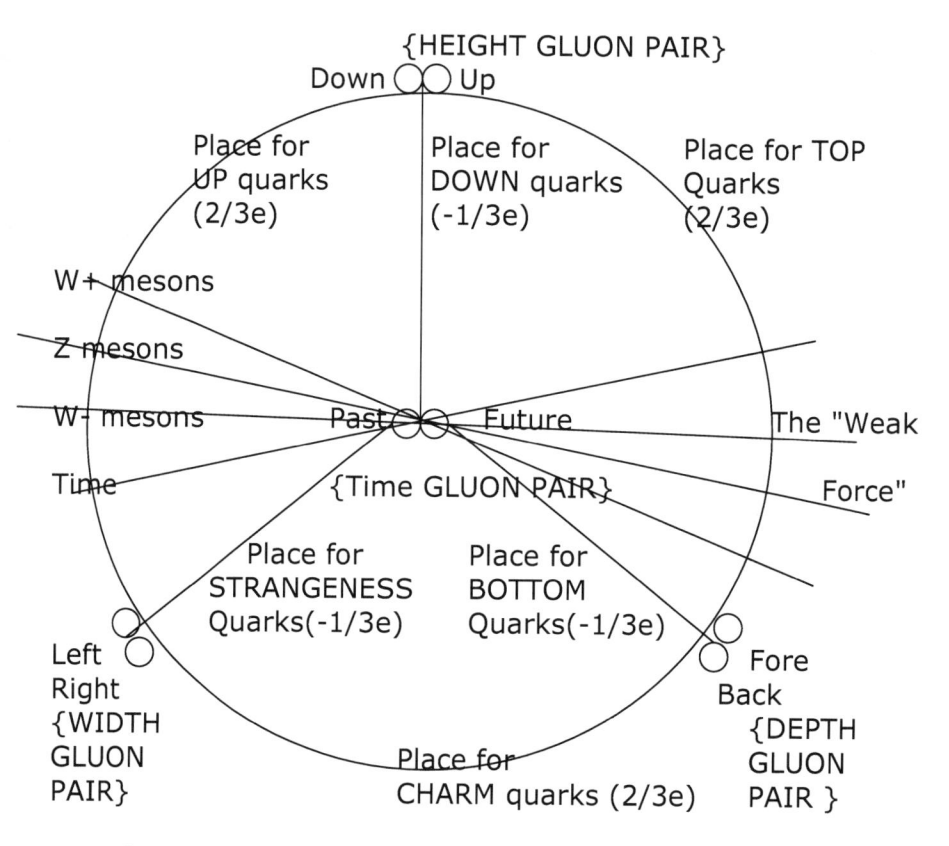

```
                    {HEIGHT GLUON PAIR}
               Down ⊙⊙ Up
         Place for        Place for          Place for TOP
         UP quarks        DOWN quarks        Quarks
         (2/3e)           (-1/3e)            (2/3e)

   W+ mesons
   Z mesons
   W- mesons         Past ⊙⊙ Future         The "Weak
   Time              {Time GLUON PAIR}       Force"

         Place for        Place for
         STRANGENESS      BOTTOM
         Quarks(-1/3e)    Quarks(-1/3e)
   Left ⊙                                    ⊙ Fore
   Right                                       Back
   {WIDTH                                     {DEPTH
   GLUON              Place for                GLUON
   PAIR}              CHARM quarks (2/3e)      PAIR }
```

On the previous page I proposed that 'dark matter' of physics today is comprised of something very familiar from the very apparently different world of FAITH – <u>Spirit (-ual Energy in seven/eleven dimensions)</u> or in particular, the HOLY SPIRIT. The problems are still vast, of what dark matter is, what goes to make it up, and how much of it there is in the Universe (in order to explain the properties of the Universe as observed by scientists' thousands of telescopes and predicted by their many very sophisticated theories). So my views expressed here are just as valid, and possibly may turn out to be more or less so, than any of the multitude of other theories floating around the scientific world at present.

A good place to look for the latest information on dark matter and the particles supposed to make it up (the 'quarks, gluons, etc' of the above diagram) is the Internet. However, be warned, when I did a search for 'dark matter' on the 'Google' search engine it returned nearly one and a half MILLION web-sites with information. Luckily after a few looks at the earlier of these in the search, I found the web-site of the University of California Riverside, and two FAQ pages there, delightfully under two pages A4 each, yet adequately summarising the world of dark matter - and 'the particle zoo': -
http://math.ucr.edu/home/baez/physics/Relativity/GR/dark_matter.html
http://math.ucr.edu/home/baez/physics/ParticleAndNuclear/particle_zoo.html

The Particle Data Book, one of the main reference books of modern physics, lists an initially intimidating 150+ different particles. Fortunately, the now largely fully accepted 'quark model' greatly simplified this forest in the 1960's, even though individual quarks are too tightly 'bound' to each other by vast forces ('other smaller particles') to be observed separately. The quark model proposes that all particles are composed of a far smaller range of three 'generations' of two quarks each, plus two other types of particle per generation, i.e. twelve basic particles including six types of quark, each with a corresponding antiparticle. Radiation 'particles' with no matter in them form a second fundamental group of 'most fundamental particles', called 'gauge bosons': -

FUNDAMENTAL PARTICLES OF MATTER

Charge
-1	electron	muon	tauon
0	electron neutrino nu(e)	mu neutrino nu(mu)	tau neutrino nu(tau)
-1/3	down quark	strange quark	bottom quark
2/3	up quark	charm quark	top quark

GAUGE BOSONS

Charge		Force
0	photon	electromagnetism
0	gluons (8 of them)	strong force
+-1	W+ and W-	weak force
0	Z	weak force

This 'quark' model of particles as related to my two earlier diagrams

1. The core feature of each diagram is the correlation of the four dimensions of the space time continuum, taken in pairs of extremes of height, width, depth and time, to the eight gluons, taken in four pairs bound together. As far as I know, this proposal that gluons work in tightly-bound pairs (held by enormous forces) and that they correspond directly to the four dimensions of space and time, is wholly new. It is a very good way, as I see it to explain how the quarks and spiritual energies that they can contain at their core as hidden 'dark matter', can be bound together by the gluons so strongly - for these comprise the very fabric or membrane of the space-time continuum! The gluons then, serve as rigid 'poles' for standing waves made up of energy flowing between them - of vast energy.

2. Quarks come in three 'generations' shown across the table above. Up and down quarks, electrons and electron neutrinos make up everyday matter; the second and third generations are more 'exotic' and increasingly so, and more massive. Likewise, 'joy and love' as spirits are very familiar, almost commonplace to us, with the media constantly blasting them out. 'Health and beauty', the equivalent in the spiritual world to second generation quarks, are much harder to attain; and the 'third generation' of Peace and Grace is virtually unheard of, increasingly so. No wonder Christians

say that Jesus had to die on the Cross in great suffering to introduce these two to the world as concepts; and that because He was the Son of God and therefore totally pure, and so innocent of his 'crime', that God was able by the Rules of Good and Evil at War to resurrect Him!

3. The **sign** of the 'charge' of quarks in the second diagram corresponds directly to the **sexual gender** of the corresponding spiritual energy as in the first diagram and others in this paper. The **magnitude of the charge of 'feminine' quarks in this view** is simply due to the fact that they are twice as far from the central axis as their male (negative charge) counterparts. Twice as complex, being female?

4. Each quark's antiparticle can be seen to arise if its 'direction' between the two gluons holding it in as a wave/particle is **reversed** and the **antiparticle** comes about. This can also be seen to happen if any two of the outermost 'spatial' gluon pairs are swapped in position as a 'pair of pairs'.

5. To carry on the parallels between physics and faith, is the 'weak force' actually equivalent to 'the Godhead'?

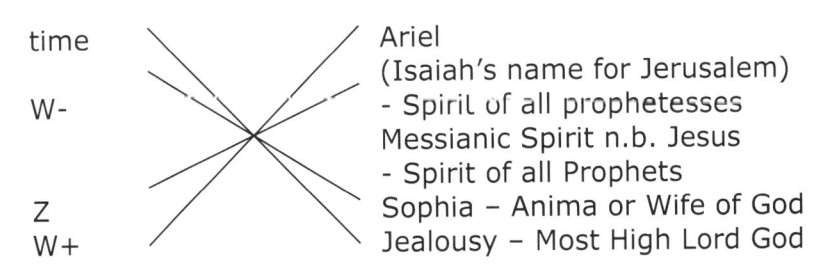

```
time                    Ariel
                        (Isaiah's name for Jerusalem)
W-                      - Spirit of all prophetesses
                        Messianic Spirit n.b. Jesus
                        - Spirit of all Prophets
Z                       Sophia – Anima or Wife of God
W+                      Jealousy – Most High Lord God
```

"What!" I hear a billion, especially Western, religious fanatics cry! "He's gone and blasphemed - and called 'our' God '*JEALOUS*'! *We know* His Name is Allah, JHWH, or Jehovah, Yahweh, etc., etc.!"

I quote the Bible in my absolute defence: -

> "For you shall worship no other God, because the LORD, *whose Name is Jealous,* is a jealous God"
>
> Exodus 34:14
> The Old Testament

6. I suggest strongly that there was originally just ONE 'QUARK' in the Big Bang – the FATHER 'QUARK' – which divided to produce the WORD and the LAW. This HOLY TRINITY then divided further to produce the whole evolution of the Universe to date – 'assisted evolution' that is! The cosmos is an energy dance of quadrillions and zillions of such quarks, each one containing a unique set of spiritual energy LANGUAGES.

7. The lines and arcs of circles in each diagram each correspond to 'strings' as in 'string theories' - and demonstrate a way in which the Universe is TWELVE-dimensional - a fact needed in any theory of everything to explain all **four** forces of nature; weak, strong, gravity & electromagnetism.

8. The 'cosmic egg pattern' explains *why* not just *how* *waves* work

There are (at least) *three* basic types of wave motion described by physics, with very different mathematical bases for *how* they arise: -
1. 'Everyday' waves like sound, and water waves like ripples and ocean waves. These all involve an *interchange of energy with matter, the energy alternating between 'potential' and 'kinetic' energy.*
2. Waves that can exist without any matter e.g. light, which can travel through a vacuum.
3. Waves due to the quantum mechanical notion of particles of matter having a 'wave particle duality' – covered more in the next section.

It is not the purpose of a purely *qualitative* paper like this, to offer any solution to the problem of any 'grand unification' of the mathematics of these – all very different types of wave – a target of physicists for decades! Rather, instead of trying to present a set of mathematical symbols trying in any way to unify physical descriptions of these three basic types of wave, I will be taking a totally qualitative – indeed, spiritual – view! However, by doing so, I *will* be offering a valid *reason* why waves are so fundamental in nature.

To quote from earlier in this part of the paper: -

"A physical dimension (like mass, length or time) is precisely equivalent to a 'fundamental spirit' "

So, rather than delve into the – essentially mathematical and symbolic – nature of *physical* waves, we instead look now at how the 'cosmic egg structure' throughout this paper, describes two 'spiritual waves', Joy and Love:

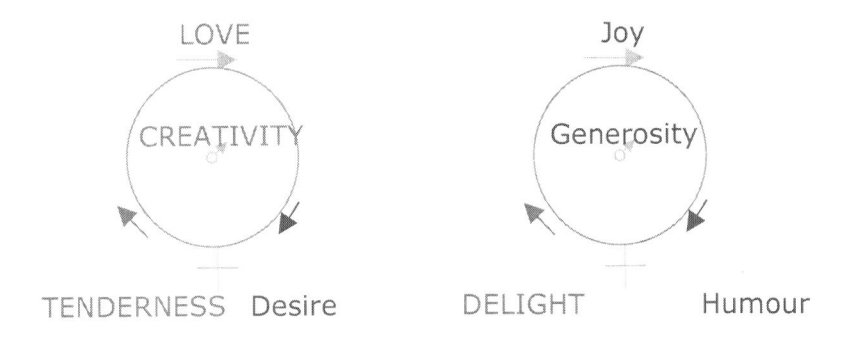

```
        LOVE                           Joy
      ─────▶                         ─────▶
     ╱       ╲                      ╱       ╲
    │CREATIVITY│                   │Generosity│
     ╲       ╱                      ╲       ╱
      ◀──   ◀──                      ◀──   ◀──

 TENDERNESS  Desire              DELIGHT    Humour
```

The four components of each 'egg' can be summarised as follows: -

Female-biased 'process'	*Male-biased 'urge'*	*male source*	*female climax*
Love	Creativity	Desire	Tenderness
Joy	Generosity	Humour	Delight

Summarising these, again in words, rather than any awkward mathematics:

"The urge to be *generous* - in Spirit - causes *Joy* i.e. *Humour* causing *Delight*".

"The urge for *creativity* leads to *Love* – i.e. the *Desire* for *Tenderness*'.

We can clearly see from the diagrams above, how the essentially *circular or cyclical* nature of waves has a 'spiritual' basis – in these and *all* 'cosmic eggs' as in this paper. Start propelling the circular ('feminine') 'shell' around – and along - the central ('male-biased') axis or nucleus, and the familiar 'sine-wave' or basic 'simple harmonic motion' of a wave as in a spring or pendulum, immediately emerges.

Yet I have claimed throughout this paper, that such 'spiritual cosmic eggs' have a distinct 'echo' as the basis of many physical phenomena. Here if we translate this spiritual concept from the seven 'spiritual dimensions' within quarks, to the four of space-time, with the final twelfth dimension of matter also being involved in the first type of *physical* wave discussed at the start of this section, a very *reason for waves emerges!*

Finally, let us turn to deal with a common feature of modern attempts to divine a 'fundamental basis for many aspects of reality' as discussed here. Namely that many aspects of nature (details of God's Creation?) follow a *spiral* pattern. This can readily be explained if the energy of the 'central urge' as above, and other 'dimensions' (spiritual and physical) tends to *grow, fuelling the wave involved.* More of this in later sections...

9. Just *why* atoms with their nucleus and orbiting electrons exist in that 'spiral-shaped' way

Firstly, an obvious remark, to any physicist or chemist reading this. The shape of the 'cosmic egg structure' of this paper is *identical* to that of the simplest atom, or structure of negatively-charged electron(s) circling a positively-charged nucleus made of positive protons and neutral neutrons, i.e. the *hydrogen atom:* -

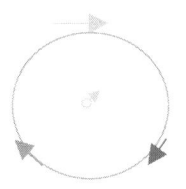

More generally, for increasingly complex types of atom, according to 'traditional' quantum mechanical models of atoms, the orbiting electrons are best represented as 'charge fields' which describe the 'chance or probability of finding an actual electron at a particular place at a particular time'.

Previous work has shown that such discussion is anathema to me! Rather I see each electron orbiting a nucleus in any atom as above, as *uniquely* subject to its own individual 'copy of the laws of physics' within its share of 11 spiritual 'dimensions' inside its material shell. Hence, all the probability and statistics of quantum-mechanical descriptions of atoms – and the fundamental particles they contain – could be *eliminated* if the *deterministic model* I proposed in section 2, of the even more basic and fundamental 'quarks', proves correct – or something very similar...

10. The 'cosmic egg pattern' explains the hot core, mantle, and shape and rotation of: - *Planets, Moons, Stars, Solar Systems, and whole Galaxies*

I now skip out completely a vast 'level of complexity' or area of science – chemistry, largely the studies of how atoms of different sorts combine together or react. We move on to larger, more 'singular' rather than 'plural or molecular' objects – astronomical ones.

Firstly, let us consider that the basis of planets, moons and stars is *all of* a 'hot', 'masculine' core within a 'cool', 'feminine' mantle or outer shell, rather like in atoms, which are far smaller. Also based on the 'cosmic egg':

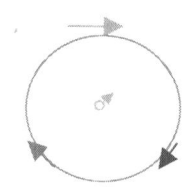

Is the rotation of all these astronomical bodies, apart significantly from our own Earth's moon, due to rotational impulses arising from the structure of the sum total of all their individual quarks above?

Secondly, how do we account for the Earth having existed for four or five billion years, according to astrophysicists, yet still has not been totally destroyed? Is the central, core, 'cosmic intelligence' of quarks, indeed going together to form a 'Mind of God' preventing such a catastrophe?

Solar systems such as our own, are clearly modelled on the 'cosmic egg structure', with a hot core (the Sun) encircled by the elliptical orbits of numerous planets, comets, asteroids and other heavenly bodies, very similar to atoms with surrounding electrons. Except that the motions of planets etc. around any star are governed by Newton's famous inverse-square law of gravitation, and by no 'statistical' quantum mechanics of the very small!

Finally on this 'giant scale of things', galaxies are usually spiral in shape. This, in my model, must correspond to a constant discharge of energy into the galaxy, making its 'cosmic egg' grow along the spiralling growth lines outlined earlier. As we said there, the spiral seems to be a common feature of a twelve-dimensional Universe. The reason? Added energy makes 'cosmic eggs' expand steadily along *all* their dimensions, spiritual as well as material.

So, how do the world's Holy Books answer scientific evidence that the Universe is around 15,000,000,000 years old, not just about 6,000-12,000 years as in say, the Bible? Let the Bible itself answer: -

'...with the Lord one day is like a thousand years, and a thousand years are like one day.'

2 Peter 3:8
The New Testament in the Bible

11. Just why *eggs, plants, trees, structures based on them like blood and nerve supplies, and so ultimately brains themselves* come about in their particular way!

The very phrase 'cosmic egg structure' tells you at once the inspiration for the main theme of this paper – is the 'egg and sperm' basis of nearly all sexual reproduction in nature. So far we have seen very many examples of how this most fundamental aspect of the Creation – or Nature – seems to apply to so many levels of that Creation or Nature. So we move on promptly to look at how an important aspect of the diagram in section eight, relates totally to so many aspects of biology. Namely the **binary** 'Tree of Life' shown there.

Binary is the operative expression, for nearly all trees and plants in zoology, and blood and nerve supplies in organisms, divide in like binary fashion virtually 100% of the time. As in the skeletal form below of the original 'Tree of Life' that can only be said to be their original *spiritual* inspiration: -

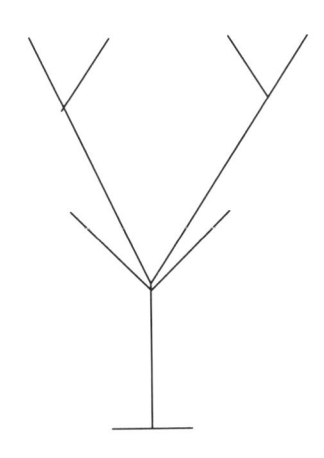

This 'Tree of Life' structure, ultimately, can be seen, simplistically, to be the very basis of all *brains*, with as you recall, Wisdom, Reason and the 'Notion of Godhead' at the base, the brainstem. Exactly as in nature.

It would be fascinating to discover if the diagram of the 'Tree of Life' in section six in fact turned out to be an *accurate map or phrenology of the brain, especially the human brain!* The Victorians sought such a 'map of the brain' – but my own is based solidly on spiritual and scriptural principles!

Scientific Proof that (God The Holy) Spirit Exists

Article Six
The Spiritual Nature of DNA
Creation v. evolution

1. Introduction. The Spiritual Nature of DNA and RNA

The 'molecules of life', DNA and RNA, operate in a hugely complex fashion, as revealed by the 'Human Genome Project'. Yet even that complexity is still far too limited to explain the human form, and above all the brain - and the bare incredible fact of our individual consciousness!

This Article challenges scientists to embrace the ideas here. To include vital notions of a 'secret spiritual life of DNA' - my own extension to their current theories that are based only on biochemistry. I argue that 'proteins are the glue between thoughts and the body', and that there are spiritual and mental components to the amino acids that make up proteins. I put the radical view that these contain spiritual energies, not just chemicals.

My own new theory argues that without these hidden spiritual components, it is impossible to claim that human beings are constructed by about just 44,000 types of protein, as the current theories argue. Computers have negative IQ and are so completely 'dumb'. Yet your average Personal Computer requires many more different component parts than that. The vastly more complex, self-contained, conscious human obviously needs hugely many more...

My own case is that spiritual energy in its hidden dimensions must accompany the bio-chemicals of DNA and RNA. By virtue of the massive information and intelligence in these spiritual energies, they could be shown by full research to explain human and animal complexity in full - even brains!

I wrote these three papers from my point of view of a fully trained scientist, trying to develop a 'Science of the Spirit' - and so the Mind. The '21st Century Spiritual Psychology' that has emerged, tries to take everything that the Bible - and other Holy Books - has to say on the subject, as far as I am concerned. These papers organise that set of information - which many billions of people around the world - 'believers' - would take as 'The Truth', into a scientific framework. This in turn enabled me throughout to consistently refer the 'Model of The Human and Holy Spirits' that I have been able to develop, against the latest scientific theories. As we have seen, astonishingly perhaps, they totally match!

As for science, its approach is different - fundamentally. A key feature of the vast majority of science is that it endeavours to be 'objective'. Scientific theories deliberately *exclude* the effect of the *mind and spirit* from what their 'approximations to truth' say about the nature of the very complex world we live in. This brings us to the second key difference between the Two Worlds of Faith and Science. People with a faith always argue that they seek The Truth - usually found in their religion's particular Holy Book or Books. For instance, the purest form of Christianity is one that relies only on an (accurate) translation of the Bible - together with inspiration from Spirit - the Holy Spirit.

It is precisely because scientific theories have no notion of Mind or Spirit, apart from more recent quantum mechanical ones like Heisenberg's Uncertainty Principle, that true scientists only ever claim that their theories are *not 'The Truth'* - merely *'an APPROXIMATION to "truth"'.* There *is* no notion as in Faith, of 'Absolute Truth' in pure, correctly applied science!

I followed the dramatic decoding of the entire length of the human 'genome' or DNA molecule, with both interest and deep concern. In particular, when I learned that the original view that it contained about 120,000 'genes', each producing one protein, had been corrected by the Mega-Buck Human Genome Project to just 44,000 or so - I immediately balked and scoffed!

Why, science reckons the adult human body contains around *100,000,000,000 cells, all different!* A sequence of 44,000 proteins is simply far too small to explain all that complexity! There MUST be, as my own thoughts in this paper would strongly suggest, in addition a strong SPIRITUAL aspect to DNA - operating in hidden 'spiritual' dimensions. In fact these dimensions must be multiplying up the complexity of the scientific view of the 'DNA/RNA genetic computer' two million times, probably much more. DNA must contain *thoughts*, to explain how treating a molecule even as vast as human DNA, *as bio-chemicals only,* completely fails to explain how human, and incidentally animal, complexity and above all consciousness, arise.

The rest of this paper, then gives first, a brief and necessarily simplistic description of the mechanism of production of complex proteins from sequences of amino-acids by RNA 'operating' on DNA molecules to unravel the 'genetic code'. Then it goes on to describe my 'spiritual' extensions to this purely biochemical theory.

It ends by suggesting various ways in which my own

extensions would require vast amounts of research to 'prove'. Possibly lasting all the way into the 22nd Century or even way beyond! In particular, how this research would need the development of a 'mind-reading or thought-reading instrument', which tongue in cheek, I will term a 'Spiritual Energy Analyser/Reader' (SEAR - pronounced 'seer' for short!) Early versions of just such a machine are being developed right now, I understand. However, they will almost certainly need years of development before they are precise and detailed enough to pick up spiritual energies *and* analyse their meaning from *any part of the body, not just the obvious place, i.e. the brain!*

So, the need for this final Paper emerges. In the body of the paper I have already challenged science to embody Mind and Spirit in its theories (to achieve a 'New Spiritual Physics' based on my "Spiritual Psychology"?) This provides a vastly more complex and to me convincing Biblical basis to intelligence than the 'logical intelligence' of computer 1's and 0's. Will 'Spiritual Computers' result? I complete this with 'Spiritual Biochemistry and so Biology'...

2. A necessarily potted and abridged summary of the current Scientific Model of how DNA and RNA supermolecules work to enable cells and organisms to reproduce

1. The chemical structures of DNA and RNA, and how these two types of supermolecule cooperate as they do, has been heavily researched since the 1950's, when two scientists, Frances Crick and James Watson, famously unravelled the now well-known 'double-helix' structure of DNA. DNA stands for *deoxyribonucleic acid,* and its cousin the simpler RNA, stands for *ribonucleic acid.* The structure of the simpler RNA molecule had been established for some time. To picture the far more complex and much longer DNA double-helix, a good analogy is to appreciate that a tape from an ordinary audio cassette has information from the A and B sides, found on either physical edge of the tape. Twist a long length of the tape so it forms a spiral, and the 'A and B' edges correspond to the double helix of DNA, in this analogy. RNA 'reads' this double helix 'genetic DNA tape' - just like the head of a tape recorder - to extract genetic information. Science to date

believes this information is solely biochemical. My own view is somewhat broader, as we will see overleaf.

2. Just as along an audio cassette there are matching magnetised particles, holding the sound or voice, in pairs corresponding to the A and B sides, the vital information of the DNA molecule occurs in pairs - of chemicals called 'nucleotides' or 'bases'. There are, perhaps surprisingly only ever just four types of these bases that feature in the two strands of DNA in any double helix, known by their initial letters of C, U, A, and G (in full - cytosine, uracil, adenine and guanine).

3. It has been found that as the RNA 'head' works along the long DNA molecule, *amino acids* are produced, which are stitched together in the sequence given by the DNA 'genetic code' of bases. The RNA 'stitches together chemically' the sequence of amino acids (complex chemicals starting with a -COOH acid group and having an -NH2 amine tail, their distinguishing characteristic) into 'peptide chains' - the larger ones called *proteins*. It was shown back in the 1960's that it takes exactly three bases on a DNA chain to be read, for the RNA to make one amino acid. With some ingenious experiments, the correspondence between these combinations of three bases, and the amino acid that each such 'codon' codes for, was found to be:

1st|2nd V ->	U	C	A	G	V 3rd
U	PHE PHE LEU LEU	SER SER SER SER	TYR TYR --- ---	CYS CYS --- TRP	U C A G
C	LEU LEU LEU LEU	PRO PRO PRO PRO	HIS HIS GLUN GLUN	ARG ARG ARG ARG	U C A G
A	ILEU ILEU ILEU MET	THR THR THR THR	ASPN ASPN LYS LYS	SER SER ARG ARG	U C A G
G	VAL VAL VAL VAL	ALA ALA ALA ALA	ASP ASP GLU GLU	GLY GLY GLY GLY	U C A G

So the sixty-four combinations of the four bases into groups of three or 'codons', codes for just 20 amino acids, the significance of which comes out overleaf in my 'spiritual extension' to all this.. There is therefore considerable redundancy or 'degeneracy' in the codons. The codons U-A-A, U-G-A and U-A-G do not code for amino-acids at all, but represent 'genetic punctuation' like 'stop reading' and 'start reading'. U-A-G is the 'full stop' codon while capital letters are more complicated...

4. A set of codons or groups of three bases, each providing one amino acid or a piece of 'genetic punctuation', that yields one protein, is called a 'gene' - hence the name of the science of genetics. Cells can either 'replicate' to replace themselves with an identical cell before they die, when only their own DNA is used in the process to guarantee an identical copy is made. In sexual reproduction, one gene from one of each of the corresponding pair from each parent's DNA molecules is 'dominant' and is used, new research indicates usually the female - the other is ignored.

5. Every cell in a body is unique; yet the DNA is identical in each!

3. A summary - once more potted - of my 'Theory of Spiritual Genetics'. How it simply extends the current simpler purely biochemical model of science we just saw, yet with adequate research could result in both Science and Faith ending up much happier - with a return to the original Universal Spiritual View.

1. As we keep saying, the complexity of the human body, and likewise that of less complex creatures, cannot solely be explained as being put together, consciousness above all, with just 44,000 proteins, with just twenty types of amino-acids making them up. I claim the 'missing factor' is supplied by the body of this paper, and is purely *spiritual*.
2. My second hypothesis in this new theory is that each type of amino acid *binds to itself a SPIRITUAL PHRASE* with the twenty spiritual qualities of each of the twenty types being given by the 'Fundamental Spiritual Fruit'. So, given the future invention of a sufficiently accurate SEAR (or mind reading machine!) we should be able to establish the precise one-to-one relationship between each of the amino acids involved in genetics with the corresponding spiritual quality of the spiritual phrase it bonds to. Proteins are strongly associated and bonded to forms of RNA molecules called 'messenger RNA' and this research would need to establish how these are involved. So we need to find out how the two seemingly vastly disparate columns below are linked by twenty one-to-one relationships: -

Amino-acid	Spiritual quality
1. PHE	Jealousy *for* (Tree of Knowledge of Good and Evil)
2. LEU	Intuition (Tree of Life – Sophia, Wife of God)
3. ILEU	Male Ultimate Quality ('The Word')
4. MET	Female Ultimate Quality ('The Law')
5. VAL	Way / Methodology (Truth leading to Life)
6. SER	Notions of Heaven (Hope leading to Comfort)
7. PRO	Reason
8. THR	Creativity
9. ALA	Generosity
10.TYR	Mercy
11.HIS	Pity
12.GLUN	Endurance
13.ASPN	Courage
14.LYS	Wisdom
15.ASP	Love
16.GLU	Joy
17.CYS	Health
18.TRP	Peace
19.ARG	Grace
20.GLY	Beauty

3. If this new spiritual theory is correct, then, three DNA bases bind to one 'spiritual phrase'.

4. It is actually one *protein* per thought - or spiritual sentence, paragraph or even tome, depending on size. Proteins it is that bind, in this hypothesis, to thoughts, and must pass them on to other chemicals and 'organelles' in building new cells, so providing the *real* intelligence to build life - that is spiritual not biochemical energy in its nature... Such *thoughts* are much more complex than the underlying merely biochemical structures, although these in turn can be fearsomely complex, like proteins and DNA!

3. Scientific and spiritual theories of evolution

It is over 100 years since Charles Darwin wrote his famous Origin of Species, based on his observations on the diversity of newly-discovered species observed on his long trip around the Pacific. He claimed that it was evident that as each generation of all species came and went, species diversified and changed –

or evolved – mostly in response to changes in their environment. This explained, he said, the great changes and diversity in species over millions of years, as observed in fossils by palaeontologists.

This notion was felt once more by the Church to be in direct conflict with the Biblical account in the Book of Genesis, and as for Galileo's work in the early seventeenth century was condemned by many in the Church as pure heresy. In particular, Darwin's view that mankind had in fact evolved from the apes instead of being 'spontaneously created by God on the sixth Day' was anathema! Personally, I feel that the notion of what a 'day' comprises in biblical accounts is very debatable, as we saw at the end of the Blue Paper. I feel that the Church of that time was in fact guilty, yet again, of over-zealously defending a whole chauvinistic tradition founded on very little, if any, actual biblical evidence.

With the discovery of the structure of the 'molecule of life', DNA, in the late 1940's, scientists felt that this offered the key to a biochemical justification and theoretical explanation for Darwin's observations. However, fifty years on, much research has been undertaken, yet is still yet to produce the much-desired basis of understanding – in purely these 'genetic terms' – of how species diversify physically over time. The precise mechanism seems to involve, once more, more than just a physical set of processes.

Once in a while in the world of science, an enigmatic character appears who is capable of providing a radically different approach to such an impasse. Such a man was the world famous French biologist and palaeontologist, Pierre Teilhard de Chardin, who brought a perhaps, unique, perspective to his work on theories of physical *and* spiritual evolution – for he was also a Jesuit father.

He died in 1955, having provided a lifetime of brilliant work to his cause – of synthesising the two approaches to evolution of science and the religious world. I cannot help feeling that my own description of the two worlds of the spiritual and physical Universe, in the previous Paper, would have greatly interested him. This is, coming as it does some 60 years after the completion in 1948 of his epic book on the subject of different forms of evolution, "The Phenomenon of Man".

In particular I feel he would have regarded with approval, my head-on assault in the previous Paper on the apparent total disparity between what he termed 'inner energy' – or spiritual energy – and external or physical energy.

Furthermore he would have been fascinated with one view I emerge with at the end of my Grand Synthesis there. This is that spiritual energy is indeed everywhere all the time, but occupies an invisible Universe 'at right angles' to the physical, observable one – and invisible because it is 'rolled up within' conventional space.

However, the advent of modern computers, which only really started to become established at the end of Teilhard's life, allows us much enhanced opportunities of looking at the whole question of 'what comprises intelligence, or psychic energy?'

Is it really a good idea to consider in the future trying to build a Really Useful Computer? One that does not just echo the thoughts of its programmers, after a great deal of labour and 'trial and error' in making the computer execute the programs correctly.

We are now thought not to be, as previously thought, the only species on Earth able to pride itself on an ability to think reflectively. Dolphins, whales and other primates have at least some measure of this supreme faculty. We are, however, unique in also having that vital digit, the thumb. In conjunction with our intellect, our thumbs have enabled us to develop great technologies and whole civilisations.

The question that is perhaps most asked in connection with the subject of evolution is how that ultimate biological organ, the brain, in particular the human brain, came to be. The evolutionary view is traditionally the same as an aspect of dialectical philosophy that I have not yet discussed.

Namely, from an enormously long and variegated series of *quantitative changes* in species, at last came a point in time when Teilhard's 'noosphere' or the Bible's Time of the End as discussed in this paper, became possible. Civilised man first emerged, it is widely thought, 12,000 years ago after the last Ice Age and for the first time made *qualitative changes* to his environment – with fire, the wheel, buildings and ultimately the first civilisations.

Dialectical thinkers usually argue that all dialectics proceed in this same way, with quantitative change and growth of things always being a necessary precursor to qualitative change. The physical aeons that preceded this vital point of the 'beginning of the noosphere', and the many lines of physical species that have led to mankind, comprise the 'workshop of civilisation'.

However, it is perfectly possible to provide an antithesis to this dialectical thesis – of dialecticians! Namely that, as we saw is my view in the previous Paper, at the very Origin of Things, the qualitative world of 'the Spirit' either preceded, or occurred in parallel to, the physical world. As indeed the spiritual world turns out to be completely *outside space and matter* – it occupies a set of dimensions 'at right angles to' both space and in particular, matter– this whole notion indeed gets rather mystical.

However, logically speaking, spirit precedes the material world; furthermore, although initially it is 'inferior' to it and *supports* it, after the 'noosphere' first appeared men developed great religions that placed it firmly 'on high' and above.

So, the line of thought of my own particular synthesis of this dialectic, about the qualitative and quantitative natures of changes, comes to this.

The Holy Spirit can be seen from the argument in the previous Paper to have had a set of dimensions to live in, before or since time began, that intersect those of the physical world 'at right angles'. To conclude an argument we need now that I only hinted at, at various points in the previous Paper, the spiritual dimensions by definition contain no matter – but psychic or Teilhardian 'inner energy'. These, by virtue of Einstein's insights, we can say gives the Holy Spirit a kind of *spiritual mass.* This then interacts with the physical world with the very familiar forces of gravity, and electromagnetic radiation – or light – to perhaps mould and change it?

The conclusion of this argument is that in synthesising religious and scientific views of evolution, my own conclusion comes down to a view that 'All evolution is *assisted* evolution'.

The Holy Spirit, then, seems to have spent literally millions of years in assisting life on Earth to proceed towards an ultimate target – brains that in turn were sufficiently, and particularly, organised. So much so that they can, since civilisation started – and perhaps earlier for other species than our own, in the view of other religions like Buddhism – act as 'vessels' in the biblical sense; or, to borrow a phrase from my own field of electronic computers, as 'amplifiers' – for the Holy Spirit.

That is, the ultimate source of our reflective capacities is the Holy Spirit Herself. She seeks to introduce us to increasing amounts of Herself, or Himself in the traditional Christian view – which I challenged strongly in the Blue Paper. The brain even mimics the 'shape' of the Holy Spirit!

The 'soul' most feel they have, is then the meeting point of their individual Spirit – the sum total of the Holy Spirit within each individual – with the Greater Body of the Holy Spirit.

The great differences between every single individual we ever meet, in that respect, can be assigned directly in this view, to the great variegation and structure I have already discussed at length in the previous Paper, of the Holy Spirit – as a set of spiritual dimensions. This is given totally uniquely via the 'template of the soul' to each and every living creature, so completely determining their unique individual **character.**

This is all about evolution – and as a scientist who studied genetics and heredity at Cambridge in my earlier studies, I fully accept evolution as a fully established mechanism for the 'development of species' over generations. However evolution cannot and does not set any **targets for the resulting design. THAT is down to the Holy Spirit – GOD!** There is a Panorama program of the famous atheist biologist Professor Richard Dawkins currently on You Tube on the Internet, proving that Darwinian evolution mechanisms produce systematic changes in species over many, many generations, with a primitive computer simulation. **However Dawkins could not explain – Darwin could not explain either – how evolution produces 'elegant, beautiful' results**. That is down to **targets** set by the HOLY SPIRIT alone – which they would both of course deny being the Ultimate Devout Fundamentalist Atheists!

This paper finally attributes the scientific fact according to a recent famous genetics book 'the Seven Eves' (I think it is called that) that all of modern humanity is descended from just **seven pairs of people.** If you are scientifically minded – only seven pairs of *homo sapiens* survived the Ice Age 12,000 years ago. According to the Bible, in Genesis, Noah and his wife and their three sons on the Ark, were joined by just three other couples to make seven pairs of all 'good' species on the Ark, if you care to read it carefully. Either way, if you equate the End of the last Ice Age, as I do, to The Biblical Flood, it was an Act of God. One which wiped out all the other humanoids science has said frequently, were wiped out then, such as *homo erectus,* Neanderthal Man, etc, etc. The Bible says they were corrupt – the 'Act of God' either way you look at it, certainly paved the way for us *homo sapiens* as the **only people.** OUR AGE is about 6,000-12,000 years since then (scientific estimates are inconclusive – but AGREES with the Bible) but the AGE OF THE UNIVERSE according to ASTRONOMY is over fourteen THOUSAND MILLION YEARS!

5. The true lengths of time of the Creations, of both the Universe and of mankind

There has been a continual debate between theologians and scientists since science began, about the likely age of the Universe and the length of the history of mankind. The purpose of the present section is to show that there is in fact no contradiction between the few statements in the Bible on the question of either age, and the discoveries of scientists.

Both religion and science now talk of a 'beginning of time', though scientists debated this amongst themselves for hundreds of years, whereas the Bible talks of an initial Creation of the Universe by God. Furthermore, the order of events described in the first chapter of the Book of Genesis, although deliberately very terse, is not greatly at variance with the much more detailed evidence of science.

However, there the similarities apparently end. Astronomers and cosmologists have shown that there are literally billions of stars and almost certainly planets in our own Galaxy, and moreover billions of such Galaxies in the Universe. This compares with the ten thousand or so stars visible in biblical times. They estimate from their complex calculations that the Universe is about fifteen BILLION years old (15,000,000,000 years). This seems to most people to conflict starkly with the Bible's Seven Days of Creation, with mankind appearing on the sixth day. The Bible itself, however, provides the answer to this apparent contradiction:

> '...with the Lord one day is like a thousand years, and a thousand years are like one day.'

2 Peter 3:8

If a day to God can seem like a thousand years, then likewise a million or a billion years (or so) can seem like a Day. So it seems quite plausible that God's Seven Days of Creation each lasted millions or billions of years, so agreeing with the scientific age of the Universe.

6. All language, thoughts, emotions and feelings, are encapsulated in microscopic 'transcendental building blocks'

'Nice thoughts' – 'male and female', in both men and women – occupy very elegant 'hyper-cubes within hyper-cubes'; which is reflected in Far Eastern traditions, especially Buddhism. All of our sublime or spiritual thoughts occupy dodecahedrons.

'Sick' thoughts, by contrast, fill jarring, nasty, triangular pyramids.

Our brain and nervous system are designed, naturally enough, to operate far better with cubic, 'nice', or 'normal', and also dodecahedral or 'sublime' or 'spiritual' thoughts – than with their opposite – 'nasty triangular pyramids'...

I was inspired to start writing this section of this paper, some years ago, after watching the first episode of a new series on BBC 2 television, called 'Brain Story'. I promptly wrote about this book, and sent a copy to the programme's narrator, Professor Susan Greenfield. The letter included the above summary, and the following paragraphs: -

I am writing to you after watching your 'Brain Story' programme on BBC2 last night, which was very interesting. It has always fascinated me, when I was a Scholar of King's College, Cambridge, studying maths, physics, and computer science, and since as a Chartered Instrument Engineer, that tera-bucks have been randomly 'lobbed' at the problem of artificial intelligence for fifty years. The result is only a very disappointing yet massive collection of *instruments* with *no sign of any* consciousness – and an IQ of precisely *zero* – *even less* given their terrible fragility – NEGATIVE IQ!!?? Their problems are the bane of the lives of many!

As a person with a deep faith that I am completely at ease with, having given it many years of thought, I can tell that by contrast, you come from the vast majority of scientists that are what I call 'devout Atheists' – especially true among scientists? You have all missed a key point – that God's 'Acts of Creation' continue forever, all the time, everywhere – because God – in the guise of The Holy Spirit – acts everywhere, all the time... I feel you should take a hard look at my own attached book that explains all this. I should very much like to hear your reaction...

The brain of all living creatures is a tera-compact, above all *conscious* organ of thought, measurement and control. How anybody can possibly imagine it 'somehow threw itself together in "evolving" by ""random chance""', when by sheer contrast to people like me it is **"God's supreme Creation!" – the very Seat of Soul, Spirit and Mind – i.e. consciousness –** is totally beyond me! If such an incredible organ, way beyond the current wit of man to build anything like a computer even vaguely approaching it, is the result of 'evolution' i.e. 'monkeys typing Shakespeare' – why is humankind manifestly completely unable to *manufacture* a conscious brain – even that of a nematode worm?

I was very stimulated by the TV programme, although as above, rather put off that the whole subject was treated totally by 'Atheist Materialist Scientists' who rather tried to explain away spiritual experiences, even, as mere brain activity i.e. purely material.

The challenge was on after I posted that letter back in July 2000. I had already realised that this book up to this point has talked about Mind and Spirit with hardly a mention of the brain itself. The onus was now on me, I felt, to bring this book to a head, and in this Part to actually attempt the long dreamed-for impossible – to give a non-material basis for thought, especially in relation to the brain. Within just twenty-four hours of posting my letter, I had been through sufficient of literally, a brainstorm, to bring the present book together and end it with a view of how mind and brain coexist...

I claim about the brain that it contains 'our portion' of the Holy Spirit. I will now be claiming that all our thoughts, feelings, emotions and moods are complex yet extraordinarily microscopic fragments of Spirit, and that: -

The brain is "a spirit-processing and spirit-memorising machine"

'Normal' or 'square' people, as the hippies called them, usually experience a pleasant-feeling mixture of 'cubic-shaped' thoughts, or 'nice thoughts', which are a subset of the overall Holy Spirit, so can be either 'male' or 'female'. Each cubic thought is composed of *spiritual dimensions containing spiritual flows*. The two male and female 'sets of dimensions' are totally different, yet complement one another perfectly. We all get a mixture of male and female thoughts, the balance largely dependent on the balance of our sexuality. *God designed* cubic *brain cells* so that *cubic* thoughts can fit precisely and so totally comfortably, physically, inside them.

Cubic thoughts can be compound, and very quickly get vastly complicated, by containing other cubic thoughts 'stacked within them'. Such compound hyper-cubes need bigger brain cells to hold them. To see the complexity, look at the 'toy' of a *Rubik's cube* – that holds just 27 'cubes within cubes' – but I for one am totally beaten by it, as are the majority of adults. Somehow children 'get the hang of' Rubik's cube, on the whole, far faster than us poor adults...

We can draw these, as I have already hinted several times in this book. By total contrast, spiky, uncomfortable, 'bad thoughts' are pyramidal and made of nasty, sharp, triangles that jar with the cells in the brain. Finally, some people experience neutral, male-and-female, thoughts, which turn out to, surprise, surprise, perhaps, immediately produce a '*child* i.e. male/female' as well. The results are rhapsodic 'spiritual thoughts'. These contain all eight of the 'jealous for' and all eight of the 'anima' spirits of Part 5 of this Volume A of this book. Also, they instantly produce the 'child' spirits above – of the Son and the Bride.

So overall 'spiritual thoughts' are very complex indeed, being made of all of the first *twenty-four* spiritual dimensions in *dodecahedrons*, nearly round objects with a high degree of symmetry, with twenty triangular faces. The four 'People' of Being (Jealousy 'for'), the Holy Spirit or Anima, Jesus and Ariel, fill such thoughts to make up the full 24 dimensions, again totally *holistically and four-square!* If cubic thoughts fit cubic brain and nerve cells easily, then rounded spiritual thoughts fit *very* comfortably, explaining physical feelings of spiritual warmth, rhapsody, awe and wonder, expressed by the Faithful...

Before going any further, I had better sketch out all four of this total of four 'possibilities of thoughts' we can have. Do they correspond to the 'four bases of the genetic code of DNA'?

MALE thought   JEALOUSY FOR

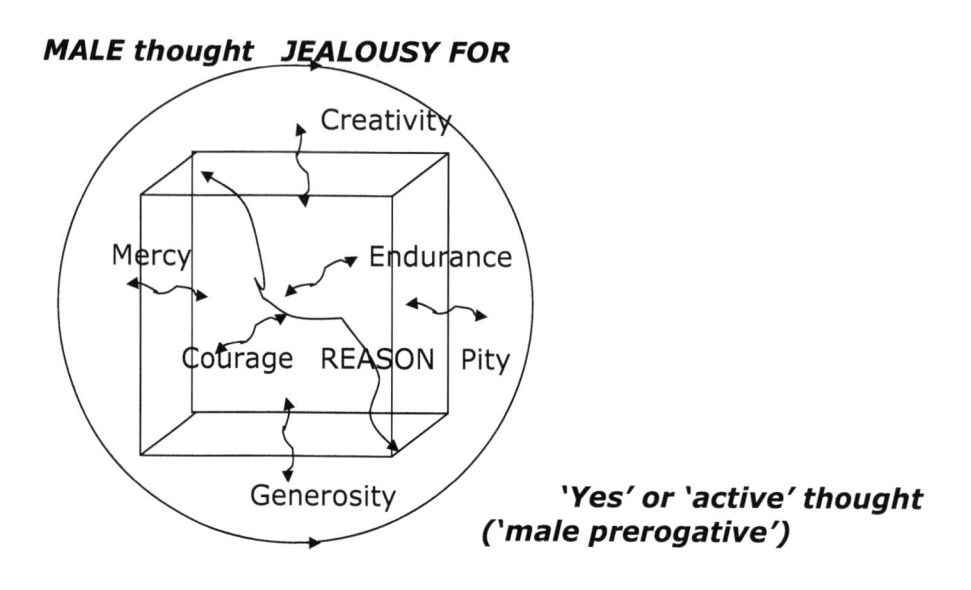

- Creativity
- Mercy
- Endurance
- Courage   REASON   Pity
- Generosity

**'Yes' or 'active' thought
('male prerogative')**

FEMALE Thought   ANIMA(true femininity/motherhood)

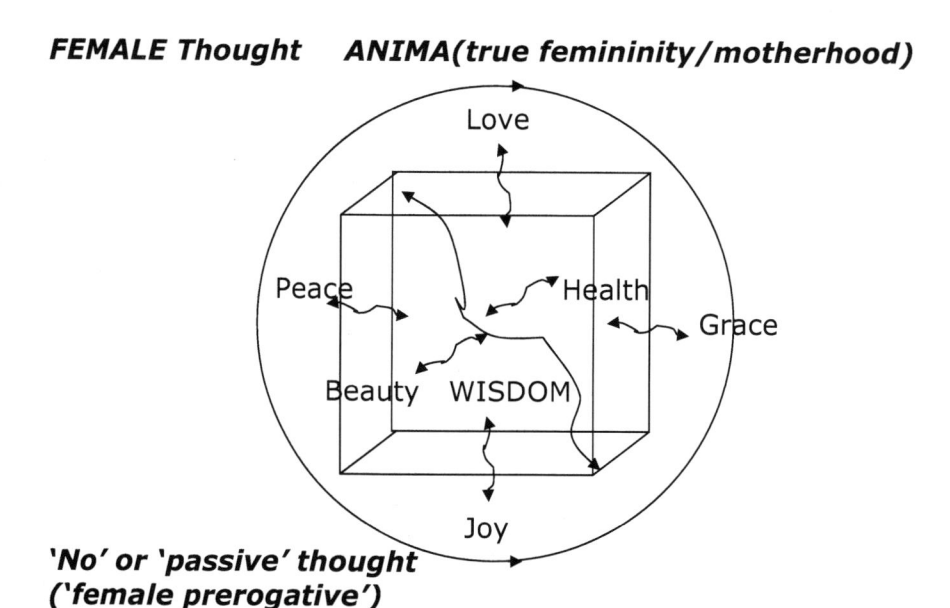

- Love
- Peace
- Health
- Grace
- Beauty   WISDOM
- Joy

**'No' or 'passive' thought
('female prerogative')**

SPIRITUAL thought | MESSIAH

Being – 'Jealousy FOR' | ANIMA or Holy Spirit

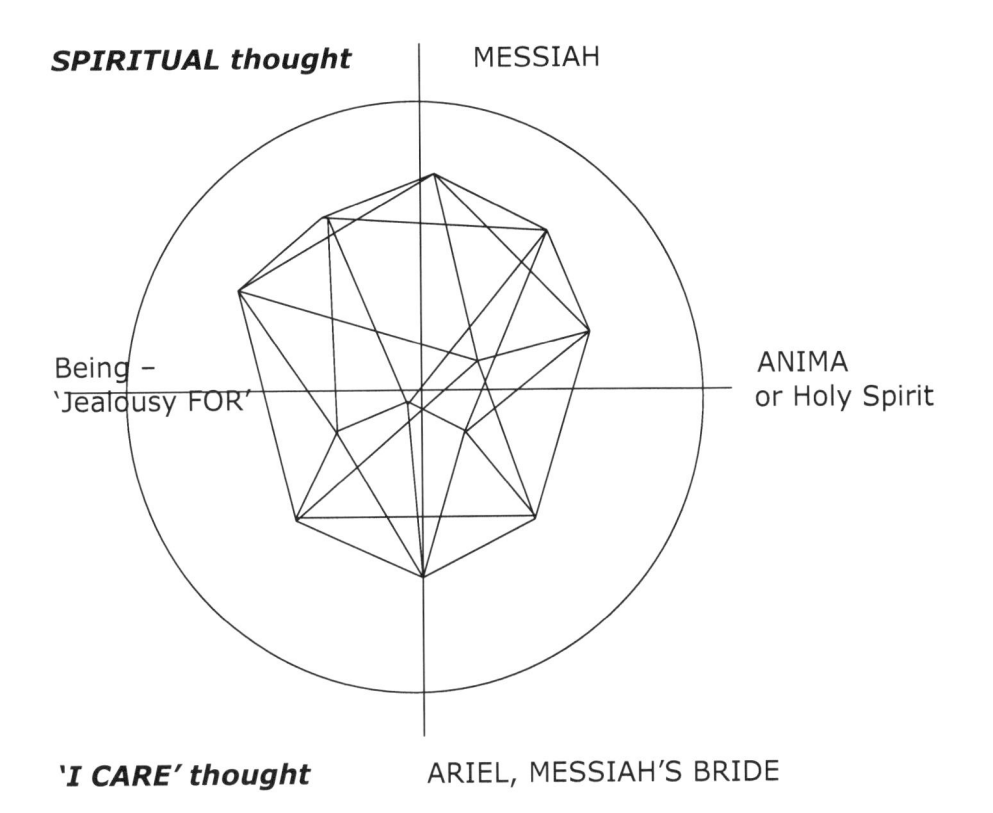

'I CARE' thought | ARIEL, MESSIAH'S BRIDE

'Awkward and spiky', nasty thought

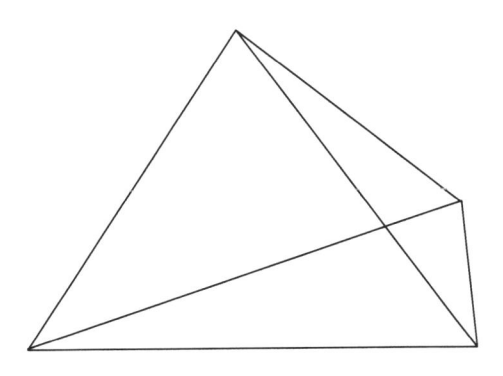

'Stuff that' or **"I don't care"** thought

7. **Backing up all these notions of 'shapes of thoughts, emotions, moods and feelings' – by appealing to my earlier discussions of Scientific Cosmology. Is all this discussion a start of a genuine Theory of Everything as in science today, embracing Religion and The Arts?**

   Clearly, if these 'thought shapes' are to fit into the tiny dendrites, or brain and nerve cells that fill the body, they are microscopic. Pretty much as you would expect for a pure thought, though, is it not? As brain cells are cubic, clearly the last diagram above, of 'nasty' thoughts, shows that they indeed will not fit comfortably into a brain cell or nerve cell. Hence their pain.

   Having worked all this out, the culmination of twenty-two years of thought and research, I can now relate all this firmly to cosmological theories of science – 'string' theories and super-gravity theory. Astonishingly, in just one table, I show, no less, that the reason all these mathematical theories require very different numbers of 'extra dimensions to work' to those of just three of space and one of time, is they are *all,* to an extent, valid. That is, each of them is correct about one of the above 'hyper-shapes of many extra dimensions than just space and time, that hold the SPIRIT'. In the process I make a major breakthrough and show, no less, how 'super-gravity theory', could be made to completely work...

Theory Number of 'extra dimensions beyond space-time'

'Strings'   Twenty-two.

This one facet of the overall 'big picture' or 'theory of Theories of Everything' on this page corresponds to 'spiritual thoughts'. These have all of twenty spiritual facets, plus the notions of 'masculinity' and 'femininity' – in particular, of God... Divine Jealousy (for) and His Anima or Wife.

'Superstrings'   Six.

These theories correspond to a view of 'cubic thoughts' only relating to their *faces*, not the notion of 'core intelligence or wisdom' that we explore overleaf. They also relate to triangular 'sick thoughts'.

'Supergravity'   Seven.

This corresponds again to cubic or 'normal' thoughts, but crucially omits the *holistic, overall* eighth spiritual dimension. I claim, and physicists reading this can verify it mathematically, that if this theory were made *holistic* with such an overall eighth dimension, it would bring up a total of twelve dimensions including space-time, as in my own model, and so would have an *even* number of dimensions. This in turn would enable the mathematics to explain all *four* fundamental forces in nature, including the weak force that this theory currently cannot explain.

This might be a major scientific breakthrough in itself...

"What is thought?" or "What is the meaning of 'meaning' itself?"

"In the beginning were God and Spirit"
   Paraphrase of Genesis I:1-2, opening the Old Testament

"In the beginning were God and the Word"
   Paraphrase of John I:1, in the New Testament

Simple, obvious conclusions: -

'ALL LANGUAGE IS MADE OF PURE SPIRIT '

"THOUGHT IS COMPOSED OF WORDS i.e. SPIRIT"

   We now turn to consider the interaction of spirits within their various spiritual dimensions that surround and occupy a space constituting a thought, of all the above types: - 'cubic, male or female', 'spiritual', and finally 'nasty' thoughts.
   First, hyper-cubic 'male' and 'female' thoughts, the easiest to discuss. They are like chords in music. Under the overall 'male or female cube-ness' of 'Jealousy FOR' or 'Anima – pure femininity' respectively, they interact to each provide a highly compact set of eight spiritual 'flows' – of letters, numbers and words. The male spirit of Reason and the female spirit of Intuitive Wisdom, respectively, are very naturally placed at the 'root' position – at the centre of such 'thought hyper-cubes'. It is of course they that compose sentences and even whole paragraphs and essays of these words drawn in each case from seven other spiritual flows of words working in unison – and add 'neutral' words of punctuation.
   So a single male or female 'thought hyper-cube' can occupy a single brain or nerve cell – but when larger cells, still cubic, start to contain 'hyper-cubes of such hyper-cubes', the situation gets massively more complicated. Spiritual sentences – thoughts or information – can of course freely pass to adjacent 'hyper-cubes', which if male is mixed with female,

produces a whole spectrum of sexual emphasis of the language produced by each 'spiritual cube'.

At this point it is good to ask the question, "What form do spiritual 'words' etc, take?" I have often said in this book that spiritual dimensions contain no matter, are completely outside our senses, especially being invisible, only containing energy. Or rather power, as that energy changes with time, and in physics power is rate of change of energy. My answer to this question is that these spiritual words are a kind of 'musical energy', perhaps answering the quest of the Ancient Greeks for a 'music of the spheres'? It is the purpose of nerve and brain cells, as designed by God, to form an interface between such 'thought energies' or psychic energies to first, other parts of the brain machinery, so utterly complex that neuro-science is still in its infancy! Beyond the brain, via the nervous system, the body, both in such a very complex way that 'free will of the Spirit' is given by God to each and every human and other conscious creature.

So, onto 'spiritual thoughts', which as one might expect have an entirely transcendent intensity and quality – and complexity or richness – due to having so many possibilities in 24 dimensions. The energy of such thoughts compared to mere 'cubic thoughts' or 'square' thoughts, is like comparing a Church organ to a triangle.

Finally, from the sublime to the ridiculous... 'Nasty' thoughts occupy a shape that is totally awkward, especially in communicating Ideas, let alone formulating them. So the words produced are often illiterate swear words, expressing the limited way that the opposites to 'nice' or even and especially, 'spiritual' thoughts, feel awkward, 'sweaty' or painful. This is quite literally the case in the brain!

8. Where is God then? SHOW HIM to us!" ask Atheists!

My answer to these desperate pleas are as follows: -

1. My book exhaustively indeed 'describes the indescribable' in giving a complete mostly very qualitative science of the Holy Spirit - and His/Her/Their/Its Enemies as well! Main conclusion - the Holy Spirit FILLS AND SUPPORTS THE ENTIRE UNIVERSE!

2. The CORRECT translation in the Bible itself if you read the original Greek is NOT 'Kingdom of Heaven' BUT 'The Kingdom of the Heavens'. (Dis)proving whether God exists only works if you answer the blatantly obvious tough question asked by any Atheist, 'WHERE is God then?'

3. My answer is there is INFINITELY more of GOD (the Holy Spirit) 'out there in the Heavens' than anywhere on Earth because I have shown that the Holy Spirit is EVERYWHERE ALL THE TIME. The Universe is obviously infinitely bigger than our tiny planet.

So the answer is 'God lives in the Heavens' ('outer space'!) Where else can 'Heaven'; or 'The Heavens' be?

9. Epilogue to this first Volume of the Book. 'The proof is in the protons – sorry, Pudding'! It is Christmas 2008 and I look to proof of all my theories up to this point - in 2009 – from the 'biggest scientific experiment ever'.

This book does not actually provide proof that (the Holy) Spirit Exists – just a lot of pointers to that fact, all starting from the notion that science only has a consistent mathematical framework, it was discovered after the string theories of the 1980's, if there are nine or ten, not just three, dimensions of space. The 'biggest scientific experiment ever' will finally get under way in 2009, after technical problems in its first few months this Autumn 2008, partly in an attempt to prove whether the Universe really has more than just the obvious three spatial dimensions.

This is the Large Hadron Accelerator at CERN, in Geneva, Switzerland. I wait with bated breath for its first results – for by those results on just how many spatial dimensions there are – all the theories up to now in this book will stand or fall! If they do detect a total of ten dimensions of space, all the avant garde theories in this book will be vindicated! Otherwise I will have to think again!

Another major aspect of 2009 that is unlikely to affect the Accelerator – it is predicted to become the harshest year economically since the Great Depression of the 1920's! Hopefully my own theories will indeed be vindicated by the above experiments with fast protons, and I can ward off the Recession by earning a few pounds for myself selling this book!

More 'conventional' approaches to Scientific Proof that God Exists – the 'Anthropic Principle' and 'Intelligent Design' 1973-2007

How incredibly precisely and universally that the Sevenfold Holy Spirit, as discussed up to now, continuously imposes, through the laws of physics that They Control at all times, the finest balances in matter, cells, life, stars and planets, and the whole Universe itself.

The evidence in this appendix is taken from the web site www.godsciencemanifesto.com by kind copyright permission of the owners of that web site.

Darwin's theory of evolution claims that the first living cell was accidentally created from just the right, random combination of ingredients over millions of years, but modern scientists from microbiologists to chemists are beginning to realize that the odds against this theory are so astronomical that it's impossible. Because of these calculations even a growing number of evolutionists are being forced to admit that because the simplest living cell is so incredibly complicated, the time it would take to be formed through purely random forces of nature would take billions and billions of years longer than the age of the entire universe!

But the origins of life aren't the only mysterious phenomena in the universe. In 1973, an astrophysicist and cosmologist by the name of Brandon Carter developed a theory called the Anthropic Principle, which states that the physical constants in the universe have been formed in the only way possible for the creation of life. Another scientist, Patrick Glynn, puts it this way:

"...the Anthropic Principle says that the seemingly arbitrary and unrelated constants in physics have one strange thing in common—these are precisely the values you need if you want to have a universe capable of producing life."

From many other recent scientific discoveries about the Universe, this evidence can be defined as a progression of phenomena, each one of which is a building block for the creation of life.

PHENOMENON 1: CREATION OF THE UNIVERSE

Scientists' Big Bang theory states that the universe was created about fifteen to twenty billion years ago from a giant explosion. Regardless of whether this theory is correct, the fact remains that the universe itself contains many physical relationships that have remained constant.

Only recently, however, are scientists beginning to discover the strange coincidence that all these physical constants are exactly what they have to be in order for all life to exist. In other words, the slightest deviation in any of these constants would prevent the existence of life anywhere in the universe.

Here are only some of these very bizarre coincidences, which have recently been discussed by many scientists:

1. Particle mass ratios. All the electrons and protons in the universe have an exact mass ratio—a proton is 1836 times more massive than an electron. If this ratio were slightly bigger or smaller, molecules could not form and life would be impossible.

2. Constant mass. If the total mass of the universe were slightly larger, too much deuterium would cause all stars to burn so fast that life wouldn't develop, and if this total mass were less, no helium would exist and stars couldn't produce the elements necessary for life.

3. Star distance. If the distance between stars in the universe were slightly less, the gravitational pull of stars would be so great that planetary orbits would be upset, creating extreme temperature changes that would destroy life. If this distance were greater than it is, the heavy fragments thrown out by exploding stars would be so thinly dispersed that no planets could ever be formed.

4. Key elements. The three elements beryllium, carbon and oxygen have exact energy levels in their atomic nucleuses. Beryllium is so unstable that it slows down the fusion rate of stars. If it were just a bit more stable, these stars would explode and many of the elements necessary for life wouldn't be formed. If beryllium were even more unstable than it is now, star fusion would be slowed down to the point where element production beyond beryllium wouldn't occur at all.

5. Carbon. The energy level of the element carbon's nucleus has an exact relationship to both helium and beryllium. If this ratio changed even slightly up or down, there wouldn't be enough carbon in the universe for life to exist.

6. Oxygen has exactly the right energy level in its nucleus to allow it to be produced from carbon in just the amount necessary for the existence of life on earth. If this energy level were greater or smaller, all carbon would be prevented from turning into oxygen, and life would not be possible.

These last three coincidences were so startling to scientist Fred Hoyle that he made this comment: "A superintellect has monkeyed with physics—as well as with chemistry and biology."

Remember, these are only some of the examples in this group; there are many more.

PHENOMENON 2 - UNSEEN FORCES

The Universe is a single, endless field of energy: the "deep space" that stretches from the inner space of atoms which make up all matter, to the outer space at the edge of the universe. In addition to making up all the visible physical reality in the universe, the Universe is also made up of four basic invisible forces: 1) The strong force that holds together subatomic particles; 2) the weak force that's involved in radioactive decay; 3) gravity, and 4) electromagnetic radiation, which includes a wide range of wave energies from mile-long radio waves at one end, to light in the middle, and to very short x-rays at the other end.

There are also some extremely odd coincidences about the exact nature of these four forces. Here are some of them.

1. Gravity. The force of gravity is constant throughout the universe. If it were just a bit stronger, stars would be larger and burn too fast, which means that none of them could support life on surrounding planets. If gravity were slightly weaker, all stars would have less mass, and the elements necessary for the formation of planets wouldn't be created, also making life impossible.

2. The strong nuclear force holds together small particles in the nucleus of all atoms. If this force were slightly weaker, these nucleuses wouldn't hold together and hydrogen would be the only element in the universe. If stronger, hydrogen would be rare in the universe, and so would most of the elements necessary for life.

3. The weak nuclear force is necessary for radioactive decay, and if it were slightly less, helium would be rare in the universe—along with other elements necessary for life. If this weak force were stronger, the elements necessary for life would be trapped forever inside the cores of stars.

4. The electromagnetic force binds electrons to protons in all atoms. If this force were slightly larger or smaller, molecules couldn't form and life would be impossible.

PHENOMENON 3: THE EARTH

The earth was created as a result of all the strangely precise physical constants outlined in Phenomena 1 and 2—and the earth itself is also very odd in many ways. For example, all the planets in our solar system are either burnt-out rocks or fiery satellites circling the sun with very little if any life. Earth is the only planet that has an atmosphere that supports millions of species. But if any one of several dozen of earth's physical constants were even slightly changed, life would vanish forever—and how our atmosphere remains exactly the way it is to support all this life has been a mystery for years.

1. Water. Unlike all other planets, which have surfaces that are either barren deserts or seething with toxic oceans, almost three-quarters of our earth is bathed in water, and if it weren't for the very unusual characteristics of this simple but amazing combination of two molecules of hydrogen and one of oxygen, there would be no life on our planet at all.

Ordinary water is anything but ordinary. In fact, it's remarkably different from all other liquids. For example, water is denser as a liquid than as a solid. If this weren't the case, ice freezing in a lake would sink to the bottom, killing all marine life. Water also has an amazing ability to store heat—without it the body temperature of the average person would soar to almost 300 degrees Fahrenheit during the day. Water can act as both an acid and as a base, and its incredibly flexible nature makes it ideally suited for the many chemical changes required for all living organisms—not to mention the fact that living organisms themselves are made up of a large part of water. In humans, the figure is 65%.

The anomalous qualities of water compared to other liquids are amazing enough—but how all these qualities combine in exactly the right way to support all life on earth is even more amazing. Needless to say, scientists really have no exact idea how this remarkable and mysterious liquid works.

2. The electromagnetic force that fills the Universe is made of a number of waves that are fatal to all life: gamma rays, x-rays, ultraviolet waves, infrared waves and microwaves. However, by the strangest of coincidences, the gases that make up earth's atmosphere soak up every one of these deadly rays like a sponge—but at the same time this same atmosphere keeps one extremely small window open to let through the one electromagnetic wave that's necessary for all life—sunlight. The size of this window is the distance between deadly ultraviolet rays at .0004 of an inch, and equally deadly infrared rays at .00004 of an inch—this means that our atmosphere opens a window only 36/100,000 of an inch wide to let through this vital sunlight—and blocks out every other ray that would destroy life.

3. The carbon dioxide and water vapour levels in our atmosphere have exactly the right balance for supporting life—if there were slightly more carbon dioxide, a disastrous greenhouse effect would exist, and if less carbon dioxide, there wouldn't be enough greenhouse effect and the earth would cool dramatically.

4. If the ozone layer were slightly thinner, too many deadly ultraviolet rays would reach earth and ground temperatures would also rise — if the ozone layer were slightly thicker, surface temperatures would drop drastically. Either way, life on earth would be destroyed.

5. The moon is very important because it stabilizes the earth as it spins around the sun--if the gravitational pull between these two bodies were slightly greater, disastrous tidal effects would be created in the oceans and atmosphere, and if this gravitational pull were less, earth's orbit would change and there would be catastrophic changes in climate.

6. The angle that the earth tilts at as it revolves around the sun is exactly what's necessary to sustain life as it is—a greater or lesser tilt in any direction would produce severe temperature changes all over the earth.

7. Atmosphere. The only other planets in our solar system that resemble earth enough to support life are Venus and Mars. But both these planets have atmospheres that are 95% carbon dioxide and their surfaces are barren rock. On the other hand, the earth's atmosphere has a ratio of 77% nitrogen to 21% oxygen, which, again, is exactly what's needed to support life. Any slight change in this ratio would have disastrous effects on all life.

PHENOMENON 4: LIFE

All of the above Phenomena #1-#3 are necessary for the existence of Phenomenon #4, life. Evolutionists claim that the first living cell was created randomly from the primordial soup of ancient seas, and that over millions of years complete organisms, including man, also evolved from this single living cell—also by sheer accident. Today scientists are beginning to realize that life itself is such an amazing phenomenon that this theory is impossible, and here's some of the evidence supporting this conclusion.

1. The first living cell. The simplest living cell has 400 linked amino acids. But even if this cell had only 100 amino acids, the probability that it would form by complete chance is about one in 10 followed by 158 zeros. To get an idea what a long shot this is, the total number of electrons in the universe is only 10 followed by 80 zeros, and the age of the universe in seconds is 10 followed by only 18 zeros! Dr. Hugh Ross thinks that even these astronomical odds are too low:

"Researchers who are both non-theists and theists and who are in a variety of disciplines have arrived at the calculation that the universe is at least 10 followed by 10 billion zeros too small or too young for life to be assembled by natural (random) processes."

And Dr. Harold Klein had this to say: "The simplest bacterium is so damned complicated from the point of view of a chemist that it's almost impossible to imagine how it happened."

Anyone who's played a Pick 10 lottery knows how difficult it is to randomly guess even ten numbers in an exact sequence—but here's how long another scientist, B.C. Ranganathan, tells us it would take for Mother Nature to win the Pick-3,000,000 lottery:

"The DNA of even the simplest form of life, such as a bacterium, has a sequential chain of 3,000,000 nucleic acids. The probability of this occurring by chance is equivalent to that of an unabridged dictionary coming into being from a monkey randomly pressing the keys on a typewriter or computer. Even the one billion years that evolutionists give for the first form of life to have come into being by chance is laughable in the light of such knowledge."

2. The first artificially produced living cell. Since Darwinists believe that the first living cell was created by a purely random combination of just the right natural ingredients over a billion years, scientists should certainly be able to come close to duplicating this process by artificially creating living cells in a laboratory. Even though these experiments would be anything but random, despite many attempts over the years, not a single such experiment has ever succeeded.

The irony of this failure is exactly the same as the absence of transitional fossils—it's completely backfired against the theory of evolution to give us an even stronger case for a Supreme Being.

3. No transitional fossils. Not one, but millions of transitional fossils should have been found since Darwin's time. In fact, he was the first to admit that if no such fossils were ever found, his theory of evolution would be invalid. But instead of admitting defeat after more than a hundred years and thousands of new fossil sites, Darwinists today keep on preaching their faith with nothing but empty rhetoric and contrived "missing links" to back it up, insisting that evolution is one of the basic facts of modem science.

4. Biology's Big Bang. The fossil record confirms that the fully developed ancestors for every species now alive suddenly appeared during biology's "Big Bang" during the Cambrian era, over 500 million years ago—still another nail in the coffin for evolutionists, who believe that such changes could only have taken place by very small, accidental changes over millions of years

The universe has been structured according to a very specific design by an entity whose intelligence is far beyond human comprehension—and because of the existence of this grand design, there must be a grand designer.

Rubik's Cube is a small plastic cube with rotating sides made up of many brightly-colored squares. Out of millions of possible combinations, there's only one combination of all squares that provides the correct solution, the perfect design. The universe is God's Cosmic Cube. Out of an infinite number of possible combinations of elements, conditions and other variables that make up this universe, they are all combined in exactly one way—and one way only—to support the existence of life.

The poet Edwin Arlington Robinson said, "We're all in a spiritual sandbox, trying to spell the name of God with the wrong blocks." For the first time in history the tools of our own exponentially growing technology are generating scientifically confirmable evidence of God's existence—a stronger and stronger light that's giving us the first real glimpse into what his worlds are really like...

Unfortunately, most of us choose to ignore this evidence.

Volume B

The Enemies of (the Holy) Spirit

The three great Apocalyptic Books of the Bible

1. The New Testament

The Book of Revelation

BACKGROUND AND INTRODUCTION

My first point is that I avoid organised religion like the plague! I prefer a deep, usually very lonely, Faith in the Lord God, the Holy Spirit of Seven Spirits, who is my main means to reach Him, and the immense richness of the Saving Grace of Jesus, all required to even *start* to read the Bible. So I am very much a 'Bible and Holy Spirit' person – as well as the Holy Books of ALL Faiths.

On 20th June 2003, with all the time in the world on my hands, I started translating the Book of Revelation *literally*, and made many interesting discoveries and so fresh interpretations. Yet that was only by reading a literal translation from the original Ancient Greek, even though I knew next to nothing of that language. "It's all Greek to me...!"

However, the Interlinear RSV New Testament that I still kept, from 1978 at Cambridge University, once dusted off, spared me that problem. It gives the original Greek of Saint John the Divine written in exile around 90 AD on the Mediterranean Island of Patmos, as well as, vitally, a word by word *literal* English translation.

Immediately I realised that: -

- The RSV (Revised Standard Version) is a bad, only about 80-90% accurate translation of the first half at least, of a very beautiful, very well-written text, which is passionate and poetic throughout. Yet the RSV is often lauded as a 'definitive translation of a very badly written text'. The complete opposite is in fact true, as any comparison of the RSV with my new translation here shows!
- The translation in this Part 1 of Volume B of this book, of the Book of Revelation, is by the chapter, with comments mostly after each section of translation. Some of great exclamation at total divergence by the RSV from the lovely language in the original, are imbedded in square brackets in the text. Revelation revisited – and for the first time? – revealed in the light of the world of the 21st Century?
- Early on, we find the author of John's Visions here has, *not* as wrongly translated in the RSV, a 'two-edged sword proceeding from his mouth' but a 'two-<u>mouthed</u> sword' – of the *Word of God* or *Jesus*! The meaning of the mystery of this peculiar phrase soon reveals itself in chapters two and three and chapters 11, 12, and 13. Good and Evil in utter, stark contrast!

REVELATION CHAPTER ONE

1. A revelation of Jesus Christ, which God gave to him, to show to his slaves things that need to occur with speed, sending signs through his angel-messenger to his slave John,
2. who bore witness of the word of God and the witness of Jesus Christ, to everything he saw.
3. Blessed is the reader and the hearers of the words of the prophecy who keep the things written in it, for the time is near.

4. John to the seven churches in Asia: Grace to you and peace from the Being and the Having Been and the Forthcoming; and from the Seven Spirits which are before His throne
5. and from Jesus Christ, the faithful witness, the firstborn of the dead, and the ruler of the kings of the earth. To the one loving us, and who released us from our sins by his blood,
6. and made us a kingdom, priests to His God and Father, whose is the glory and the might unto the ages of the ages. Amen.

7. Behold, he comes with the clouds, and every eye will see him, everyone who pierced him; and all the tribes of the earth will wail over him. Yes, Amen.

8. "I am the Alpha and the Omega", says the Lord God, the Being and the Having Been and the Coming, The Almighty.

9. I John, your brother and fellow slave in the affliction and kingdom and endurance in Jesus, came to be on the island called Patmos on account of the word of God and the witness of Jesus.
10. I came to be in spirit on the imperial day, and heard behind me a great voice like a trumpet, saying;
11. "What you see write in a scroll and send it to the seven churches, to Ephesus, Smyrna, Pergamum, Thyatira, Sardis, Philadelphia and Laodicea".
12. And I turned to see the voice which spoke with me, and on turning I saw seven golden lampstands,
13. and in the midst of the lampstands one like the Son of Man, clothed to the feet and with a golden girdle around his breast;

14. his head and his hair white as wool, white as snow, and his eyes like a flame of fire,
15. his feet like burnished brass fired as in a furnace, and his voice like the sound of many waters;
16. and he held seven stars on his right hand, out of his mouth proceeded a sharp two-mouthed sword, and his face was as if the power of the sun shone in it.
17. When I saw him, I fell at his feet as if dead; and he placed his right hand on me saying, "fear not: I am the first and the last
18. and the living, and I became dead, and behold, I am living unto the ages of the ages, and I have the keys of death and of Hades.
19. Therefore write you the things which you saw and the present things and the things which are to occur after these things.
20. The mystery of the seven stars which you saw on my right hand, and the seven golden lampstands; the seven stars are the angel-messengers of the seven churches, and the seven lampstands are the seven churches".

Notes on Revelation Chapter One

1. The translation above is very different to that of the Revised Standard Version – and we will see it only starts to get much closer after Chapter Nine of the Book of Revelation!

2. The two chapters of the Book of Revelation that follow, where the 'angel-messenger' Jesus figure addresses his 'slaves' ('servants' in the RSV translation) of the seven churches of Asia Minor, and mostly tells them off, has a message for each church that are *distinctly* all ended with the first of many phrases with 'two-mouthed' meanings! These are addressed to 'the one who overcomes', the literal translation, not 'the one who conquers' as in the RSV.

3. The whole of Volume A of this book is devoted to 'the seven spirits' of this chapter – and just what each one is – and how they, Time, Space, God, and Jesus fit together and work together – scientifically!

REVELATION CHAPTER TWO

1. "To the angel-messenger of the church in Ephesus write you: 'The one holding the seven stars on his right hand says these things, the one walking in the midst of the seven golden lamp-stands.
2. I know your works and toil and your endurance, and that you cannot bear bad men, and tested those saying, "We are apostles" and are not, and found them liars;
3. and you have endurance, because of bearing my name, and have not grown weary.
4. But I have it against you that you did leave your first love.
5. Remember therefore from whence you have fallen, and repent and do the works as at first. If not, I will come to you and remove your lamp-stand out of its place, unless you repent.
6. But this you have, that you hate the works of the Nicolaitans, which I also hate.
7. The one with an ear, let him hear what the Spirit says to the churches. To the one who overcomes, I will grant to eat of the tree of life, which is in the paradise of God.'

8. To the angel-messenger of the church in Smyrna write you: 'The first and the last says these things, who became dead yet lives.
9. I know your affliction and poverty, but you are rich, and the ones who call themselves Jews rail against you, yet they are not, only a synagogue of Satan.
10. Do not fear the things you are about to suffer. Behold, the devil is about to cast some of you into prison, in order to try you, and you will have ten days of affliction. You be faithful unto death, and I will give you the crown of life.
11. The one with an ear, let him hear what the Spirit says to the churches. The one who overcomes will by no means be hurt by the second death.'

12. To the angel-messenger of the church in Pergamum write you: 'The one with the sharp two-mouthed sword says these things:
13. I know where you dwell, where Satan's throne is; you hold onto my name, and did not deny your faith in me, even in

the days of Antipas my witness, who was faithful in me, who was killed among you, where Satan dwells.
14. But I have a few things against you, because you have there ones holding the teaching of Balaam, who taught Balak to cast a stumbling-block before the sons of Israel, to eat idol sacrifices and to commit fornication.
15. So you have also some holding the teaching of the Nicolaitans likewise.
16. Repent, therefore. Otherwise, I am coming to you quickly, and will fight with them with the sword of my mouth.
17. The one with an ear, let him hear what the Spirit says to the churches. To the one who overcomes, I will reveal hidden manna, and I will give him a white stone, and a new name written on the stone, which no-one knows except the one receiving it.'

18. To the angel-messenger of the church in Thyatira write you: 'The Son of God says these things, who has eyes like a flame of fire, and whose feet are like burnished brass.
19. I know your works, your love and faith and ministry and endurance, and that your last works exceed the first.
20. But I have it against you, that you permit the woman Jezebel, who calls herself a prophetess, and teaches and deceives my slaves to commit fornication and to eat idol sacrifices.
21. I gave her time to repent, and she will not repent of her fornication.
22. Behold, I am casting her into a bed, and those who commit adultery with her into great affliction, unless they repent of her works;
23. I will put her children to death. And all the churches will know that I am the one who searches kidneys [NOT 'minds'!] and hearts, and I will give to each one of you, according to your works.
24. But to the rest in Thyatira this I say to you, who do not have the so-called teaching of the deep things of Satan, I am not casting on you another burden;
25. Nevertheless hold what you have until I shall come.
26. And to the one who overcomes and who keeps my works until the end, I will give him authority over the nations,
27. and he will shepherd them with an iron staff, as the clay vessels are broken, as I also have received from my Father,

28. and I will give him the morning star.
29. The one with an ear, let him hear what the Spirit says to the churches'.

REVELATION CHAPTER THREE

1. And to the angel-messenger of the church in Sardis write you: 'The one says these things, who has the seven spirits of God and the seven stars. I know your works, that you have a name that you live, yet you are dead.
2. Be you watching, and establish the remaining things, which were about to die; for I have not found your works fulfilled before my God.
3. Remember then what you received and heard, and keep and repent. If therefore you do not watch, I will come as a thief, and you know by no means, at what hour I will come upon you.
4. But you have a few names in Sardis which did not defile their garments, and they shall walk with me in white, because they are worthy.
5. The one who overcomes, thus shall be clothed in white garments, and by no means shall I blot his name out of the scroll of life, and I will confess his name before my father and his angel-messengers.
6. The one with an ear, let him hear what the Spirit says to the churches'.

7. To the angel-messenger of the church in Philadelphia write you: 'The holy one, the true one, says these things, the one who has the key of David, the opening which no one shall shut, and on shutting, no one opens.
8. I know of your works; behold, I have given you a door already opened, which nobody can shut; because you have a little power, and kept my word and did not deny my name.
9. Behold, I may make some of the synagogue of Satan, the ones calling themselves Jews, who are not, but they lie – behold, I will change them so that they come and worship God before your feet, and they shall know that I loved you.

10. Because you did keep the word of my endurance, I will also keep you out of the hour of trial to come on all the inhabited earth.
11. I am coming quickly; hold onto what you have, so no one takes your crown.
12. The one who overcomes, I will make him a pillar in the shrine of my God, and he will never leave it. I will write on him the name of my God and the name of the city of my God, of the New Jerusalem descending out of heaven from my God, and my new name.
13. The one with an ear, let him hear what the Spirit says to the churches'.

14. To the angel-messenger of the church in Laodicea write you: 'The Amen says these things, the faithful and true witness, the head of the creation of God:
15. I know your works, that you are neither cold nor hot. I wish you were cold or hot!
16. So because you are lukewarm, and neither cold nor hot, I am about to vomit you out of my mouth.
17. For you say, I am rich, I have become rich and I have no need, and you know not that you are wretched and pitiable and poor and blind and naked.
18. I counsel you to buy from me gold that has been refined by fire in order that you may be rich, and white garments so that you may be clothed and hide the shame of your nakedness, and eye-salve to anoint your eyes so that you may see.
19. As many as I love, I rebuke and I chasten; therefore you be hot and repent.
20. Behold, I stand at the door and I knock; if anyone hears my voice and opens the door, I will come in to them and dine with them, and them with me.
21. The one who overcomes, I will grant him to sit on my throne with me, as I also overcame, and sat with my father on his throne.
22. The one who has an ear, let him hear what the Spirit says to the churches'. "

Notes on Revelation Chapters Two and Three

This 'angel-messenger Jesus' dictates seven messages to each of the then seven Churches in Asia Minor. Only two, Smyrna and Philadelphia, are at all praised! A common key phrase is repeated to each: -

'The one who has an ear, let him hear what the Spirit says to the churches'. (see 2:7, 2:11, 2:17, 2:29, 3:6, 3:13, and 3:22). Each church is either told that it is making the right choice of a pair of opposites confronting them, or to very decisively make that choice! As we said before, only Smyrna and Philadelphia come into the former 'approved' category.

Finally the message to each church ends with a very encouraging 'spiritual message' to 'he who overcomes'.

We can very easily and conveniently summarise the seven messages to the seven churches in a table, as follows:

Letter	Church	Choice Between	Current Choice	Promise
2:1-7	Ephesus	love / hate	hate - love forgotten	2:7
2:8-11	Smyrna	rich / poor free / suffering	poor suffering **(approved of!)**	2:11
2:12-17	Pergamum	true worship / false worship	mixture (hypocrisy)	2:17
2:18-29	Thyatira	'works for Jesus' / 'works for Satan'	mixture (hypocrisy)	2:26-28
3:1-6	Sardis	live / dead	zombie!	3:5
3:7-13	Philadelphia	weak / resisting open / shut	weak / yet resisting 'shut yet open' **(approved of!)**	3:12
3:14-22	Laodicea	cold / hot	lukewarm	3:21

The message to most Churches then is to make a positive, powerful choice between two 'opposing states' confronting them. Typically, Jesus doesn't mess around!

Astonishing yet amusing 'worst bad translation' first! Revelation 2:23 should read **not** like the RSV, 'I search mind and heart' but 'I search kidneys and heart'! Since William Harvey discovered the circulation of the blood in the nineteenth century, the heart has been known to continually pump blood around the body; while the kidneys, equally importantly, continually cleanse the blood in the body. The RSV originated from the 'Standard' King James version of 1611, two whole centuries before Harvey's crucial discoveries, so vital to Western medical science. That is its only excuse for such an appalling mistranslation as 'kidneys' into 'mind'!

The promises to 'the one who overcomes' (**not** 'conquers' – the RSV version as often is far too inflammatory a translation!) start off seeming to mostly be open to anybody who 'overcomes'. However, the promises in Revelation 2:26-28 echo Revelation 12 onwards, in only applying to 'him who overcomes, who will shepherd (**not** 'rule' – wrong again, RSV!) the nations with the authority of his iron staff'. Likewise only *one* man can 'be given the morning star', etc.

REVELATION CHAPTER FOUR

1. After these things I saw, and behold, a door had opened in the heavens! And the first voice, which I heard speaking with me like a trumpet, was saying: "Come up here, and I will show you things which must occur after these things."
2. Immediately I became in Spirit, and behold, a throne was set in the heavens, with one seated on the throne!
3. And the one who sat there appeared like stone of jasper and sardius [carnelian – the colour of 'white' skin; as jasper is *any shade* of orange, red, brown, or black skin. Any colour skin at all *except the grey of Death!*] and there was a rainbow round the throne, like an emerald in appearance.
4. And round the throne I saw twenty-four thrones, and on these thrones sat twenty-four elders clothed in white garments, with golden crowns upon their heads. [Symbolising the twenty-four hours of each day. Nobody has ever said who invented the 24-hour clock. God did...]
5. Out of the throne come forth lightnings and sounds and thunders; and seven lamps of fire burn before the throne, which are the seven spirits of God; and
6. before the throne there is a glassy sea, like crystal; and in the midst of the throne and round the throne, are four living creatures, full of eyes before and behind:
7. the first living creature like a lion, and the second living creature like an ox, and the third living creature with the face of a man, and the fourth living creature like a flying eagle.
8. And the four living creatures, one by one in turn, each with six wings, and full of eyes around and within, with no respite, day and night they say:

    'Holy, Holy, Holy,
    Lord God Almighty,
    the Having Been, the Being, and the Coming'.

9. And whenever the living creatures shall give glory and honour and thanks to the one sitting on the throne, to the living unto the ages of the ages,
10. the twenty-four elders will fall before the one sitting on the throne, and worship the living unto the ages of the ages, and will cast their crowns before the throne, saying :

11. "Worthy are You, our Lord and God, to receive the glory and the honour and the power, because You did create all things, and because of your will they were, and were created".

Notes on Revelation Chapter Four

Chapter One of the Book of Revelation featured an 'angel-messenger Jesus' with an often 'double-mouthed' or dual-edged meaning to the message which He then gave to the seven churches of Asia Minor in the next two Chapters of Revelation, Two and Three.

My commentary on this last brief 'sally into Heaven through, of all things, a *door*' adds some now suddenly transparently obvious 'spiritual equations' to the symbolism in Revelation: -

- <u>Twenty-four</u> elders – the 24 hours of each terrestrial day. No culture claims to have invented the 24-hour clock. None other than the Lord God did so! Who else could have done so?

- <u>Seven</u> Spirits of God. "Sophia" or *Divine Wisdom* – the Anima, the *Bride* of the Lord God. As reverently and very gradually introduced with all her 'hidden manna' or qualities – or as *Mother Nature or 'Mother Quality'* - in Volume A of this book.

- This is also the obvious inspiration for another invention by God, as in the Book of Exodus in the Bible as instructed to Moses, *the seven-day week.*

- <u>Four</u> 'living creatures' each with *six* wings i.e. *three pairs* of wings. The *four seasons*, each of *three* months, of two original 15-day fortnights taken in a pair per month of 30 days.

- The Great Mystery of the Lord God is completed with those of His seven-fold Spirit. 'Mother Nature, Divine Wisdom made of Qualities or Virtues' – the Holy Spirit, in Person. I showed conclusively in Volume A of this present book, that the *seven spirits* are principally: -

1. Wisdom, comprising: -
2. Joy and
3. Love
4. Health and
5. Beauty
6. Peace and
7. Grace

I call the Spirit 'She' but Spirit is fundamentally *neutral in gender.* The explanation for this, as in Volume One of this book, is that Spirit is made up of equal numbers of male and female component spirits!

REVELATION CHAPTER FIVE

1. And I saw on the right hand of the one sitting on the throne, a scroll which had been written within and on the reverse side, which had been sealed with seven seals;
2. and I saw a strong angel-messenger proclaiming in a great voice, "Who is worthy to open the scroll and loosen its seals?"
3. And no one in heaven nor on earth nor underneath the earth was able to open the scroll nor to look at it.
4. And I wept much, because no one was found worthy to open the scroll nor to look at it.
5. And one of the elders said to me, "Weep not; behold, the lion of the tribe of Judah, the root of David, overcame to open the scroll and its seven seals".
6. And I saw in the midst of the throne, and of the four living creatures, and in the midst of the elders, a lamb standing as though it had been slain, with seven horns and seven eyes, which are the seven Spirits of God previously sent forth into all the earth.
7. And he came and took the scroll out of the right hand of the one sitting on the throne.
8. And when he took the scroll, the four living creatures and the twenty-four elders fell before the lamb, each one having a harp, and with golden bowls full of incenses, which are the prayers of the saints;
9. And they sing a new song, saying, "Worthy are you to receive the scroll and to open its seals, because you were slain and by your blood did purchase men to God out of every tribe and tongue and people and nation,
10. and did make them a kingdom and priests for our God, and they will reign over the earth".
11. And I saw, and I heard a sound of many angel-messengers round the throne and the living creatures and the elders, in numbers myriads of myriads and thousands and thousands,
12. saying with a great voice: "Worthy is the slain lamb to receive the power and riches and wisdom and strength and honour and glory and blessing".
13. And I heard every creature which is in heaven and on the earth and underneath the earth and on the sea, and in them all things, saying: "To the one sitting on the throne and to

the lamb be the blessing and the honour and the glory and the might unto the ages of the ages".
14. And the four living creatures said, 'Amen', and the elders fell and worshipped.

REVELATION CHAPTER SIX

1. Now I saw when the lamb opened one of the seven seals, and I heard one of the living creatures saying with a voice of thunder: 'Come!'
2. And I saw, and behold, a white horse, and the one sitting on it had a bow, and was given a crown, and he went forth overcoming and in order that he might overcome.
3. And when he opened the second seal, I heard the second living creature saying: 'Come!'
4. And another horse went forth, red, and the one sitting on it was permitted to take peace out of the earth, in order that they should slay one another, and he was given a great sword.
5. And when he opened the third seal, I heard the third living creature saying 'Come!' And I saw, and behold, a black horse, and the one sitting on it had a balance in his hand.
6. And I heard a voice in the midst of the four living creatures, saying:
"A choenix [quart or two pints] of wheat for a denarius, and three choenixes of barley for a denarius; and the oil and the wine do no harm!"
7. When he opened the fourth seal, I heard the voice of the fourth living creature saying: 'Come!'
8. And I saw, and behold, a pale green horse, and the name given to the one on it was death, and Hades followed with him, and authority was given to them over the fourth part of the earth, to kill with sword and with famine, and with death by the wild beasts of the earth.
9. And when he opened the fifth seal, I saw underneath the altar the souls of the ones who had been slain on account of the word of God and of the witness which they had.
10. And they cried with a great voice, saying, "O Holy and true Master, until when will you not judge and avenge our blood of those dwelling on the earth?"

11. Each one of them was given a white robe, and they were told that they should rest yet a little time, until their fellow-slaves and their brothers should also reach the fulfilment to be killed like them.
12. I saw when he opened the sixth seal, and a great earthquake occurred, and the sun became black as sackcloth made of hair, and the whole moon became like blood,
13. and the stars of the sky fell to the earth, as a fig-tree casts its unripe figs when shaken by a strong wind,
14. and the heaven departed like a scroll rolling up, and every mountain and island were moved out of their places.
15. And the kings of the earth and the great men and the chiliarchs [generals] and the rich men and the strong men and every slave and free man hid themselves in the caves and in the rocks of the mountains,
16. calling to the mountains and the rocks: "Fall on us and hide us from the face of the one sitting on the throne and from the wrath of the lamb, because the great day of their wrath came, and who can stand?"

Notes on Revelation Chapters Five and Six

From the sublime in Chapter Five, to the plain 'ridiculous' in chapter 6:1-8, revealing that GOD has a truly awesomely black and rich vein of humour! In the four PANTOMIME 'horsemen of the apocalypse' – before the serious stuff resumes in chapter 6:9-16!

Chapter five is clearly extremely serious, and very moving, before there is immediately to me at least, some extraordinary light relief with the four traditionally feared 'Horsemen of the Apocalypse' of chapter 6:1-8. So: -

Revealed - how God has a truly awesome sense of Humour! A procession of four *pantomime* horsemen, far from the traditional view of Revelation chapter 6:1-8 as 'the Four Horsemen of the Apocalypse'. Rather, I reveal them in their true guise, as a choice selection of Graeco-Roman *demigods*, whistling variations, as they ride, to a theme of Vivaldi's *'Four Seasons'*?

Rev 6:1-2. *Spring* in the Pagan (Roman) calendar, 21st March to 20th June.
'When spring is in the air, a young man's thoughts turn to Love'.
The horse is white – colour of virginity and courtship, and Love. The rider with a bow and a crown can only be *Cupid*, Graeco-Roman demigod of love, *'overcoming all and going out to overcome all'*.

Rev 6:3-4. *Summer*. 21st June – 20th September.
The horse is red, the colour of blood *or* of red wine. The rider is the Graeco-Roman demigod *Bacchus*, famous for his 'rites' where men got drunk, had orgies with each other and women, and had fights to the death.

Rev 6:5-6. *Autumn*. 21st September – 20th December.

So we have had an upbeat note, then a downbeat note, and the short 'Four Seasons concerto' ends with the pattern repeated with the last two seasons.

The 'black horse' could be called a 'dark horse', certainly in view of all the horse-trading with the rider's balance, going on here! For this is a picture of all the market trading that goes on in the autumn, once the harvest is in, and the granaries are all full. Hence the wheat and barley, and the statement that 'oil and wine do no harm!'

Rev 6:7-8. *Winter*. December 21st – March 20th.

The horse is pale green, the colour of the landscape in winter, with few trees with leaves, and the grass starved of sunshine, hence going pale. 'Sleep, close cousin of death' wrote the Roman poet Virgil in the Aeneid of the Morphius and Morbius pair of "doom-bringers" in winter here – the Roman demigods of sleep and death respectively.

Rev 6:9-11. Onto the opening of the fifth seal. An awesome question begs. This vast number of 'slain souls' is *nowhere* specified as just *human*. Is it actually the entire abused and slaughtered number of animals, birds and fish, not just people, of the world's entire *Creation* that await God's vengeance?

Rev 6:12-16. I have, as you have already seen, always taken the view that the rest of the Book of Revelation is in date order. So has this part happened already? A similar event is described in the gospels, saying that the sky went black for three hours after Jesus died on the cross (and the curtain of the temple was rent in two).

No. Later in the Revelation God states, "Behold, I make all things new!" So this darkening of the sky may have passed unrecorded in the Dark Ages, around the First Millennium, at 1000 AD. It could happen again – any time!

REVELATION CHAPTER SEVEN

1. After this I saw four angel-messengers standing on the four corners of the earth, holding back the four winds of the earth, so that no wind should blow on the earth nor on the sea nor on any tree. [i.e. they stand on one spot!]
2. Then I saw another angel-messenger coming up from the rising of the sun, with a seal of the living god, and he cried with a great voice to the four angel-messengers to whom it was given to harm the earth and the sea, saying:
3. "Do not harm the earth nor the sea nor the trees, until we have sealed the slaves of our God on their foreheads".
4. And I heard the number of the sealed, a hundred and forty-four thousands, sealed out of every tribe of sons of Israel:
5. twelve thousands sealed out of the tribe of Judah, twelve thousands sealed out of the tribe of Reuben, twelve thousands sealed out of the tribe of Gad,
6. twelve thousands sealed out of the tribe of Asher, twelve thousands sealed out of the tribe of Naphtali, twelve thousands sealed out of the tribe of Manasseh,
7. twelve thousands sealed out of the tribe of Simeon, twelve thousands sealed out of the tribe of Levi, twelve thousands sealed out of the tribe of Issachar,
8. twelve thousands sealed out of the tribe of Zebulun, twelve thousands sealed out of the tribe of Joseph, twelve thousands sealed out of the tribe of Benjamin. [There are calculated to be 144,000 distinct languages and dialects in the world today as reckoned by top philologists!]
9. After this I saw, and behold, a great multitude which no one could number, out of every nation and tribe and people and tongue, standing before the throne before the lamb, clothed with white robes, and palms in their hands,
10. and they cry with a great voice, saying, "Salvation to our God sitting upon the throne, and to the lamb!"
11. And all the angel-messengers stood round the throne and the elders and the four living creatures, and fell before the throne on their faces and worshipped God, saying,
12. "Amen, blessing and glory and wisdom and thanks and honour and power and strength to our God, unto the ages of the ages: Amen".

13. And one of the elders answered, saying to me, "These ones clothed in white robes, who are they and where have they come from?"
14. I said to him, "My lord, you know". And he told me, "These are those who have come out of the Great Holocaust, and washed their robes and whitened them in the blood of the lamb.
15. Therefore they are before the throne of God, and serve him day and night in his shrine, and the one sitting on the throne will spread his tent over them.
16. They will not hunger any longer nor will they thirst any longer, neither will the sun nor any heat fall on them.
17. Because the lamb in the midst of the throne will shepherd them and will lead them upon fountains of waters of life; and God will wipe every tear out of their eyes."

REVELATION CHAPTER EIGHT

1. Whenever he opened the seventh seal, there was silence in heaven for about half an hour.
2. Then I saw seven angel-messengers who stood before God, and they were given seven trumpets,
3. and another angel-messenger came and stood on the altar with a golden censer, and was given many incenses to give with the prayers of the saints on the golden altar before the throne.
4. The smoke of the incenses with the prayers of the saints went from the hand of the angel-messenger before God.
5. And the angel-messenger took the censer, filled it with fire from the altar and cast it into the earth; and there were thunders and sounds and lightnings and an earthquake.

6. Now the seven angel-messengers with the seven trumpets prepared themselves to blow them.
7. The first trumpeted, and there was hail and fire mixed with blood, and it was cast to the earth, and the third part of the earth was burnt down, and the third part of the trees was burnt down, and all green grass was burnt down.
8. The second angel-messenger trumpeted, and a great mountain, burning with fire, was cast into the sea; and the third part of the sea became blood, and
9. the third part of the creatures in the sea died, those with souls, and the third part of all ships were destroyed.
10. The third angel-messenger trumpeted, and a great star fell out of heaven burning like a lamp, and it fell onto the third part of the rivers and onto the fountains of the waters.
11. The name of the star is absinth [Wormwood]. The third part of the waters turned into absinth, and many men died from the waters because they were made bitter.
12. The fourth angel-messenger trumpeted, and the third part of the sun and the third part of the moon and the third part of the stars were struck, so that the third part of them was darkened; and the third part of the day could not appear, and likewise the night.
13. Then I looked, and I heard a lone eagle flying in mid-heaven, saying with a great voice, "Woe, Woe, Woe to those dwelling on the earth from the voices of the remaining three trumpets of the three angel-messengers about to trumpet!"

Notes on Revelation Chapter Eight

Chapter eight of Revelation concludes the 'opening of the seven seals' with the last one – which seems to be the most important, as its effects run into the next four chapters 8-11 of the book. A large number of 'angels' are involved in these, but there is principally a 'jazz band' of just seven, who each blow a trumpet they have been given, in turn!

For the first time in this strange book I believe it is possible to relate the account by John to historical events that happened hundreds of years later. Note that most people, however, prefer a version of the prophetic account in Revelation that makes it all appear to have 'come true' in the first century AD. I believe that a far more recent 'fulfilment of these strange visions' is just as valid if not more so.

Certainly, as we go through this chapter of Revelation and the one that follows it, you will see that I have identified striking parallels between the visions in these two chapters eight and nine, and various scientific discoveries and inventions, especially in the 20th century!

The first angel involved in chapter eight is not one of the seven with a trumpet. In verse 5 he throws a 'prayer censer' on the earth, which results in 'peals of thunder, rumblings, flashes of lightning and an earthquake'! I believe that this vision that John saw is of something invented hundreds of years later and thousands of miles away. Gunpowder, the first **explosive** invented, was discovered in China, and rapidly revolutionised warfare. It was of course swiftly taken up by all the armies and navies in the world.

I believe that the remaining trumpets blown by the other four 'angels' in this chapter, actually correspond to scientific developments in the last century and this. Highly significantly, in this chapter, as each angel blows their trumpet, exactly one third of some vital aspect of the earth gets 'destroyed'. My case rests that this vital 'one third' is not an exact one-third measure, but a one-third portion – I believe these four angels each symbolise a scientific invention or development that removed the **'andedness'** of a previously three-part concept – and so made it less dualistic.

The first angel blows his trumpet in verse 8:7. I believe what is described there corresponds to the work of the scientist and monk, **Gregor Mendel**, in the late 1800's. His pioneering experiments in **genetics** led to the mystery of sexual reproduction – the 'and' in 'male and female' to be largely destroyed.

His work had immediate political consequences! Politicians of a racist bent eagerly seized on his innocent investigations into genetics, very much as the 'Father of Genetics', to 'prove' their notions of the supremacy of their own race. This obviously had a bearing on the Second World War, but also to a large extent on the First World War as well. Mendel's experiments took place in a garden, and the mention of blood, earth, trees and grass in this verse 8:7 all fit with his 'monastery garden' investigations into lines of descent – or 'blood lines' in animals and humans.

Verses 8:8-9 remind me strongly of parallels in physics, to the splitting of the atom, by bombarding one with highly energetic subatomic particles. This was first done by **Ernest Rutherford** at Cambridge in 1916, and finally destroyed the 'and' in 'energy and matter' – so validating Albert Einstein's theories. This led in the end to the development of atomic weapons at the start of the Second World War, and their use to end the war in Japan in 1945.

The effect of 'the great star Wormwood' (in English, the bitter-tasting plant absinth) in verses 10-11 is to make all water 'bitter' so that people die from drinking it. This seems to be a simile for radioactivity, much investigated by **Albert Einstein** in working out his two theories of Special and General Relativity. These two theories certainly made the very complacent scientific community of his day, convinced that 'physics was almost completed' have a very strong and shocked reaction when he introduced relativity to the world.

These theories attempted the unthinkable – to remove the 'and' from both 'space and time' and 'energy and matter'.

Although Einstein was deeply upset when his work led to the development of nuclear weapons, since his theories enabled their invention, hundreds of thousands of people have died from radiation – the 'bitterness' of 8:11? Finally, the development of nuclear power for 'peaceful purposes' as in power stations, has inevitably killed thousands more from leaked radiation, notably after the disasters at Three Mile Island in New York and Chernobyl in Georgia.

181

In 8:12, the fourth angel blows his trumpet, and I see in this vision, all about light and darkness, the 'and' in 'electricity and magnetism' being destroyed. This was after Michael Rutherford carried out memorable experiments on electricity and magnetism, to make light, in the nineteenth century.

Then **James Clerk Maxwell** formulated theories that fully explained, totally precisely, all of Rutherford's findings.

If this matching 'prophecy to scientific developments' actually fits the facts, then these discoveries can all be seen to have come within 50 years, so it is highly apt that these first four angels blow their trumpets all in one chapter. The last three take longer – with two in the next chapter, chapter nine, and the last in chapter 11.

REVELATION CHAPTER NINE

1. The fifth angel-messenger trumpeted, and I saw a star fallen from heaven onto the earth, given the key of the shaft of the abyss.
2. He opened the shaft of the abyss, and there went up from the shaft smoke like the smoke of a great furnace, and the sun and the air were darkened by the smoke of the shaft.
3. Then out of the smoke came forth locusts to the earth, given authority as the scorpions of the earth have authority.
4. And they were told not to harm the grass of the earth nor any green stuff nor any tree, only the men who do not have the seal of God on their foreheads.
5. They were not allowed to kill them, but to torment them for five months, and their torment is like that of a scorpion, whenever it stings a man.
6. And in those days men will seek death and by no means at all find it, and they will long to die but death will fly from them.
7. In appearance the locusts were like horses prepared for war, with crowns of gold on their heads, with faces like men,
8. hair like women's hair, teeth like lions' teeth,
9. breastplates like iron breastplates, and the sound of their wings like the sound of chariots with many horses, running to war.
10. They have tails like scorpions, and stings, and with their tails lies their authority to harm men for five months.
11. They have over them a king, the angel-messenger of the abyss; his name in Hebrew is Abaddon, and in the Greek he is called Apollyon. ['the destroyer']

12. The first woe passed; behold, here are two woes after these things.

13. The sixth angel-messenger trumpeted, and I heard a voice out of the four horns of the golden altar before God,
14. saying to the sixth angel-messenger with the trumpet, "loose the four angel-messengers who are bound at the great river Euphrates".
15. And the four angel-messengers were loosed, who had been prepared for the hour and day and month and year, in order to kill the third part of men.

16. And the number of bodies of soldiers of the cavalry was two myriads of myriads [200,000,000!] – I heard their number.
17. Thus I saw the horses in the vision and the ones sitting on them: they had fire-coloured, also dusky red and sulphur-coloured breastplates, and the heads of the horses were like lions' heads, and fire and smoke and sulphur came out of their mouths.
18. By these plagues the third part of men were killed, by the fire and the smoke and sulphur coming out of their mouths.
19. For the authority of the horses is in their mouths and in their tails; for their tails are like serpents, with heads, and with them they do harm.
20. The rest of mankind, who were not killed by these plagues, did not even repent of the work of their hands, so still worshipped demons and idols of gold and silver and bronze and stone and wood, which can neither see nor hear nor walk.
21. And they did not repent of their murders nor their sorceries nor their fornication nor their thefts.

Notes on Chapter Nine of Revelation

Chapter nine contains two distinct sections, 9:1-11 and 9:13-21, corresponding to the blowing of the fifth and sixth trumpets. In each section, a 'plague' of very strange creatures is unleashed on the earth.

After the last section, it will come as no surprise that I can see these two 'plagues' as resulting from further scientific inventions, in the 20th Century. This chapter, in being described as 'two woes' whereas the even more apocalyptic visions of the previous chapter are not, further convinces me that the 'first four trumpets' of that chapter eight are indeed all 'spiritual analogies' for scientific inventions and theories.

These removed 'andedness' from previously dualistic concepts, and made them into a 'threefold continuum' – a dialectic rather than a dualistic notion, of great impact on the world of science, and then the modern world as a whole.

Chapter nine of Revelation divides into two distinct sections, each corresponding to the blowing of the next two of the seven trumpets by their angels – the fifth and sixth angels in the sequence. In verses 9:1-11 the blowing of the fifth trumpet unleashes a 'first woe' or plague of creatures of remarkable appearance and faculties, that remind John most of a plague of locusts. In verses 9:13-21, a second plague is unleashed by the sixth trumpeter that is even more dramatic in its effects, and if that were possible, comprised of even stranger creatures. Both visionary images are very weird!

I expressed my unorthodox yet inspired views above, that chapter eight describes scientific discoveries or inventions of the last two centuries. You will therefore not be surprised to learn that I believe that these two plagues both correspond to scientific images of the 20th century.

The team of the 'fifth angel' and a 'fallen star' in verses 9:1-2, seem to me to correspond uncannily well, given the rest of this section 9:3-11, to the scientific duo of Francis Crick and James Watson. They were the first to discover the structure of the famous 'double-helix molecules of life', DNA and RNA, in the 1950's. Indeed, by so doing, they 'opened the bottomless pit (of genetics and sexual reproduction)' as in verse 9:2. At about that time the first electron microscopes were invented, and were able to verify their theories about the structure of

DNA and RNA with total accuracy, by photographing the structure of DNA and RNA molecules, with both unprecedented magnification and resolution.

These massively powerful electron microscopes also revealed the shape and structure of cells, bacteria and **viruses**, the most minute 'specks' of matter able to reproduce. However, viruses achieve their reproduction – or rather, replication – in a very 'fiendish' way compared to bacteria or living cells, which simply divide in two yet in a very complex fashion. This is why viruses are regarded by all scientists as parasites. In order to replicate, they inject their characteristic RNA into the DNA of a host cell or bacterium. When the time comes for that cell or bacterium to replicate, as a result of now containing alien RNA from the virus, both new cells die, and instead, a host of new copies of the virus are released.

John attempts to describe what he saw in his remarkable vision, in verses 9:7-11. He is obviously horrified and confused by the 'locusts', as in the opening phrase of verse 9:7 he describes them as resembling horses! However, this vision, taking the elements of the 'locust-horses' together, can be seen to totally accurately correspond to a type of virus only revealed to mankind in the 1950's by electron microscopes. This is the **phage** virus, also called an 'icosahedral virus' because the 'sac' holding its parasite RNA is made of twenty triangular plates. Overleaf I give a diagram, along with a modern-day parallel to the second plague of Revelation chapter nine, relating John's vision to the structure of phage viruses.

The work of scientists on these viruses and RNA and DNA, and also on bacteria, has been cynically hi-jacked and used to develop germ warfare all around the world by the military. The most infamous, AIDS, virus that emerged about 15 years ago, may well have arisen from such deadly research. This causes death from a secondary infection in the final stages of the viral infection, about five months after the start of this final stage of this fatal illness. Although not a phage virus – AIDS is shaped like a dumb-bell – verses 9:5-6 describes vividly the agonies that sufferers from these viruses go through – for the same five months as in John's vision!

The extraordinary parallel between John's vision and phage viruses even continues in 9:10 – the 'tails' of phages are indeed the place holding their power to inject, and harm!

That completes our look at Revelation 9:1-11, in relation to phage viruses and viruses in general, except to say that they are indeed nearly invincible foes for medicine. They cause many diseases in people, animals and plants, and the faster the medical scientists find a cure for one, the faster they mutate into new, slightly different, more 'resistant' to cure, forms. A particularly nasty enemy of man, whose true nature was only first revealed by electron microscopes in the nineteen-fifties! Before and since then there has been no true cure found for AIDS (HIV) or any other type of virus...

So, on to Revelation 9:13-19, the description of the 'second woe' of this chapter, the other 'plague of strange creatures'. These seem to be equally strange creatures – as they are to be equated in the modern world, starting from the 1960's – with equally inanimate 'objects'. Once again, my personal interpretation will surprise you, for I see these no less than 200,000,000 strange 'cavalry' equating directly, as the 'locusts' equate to 'phages', to colour screens of TV's and computers! These only existed from the 1960's!

If you first read 9:17-19 and then look at the diagram overleaf and bottom, you should see the uncanny analogy between John's 'cavalry' and colour monitors or screens! Further 'prophetic evidence' comes from verses 9:15-9:19. In 9:15 'a third of mankind is killed' at a precise 'the hour, the day, the month and the year'. This precision corresponds to the average daily mediochre TV schedule! The 'one-third' is, again, not a quantity! It is the 'andedness' or inter-personal relations between people, which when watching TV, or a computer screen, is totally disrupted. 9:16 says there are a massive total of 200,000,000 'cavalry' – about the same as the number of colour screens in the world!

In verse 9:17, note that fire is bright red, hyacinth or smoke is bright blue, and sulphur is bright yellow. These then correspond to primary colours, as used a great deal on TV sets and computer monitors. Verse 9:18 indicates that the picture of a TV set or monitor, using these primary colours, is what does the damage. Verse 9:19 literally indicates about such devices today that their – electrical – power comes in through their two 'tails' – one supplying the 'signal power' for the sound and picture and the other, mains power! Again, each set has two 'mouths' – one for sound, one for the picture, and these when powered up destroy conversation and all relations – the 'one-third of humanity'!

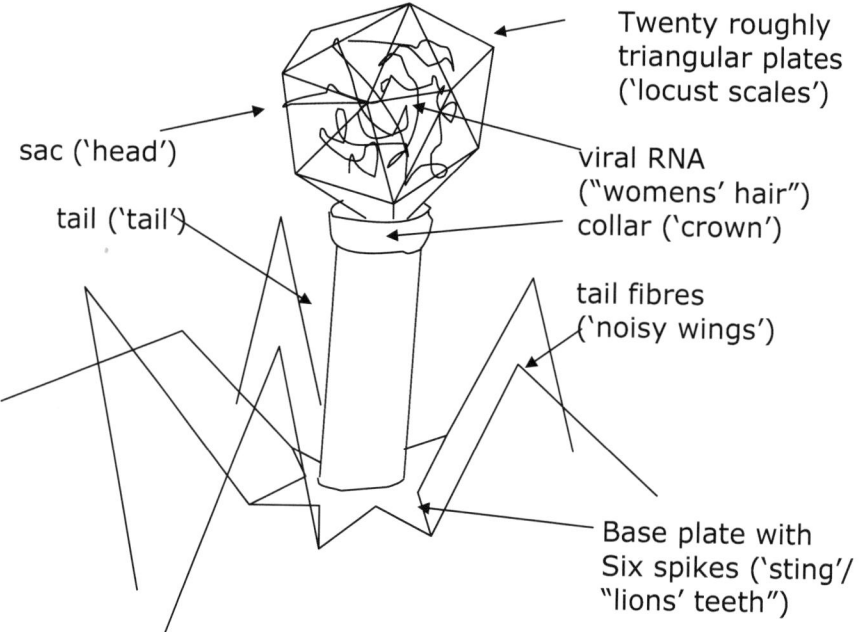

The 'locust-horses' of Revelation 9:3-11 ?

- sac ('head')
- tail ('tail')
- Twenty roughly triangular plates ('locust scales')
- viral RNA ("womens' hair")
- collar ('crown')
- tail fibres ('noisy wings')
- Base plate with Six spikes ('sting'/ "lions' teeth")

The 'cavalry' of Revelation 9:13-19 ?

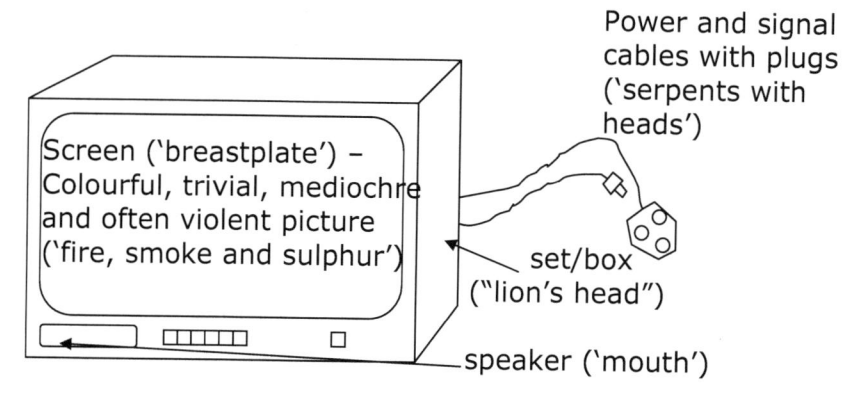

- Screen ('breastplate') – Colourful, trivial, mediochre and often violent picture ('fire, smoke and sulphur')
- Power and signal cables with plugs ('serpents with heads')
- set/box ("lion's head")
- speaker ('mouth')

This chapter then seems to predict computers and their main enemies – viruses!

REVELATION CHAPTER TEN

1. I saw another strong angel-messenger coming down out of heaven, clothed with a cloud, with a rainbow over his head, and his face was like the sun, and his legs like pillars of fire.
2. He had a little scroll opened in his hand. And he placed his right foot on the sea, and his left foot on the land,
3. and cried with a great voice like a lion roaring. When he cried, the voices of the seven thunders uttered themselves.
4. When the seven thunders spoke, I was about to write; and I heard a voice out of heaven saying, "Seal you the things the seven thunders spoke, and do not write them down".
5. And the angel-messenger, whom I saw standing on the sea and on the land, lifted his right hand to heaven,
6. and swore by the one living unto the ages of the ages, who created heaven and the things in it and the earth and the things in it and the sea and the things in it, that there should be no more delay,
7. But in the days of the voice of the seventh angel-messenger, whenever he is about to trumpet, the mystery of God should be ended, as he told his slaves the prophets.

8. Then the voice which I heard out of heaven, again spoke with me and said, "Go, you take the scroll, opened in the hand of the angel-messenger standing on the sea and on the land."
9. So I went up to the angel-messenger, and told him to give me the little scroll. And he said to me, "Take and devour it; it will make your stomach bitter, but will be as sweet as honey in your mouth".
10. I took the little scroll out of the hand of the angel-messenger and devoured it, and when I ate it, my stomach was made bitter.
11. They said to me, "You must prophesy again before many peoples and nations and tongues and kings".

REVELATION CHAPTER ELEVEN

1. Then I was given a reed like a staff, and they said, "Rise and measure the shrine of God and the altar and those worshipping in it.
2. But leave out completely the court outside the shrine and do not measure it, because it was given to the nations, and they will trample over the holy city for forty-two months.
3. And I will grant to my two martyrs, and they will prophesy for one thousand two hundred and sixty days, clothed in sackcloth".
4. These are the two olive-trees and the two lamp-stands standing before the lord of the earth.
5. If anyone wishes to harm them, fire comes out of their mouths and devours their enemies; and if anyone should wish to harm them, thus they must be killed.
6. They have the authority to shut heaven, so that rain may not fall during the days of their prophecy, and they have authority over the waters, to turn them into blood, and to strike the earth with every kind of plague, as often as they may wish.
7. When they finish their witness, the beast coming up out of the abyss will make war with them and conquer them and kill them,
8. and their dead bodies will lie in the open street of the great city, which is spiritually called Sodom and Egypt, where indeed their lord was crucified.
9. For three and a half days, some of the peoples and tribes and tongues and nations will look on their corpses, and refuse to let their corpses be placed in a tomb,
10. and those who dwell on the earth will rejoice over them and be glad, and will send presents to one another, because these two prophets tormented those dwelling on the earth.
11. And after the three days and a half, a spirit of life out of God entered them, and they stood on their feet, and great fear fell on their onlookers.
12. They heard a great voice out of heaven saying to them, "Come you up here!", and they went up to heaven in the cloud, in the sight of their foes.
13. And in that hour occurred a great earthquake, and a tenth of the city fell; seven thousand people were killed in the

earthquake, and the rest became terrified and gave glory to the God of Heaven.

14. The second woe passed away; behold, the third woe is coming quickly.

15. Then the seventh angel-messenger trumpeted; and there were great voices in heaven, saying, "The kingdom of the world has become the world of our Lord and of his Christ, and he shall reign unto the ages of the ages".
16. And the twenty-four elders sitting on their thrones before God, fell on their faces and worshipped God, saying,
17. "We thank you, O Lord God the Almighty, the Being and the Having Been, because you have taken your great power and did reign;
18. and the nations were wrathful, and your wrath came and the time of the dead to be judged, and to give rewards to your slaves, the prophets and the saints and those who fear your name, to the small and to the great, and to destroy those destroying the earth".

19. Then the shrine of God in heaven was opened, and the ark of his covenant was seen in his shrine, and there were lightnings, sounds and thunders and an earthquake and great hail.

REVELATION CHAPTER TWELVE

1. A great sign was seen in heaven, a woman clothed with the sun, and the moon under her feet, and on her head a crown of twelve stars;
2. she was pregnant and cried out suffering birth pangs, and distressed to bear.
3. And there was seen another sign in heaven, and behold, a great red dragon, with seven heads and ten horns, and on his heads ten diadems,
4. and his tail drew the third part of the stars of heaven, and cast them to the earth. The dragon stood before the woman in labour, so that when she gave birth he could devour her child.

5. She bore a son, a male, who is about to shepherd all the nations with an iron staff; but her child was seized to God and his throne.
6. The woman fled into the desert, where she has there a place prepared by God, so that there they can nourish her for a thousand two hundred and sixty days.

7. Now war broke out in heaven, Michael and his angel-messengers making war with the dragon. And the dragon and his angel-messengers fought yet
8. did not prevail; and no place was found for them still in heaven.
9. So the great dragon was cast down, the old serpent, called the Devil and Satan, the deceiver of the whole inhabited earth was cast to the earth, and his angel-messengers were cast down with him.
10. And I heard a great voice in heaven saying, "Now the salvation and the power and the kingdom of our God and the authority of his Christ have come, for the accuser of our brothers has been cast down, who was accusing them day and night before our God.
11. They overcame him because of the blood of the lamb and because of the word of their witness, and they loved not their lives unto death.
12. Therefore be glad, O heavens and those who tabernacle in them! Yet woe to the earth and the sea, because the Devil has come down to you in great anger, knowing he has little time."
13. When the dragon saw that he was cast to the earth, he pursued the woman who had given birth to the male child.
14. Yet the woman was given the two wings of the great eagle, so that she might fly to her place in the desert, there to be nourished for a time and times and half a time, away from the face of the serpent.
15. The serpent poured water like a river from his mouth behind the woman, to make her be carried off by the river.
16. The earth helped the woman, and the earth opened its mouth and swallowed the river, which the serpent poured out of its mouth.
17. The dragon was enraged over the woman, and went away to make war with the remainder of her seed, keeping the commandments of God and having the witness of JESUS.

REVELATION CHAPTER THIRTEEN

1. I stood on the sand of the sea, and I saw a beast coming out of the sea, with ten horns and seven heads, and ten diadems on its horns, and on its heads, names of blasphemy.
2. And the beast which I saw was like a leopard, its feet like those of a bear, and its mouth like a lion's mouth. To it the dragon gave its power and its throne and great authority.
3. One of its heads was as if slain to death, yet the stroke of its death was healed. All the earth wondered after the beast,
4. and they worshipped the dragon, because he gave the authority to the beast. They worshipped the beast, saying, "Who is like the beast, and who can make war with it?"
5. And it was given a mouth speaking great things and blasphemies, and it was given authority to act for *forty-two months*.
6. It opened its mouth in blasphemies against God, to blaspheme his name and his tabernacle, and those who tabernacle in heaven.
7. Authority was given to it over every tribe and tongue and nation.
8. Everyone on the earth will worship it, whose names have not been written from the foundation of time ['the word of God' in other words] in the scroll of life of the lamb that was slain.
9. If anyone has an ear, let him hear.
10. If anyone is to be made captive, to captivity he goes; if anyone makes to kill with a sword, he must be killed by a sword. Here is the endurance and the faith of the saints.

11. And I saw another beast coming up out of the earth, and it had two horns like a lamb, and spoke like a dragon.
12. It exercises all the authority of the first beast before it. It makes the earth and those dwelling in it worship the first beast, whose stroke of death was healed.
13. And it does great signs, even making fire come out of heaven down onto the earth before men.
14. By the signs it can make before the beast, it deceives those dwelling on the earth, telling them to make an image for the beast, which had the stroke of the sword yet lived again.
15. It was allowed to give spirit to the image of the beast, so that the image of the beast might even speak, and to cause

those who would not worship the image of the beast to be killed.
16. It makes all, the small and the great, both the rich and the poor, both free men and slaves, accept a mark on their right hand or their forehead,
17. so that nobody can buy or sell without having the mark, the name of the beast or the number of its name.
18. Here is wisdom. The one with reasoning reckon the number of the beast; for it is the number of a man, and the number is six hundred and sixty-six.

Notes on Revelation Chapter Ten

"Curiouser and curiouser!" said Alice in Wonderland. "Six out of seven angel-messengers have blown their trumpets when this **eighth** angel messenger appears like thunder! Who is he?"

"My own singular contention, my dear little friend, is that he was the late great **Prime Minister of Britain – Winston Churchill.** Some say the greatest PM we ever had! Here is the evidence for saying that he alone fulfilled this prophecy."

Churchill was constantly at war, or shouting great words of oratory! He was a journalist and was captured by the Boers in South Africa in the Boer War of the late 19th Century. He fought at Gallipoli in the First World War, and was recalled from years 'in the political wilderness' to lead the wartime coalition government to great victory in the Second World War.

The 'seven thunders', apparently too terrible for St. John to be allowed to write them down, almost certainly said: -
"First World War And Second World War!"

Churchill is depicted as standing one foot on the land and one foot on the sea. Indeed, he famously suffered acute mood swings of 'manic depression' – a sea of depression, punctuated by glorious 'hard, like the land' highs especially when speaking!

It goes on – a rainbow over his head symbolising a genius of a leader. A famously round face 'like the sun'. A great and fast walker – 'legs like pillars of fire'.

Finally – he just adored Cuban cigars. If you have never smoked one, these are dipped in a sugar solution at the mouth end.

So – the little scroll was a **cigar** – sweet in St. John's mouth but bitter to his stomach when he ate (smoked!) it...

The atrocities in the USA and especially New York on '9/11' – Tuesday 11th September 2001

Were these compellingly and chillingly accurately prophesied in the Bible in 90 AD, 2,000 years ago, in the book of Revelation Chapter 11?

This Chapter Eleven of Revelation has been 'bugging me' for twenty-three years, ever since my discovery in that book that the Holy Spirit is 'Seven Spirits, or a Seven-Fold Spirit'. However I firmly believe that the Book of Revelation is an 'account of the future – in *strict* chronological order of events'. So here is my interpretation of Revelation 11: -

"Then I was given a reed like a staff, and they said, "Rise and measure the shrine of God and the altar and those worshipping in it. But leave out completely the court outside the shrine and do not measure it, because it was given to the nations, and they will trample over the holy city for forty-two months. And I will grant to my two martyrs, and they will prophesy for one thousand two hundred and sixty days, clothed in sackcloth".

Revelation 11:1-3

- This chapter 11 is about buildings! 'Temples' – secret, sacred, buildings, too! The 'court outside the temple' is New York City, especially Manhattan, a leading world tourist attraction for visitors from 'the nations' (the United Nations even used to be based in a building on Manhattan at the time the World Trade Centre was built, 1970-1977). Yet, it is a city 'HOLY to mammon' – money, the 'root of all evil' – containing Wall Street, the world's largest stock exchange, of which until '9/11' the World Trade Centre formed a huge portion!

- For '42 months' in the Bible is always an omen of Evil or 'spiritual warfare'! It is half the Holy cycle of seven years. Seven is in fact the ultimate Holy number in all religions, and two in Occult circles the number of the Devil – Seven versus two spells trouble! 1,260 days only corresponds to 42 months of 30 days each if one works out 30 days per month as according to the 'Numera-logical Calendar' in Volume C Part 1 of this book... A total of seven years is indicated here by 42 months and 1,260 days each appearing. It took 7 years to build the World Trade Centre, 1970-1977, as I said above...

- The two martyrs of the World Trade Centre were indeed steel-grey in colour ('clothed in sackcloth') and indeed took 1,260 days to build – times two, the Devil's number – 1970-1977...

"These are the two olive-trees and the two lamp-stands standing before the lord of the earth."

Revelation 11:4

Strip away the façade, and the twin towers were filled with literally hundreds of thousands of miles of electrical, computer and communications cables – for as well as being computer centres for Wall Street they were also communications towers. Just like well-dressed olive trees... The largest buildings in the world at nearly a mile high and an acre each in area when built. At night they lit up the Manhattan skyline – like lampstands on a vast scale... I went to their top floor in 1980, and got a real impression of them at the south tip of the island, 'standing before the lord of the earth' i.e. Wall Street, Manhattan; and/or the United States of America!

"If anyone wishes to harm them, fire comes out of their mouths and devours their enemies; and if anyone should wish to harm them, thus they must be killed. They have the authority to shut heaven, so that rain may not fall during the days of their prophecy, and they have authority over the waters, to turn them into blood, and to strike the earth with every kind of plague, as often as they may wish."

Revelation 11:5-6

The World Trade Centre headed up Wall Street, which headed up the economic might of the USA. These verses indicate how these forces protected themselves militarily till '9/11', greatly helped by the geographical separation of that country and them, from enemies.

"When they finish their witness, the beast coming up out of the abyss will make war with them and conquer them and kill them, and their dead bodies will lie in the open street of the great city, which is spiritually called Sodom and Egypt, where indeed their lord was crucified. For three and a half days, some of the peoples and tribes and tongues and nations will look on their corpses, and refuse to let their corpses be placed in a tomb, and those who dwell on the earth will rejoice over them and be glad, and will send presents to one another, because these two prophets tormented those dwelling on the earth."
Revelation 11:7-10

- The beast from the bottomless pit – insane suicidal terrorism born of pure malignant hatred and possibly envy of the USA.
- Sodom and Egypt – same metre as Manhattan Island in New Amsterdam – New York's original Dutch name when founded by Peter Stuyvesant in the 17th Century
- It took till Friday – three and half days – for the dust to settle over this atrocity, and those in Washington and Pittsburgh, Pennsylvania, that same awful morning
- Only the 'earth people' celebrated in this way – spiritual people, even including all True Muslims, mourned this tragedy

" And after the three days and a half, a spirit of life out of God entered them, and they stood on their feet, and great fear fell on their onlookers. They heard a great voice out of heaven saying to them, "Come you up here!", and they went up to heaven in the cloud, in the sight of their foes. And in that hour occurred a great earthquake, and a tenth of the city fell; seven thousand people were killed in the earthquake, and the rest became terrified and gave glory to the God of Heaven. The second woe passed away; behold, the third woe is coming quickly."
Revelation 11:11-14

Current estimates are that around 7,000 people will indeed have died as a result of those awful events, at the Pentagon, Pittsburgh, Pennsylvania, and above all Manhattan Island.

Again, indeed, the island of Manhattan was so badly damaged by the earthquake resulting from the collapse of the World Trade Centre, that a tenth of all its buildings have been made unsafe and so uninhabitable. All this happened after the dead indeed went to Heaven ('in a cloud' – of dust and flames), and their photographs were produced by grieving relatives in the streets ('they stood on their feet').

Notes on Revelation Chapter Twelve

Revelation 12:3
The seven heads and the ten horns of the dragon symbolize Satan's names: -

LUCIFER BE'ELZEBABL

Revelation 12:4
We note in passing, returning to it when discussing Chapter 13, concerning the 'third part' of the stars, that SATAN has THREE heads (like Cerberus and Tartarus, the mythological dogs guarding Hell) whereas God is three-in-one.

Revelation 12:7-12
The same time period of 1,260 days or 'a time, times and half a time' – a 360-day (ideal) year being a 'time' – occurred in Chapter 11, here, and again in chapter 13. HALF the 'ideal cycle' of seven years...

Notes on Revelation Chapter Thirteen

The 'beast 666' is now fully developed in our 21st century world, the beast of '(global) wanton materialism' (seven heads – vowels – and ten horns – consonants) supported viciously by a second beast - (information) technology (IT) and the related television (TV). We look at this beast again in Part 2 of this Volume B – the Book of Daniel – and Part 3 – the Second Book of Esdras – where the full meaning will become clear. In the meantime, parallels can be drawn with George Orwell's '1984' – the three heads of the modern world are three superpowers, each described by words of *six* letters. 'United States'; 'Briton-Europe'; 'Asians'. Each has in turn three heads, again of *six* letters, that originated in the Latin phrase of the Roman empire 2,100 years ago:
CIVITA-TEMPLA-CAESAR
'State(s)-Temple(Church)-Leader(Crowns)'
- the three-headed, Satanic, very confusing basis of all modern 'civilised' countries
- the 'beast 666'!

So, where are we now? In a world where most of my daughter's friends, all around the tender age of sixteen, are convinced this planet is *Hell*! No wonder:-

- The Holy Spirit (Wisdom, Joy and Love, Health and Beauty, Peace and Grace) has now been nearly totally supplanted by Her polar opposite – *Money*
- Love has been replaced by the pornography of sex and worse, pornography of violence
- Peace has been replaced by Paranoia and constant reports and rumours of global warfare
- Most countries, even Britain and the USA, now have heavily censored 1984-style 'news', really propaganda, and all the above Devilish elements occupy TV and to an extent, radio. Children cannot really escape what used to be 'X Certificate' until a few years ago.
- A totally sick-sick-sick 21st Century world!

REVELATION CHAPTER FOURTEEN

1. And I saw, and behold, the lamb standing on Mount Sion, with a hundred and forty-four thousands with his name and the name of his Father written on their foreheads.
2. And I heard a sound out of heaven like the sound of many waters and like the sound of loud thunder, and the sound which I heard was like harpists playing on their harps,
3. and they sing a new song before the throne and before the four living creatures and the elders; no man could learn the song except the hundred and forty-four thousands, those ransomed from the earth.
4. These have not been defiled with women; for they are celibate. They follow the lamb wherever he may go. They were ransomed from mankind as first fruits for God and the lamb,
5. and in their mouths were no lies, for they are unblemished.
6. I saw another angel-messenger flying in mid-heaven, with an eternal gospel to preach over those on the earth and over every nation and tribe and tongue and people,
7. saying in a great voice, "Fear God and give him glory, because the hour of his judgement came, and worship him who had made the heavens and the earth and sea and fountains of waters".
8. Another angel-messenger, a second, followed, saying, "Fallen, fallen is Babylon the Great, she who made the nations drink of the wine of the anger of her fornication".
9. Another angel-messenger, a third, followed them, saying in a great voice, "If anyone worships the beast and its image, and receives a mark on their forehead or on their hand,
10. they shall drink the wine of the wrath of God, mixed undiluted in his cup of wrath, and will be tormented with fire and sulphur before the holy angel-messengers and the lamb.
11. The smoke of their torment goes up for ages of ages, and they have no rest day and night, those worshipping the beast and its image, anyone receiving the mark of its name.
12. Here is the endurance of the saints, those keeping the commandments of God and the faith of Jesus".
13. I heard a voice out of heaven saying, "Write you, Blessed are the dead in the Lord who die from now". Yes, says the Spirit, so that they shall rest from their labours, for their work follows with them.

14. I saw, and behold, a white cloud, and on the cloud one sitting like the Son of Man! - with a golden crown on his head and a sharp sickle in his hand.
15. And another angel-messenger went out of the shrine, crying in a great voice to the one sitting on the cloud, "Send your sickle and reap, because the hour has come to reap, because the harvest of the earth has dried."
16. The one sitting on the cloud thrust his sickle over the earth, and the earth was reaped.
17. Another angel-messenger went forth out of the shrine in heaven, also with a sharp sickle.
18. Another angel-messenger went out of the shrine, the one with authority over the fire, and spoke in a great voice to the one with the sharp sickle, saying, "Send your sharp sickle and gather the clusters of the vine of the earth, because its grapes are ripened".
19. The angel-messenger thrust the sickle into the earth, and gathered the vine of the earth and cast it into the great winepress of the wrath of God.
20. The winepress was trodden outside the city, and blood left the winepress, as high as a horse's bridle, for two hundred miles.

REVELATION CHAPTER FIFTEEN

1. Then I saw another sign in heaven, great and wonderful, seven angel-messengers with seven last plagues, for with them the wrath of God is ended.
2. I saw something like a glassy sea mingled with fire, and those who had conquered the beast and its image and the number of its name, standing on the glassy sea, with harps of God. [The glassy sea mingled with fire, is a description of all _semiconductor_ as in all computers! They stand _on_ it – i.e. have _defeated_ it!]
3. They sing the song of Moses, the slave of God, and the song of the lamb, saying, "Great and wonderful are your deeds, O

Lord God the Almighty; righteous and true are your ways, king of the nations!
4. Who will not fear and glorify your name, O Lord? Because only you are holy, because all the nations will come and worship before you, because your ordinances were made manifest".
5. After these things I saw, and the shrine opened in heaven of the tabernacle of the testimony,
6. and the seven angel-messengers came forth out of the shrine, with the seven plagues out of the shrine, clothed in bright clean linen, with golden girdles round their breasts.
7. One of the four living creatures gave the seven angel-messengers seven golden bowls full of the anger of God, the living unto the ages of the ages.
8. The temple was filled with smoke from the glory of God and from his power, and no one could enter the shrine until the seven plagues of the seven angel-messengers were ended.

REVELATION CHAPTER SIXTEEN

1. Then I heard a great voice out of the shrine saying to the seven angel-messengers, "Go and pour out the seven bowls of God's anger on the earth".
2. The first went away and poured out his bowl on the earth, and a foul and evil sore came on the men with the mark of the beast and worshipping its image.
3. The second poured out his bowl onto the sea [i.e. the glassy sea of semi-conductor!] and it became like the blood of a dead man, and every living soul died, of the things in the sea. [i.e. all programs and 'artificial intelligence'!]
4. The third poured out his bowl onto the rivers and the fountains of the waters; and they became blood [i.e. all *circuitry* in computers!]
5. And I heard the angel-messenger of the waters saying, "Righteous are you, the Being Now and the Having Been, the holy one, over those you judge,
6. because they shed the blood of saints and prophets, and you have given them blood to drink. It is their due!"
7. And I heard the altar saying, "Yes O Lord God the Almighty, true and righteous are your judgements".
8. The fourth poured out his bowl onto the sun, and it was allowed to scorch men with fire. [as the computers melt as above]
9. They were burnt with a great heat, and they blasphemed the name of God, who had the authority of these plagues, and did not repent and give him glory.
10. The fifth poured out his bowl onto the throne of the beast, and its kingdom became darkened, and they gnawed their tongues from the pain,
11. and they blasphemed the God of heaven from their pains and sores, and did not repent of their works.
12. The sixth poured out his bowl onto the great river Euphrates, and its water was dried up to make way for the kings from the rising of the sun.
13. I saw, issuing out of the mouth of the dragon, and the mouth of the beast, and the mouth of the false prophet, three unclean spirits like frogs;
14. for they are demonic spirits performing signs, which go forth to the kings of the whole earth, to assemble for the war of the great day of God the Almighty.

15. Behold, I am coming as a thief! Blessed is he who watches and keeps his garments, lest he walk naked and men see his shame.
16. They assembled in the place called in Hebrew Armageddon.
17. The seventh poured out his bowl on the air; and a great voice came out of the shrine from the throne saying, "It has happened!"
18. There were lightnings and voices and thunders, and a great earthquake occurred, such as has never been since men were on the earth, so great was that earthquake.
19. And the great city was split in three parts and the cities of the nations fell. And God remembered Babylon the Great, and gave her the cup of wine of his anger and wrath.
20. Every island fled, and no mountains were found.
21. A great hail, a talent in size [50 kg!] came out of heaven on men; and men blasphemed God for the plague of the hail, because the plague was exceedingly great.

REVELATION CHAPTER SEVENTEEN

1. Then one of the angel-messengers who had the seven bowls came to me, and said, "Come, I will show you the judgement of the great harlot seated on many waters,
2. with whom the kings of the earth committed fornication, and the dwellers on earth became drunk on the wine of her fornication."
3. He carried me away in Spirit into a desert. I saw a woman sitting on a scarlet beast, filled with names of blasphemy, with seven heads and ten horns.
4. The woman was clothed in purple and scarlet, gilded with gold and precious stone and pearls, with a golden cup in her hand full of abominations and the unclean things of her fornication,
5. And on her forehead was written a name of mystery, BABYLON THE GREAT, THE MOTHER OF THE HARLOTS AND OF THE ABOMINATIONS OF THE EARTH.

6. I saw the woman being drunk from the blood of the saints, and from the blood of the witness of Jesus. When I saw her, I wondered greatly.
7. But the angel-messenger said to me, "Why wonder? I will tell you the mystery of the woman and of the beast carrying her with the seven heads and the ten horns. [the beast is the phrase *wanton materialism (seven vowels – heads – and ten horns – consonants)* with the double meaning of the 'beast and false prophet' of Revelation 13 – the empire of materialism 'witnessed' by its sister empire of IT or television. Overall, mass production has evolved in the last two centuries out of manual labour to produce the modern 'Babylon' materialistic Empire of 'the world' – as opposed to 'Israel' – i.e. the 'true good spirit of humanity' in its most global meaning].
8. The beast which you saw was and is not, and is about to come up out of the abyss and go to destruction.
9. This needs a mind with wisdom. The seven heads are seven mountains, where the woman sits, and seven kings:
10. Five have fallen, one is, the other has not yet come, and whenever he comes he remains only a little while. [The seven mountains are the seven hills of Rome, which as we soon come to see in Parts 2 and 3 of this Volume B of this book, is where the modern "Empire of Babylon of wanton materialism" started. The seven kings are *prophets*. The first five are the great prophets of the Old Testament: Elijah, Isaiah, Jeremiah, Ezekiel and Daniel. The one 'who is' – Jesus. The seventh is *Father Christmas!*]
11. The beast which was and is not, even he is an eighth, and is of the seven, and goes to destruction. [astrology/alchemy/witchcraft]
12. The ten horns which you saw are ten kings, who have not yet received a kingdom, but are to receive authority as kings for one hour with the beast.
13. These have one mind, and give their power and authority to the beast.
14. They will make war with the lamb, and the lamb will overcome them, because he is lord of lords and king of kings, and those with him are called and chosen and faithful".
15. He said to me, "The waters where the harlot sits, are peoples and crowds and nations and tongues.

16. The ten horns which you saw will hate the harlot and make her desolate and naked, and eat her flesh, and consume her with fire;
17. for God has put it into their hearts to do his will, by having one mind and give their kingdom to the beast, until the words of God are accomplished.
18. The woman which you saw is the great city which has dominion over the kings of the earth". [Babylon is MONEY, THE ROOT OF ALL EVIL]

Notes on Revelation Chapters Eighteen to Twenty-Two

From now on the translation in the RSV Revised Standard Version is much more accurate, so I follow it closely with two main exceptions: -
1. I continue to say 'angel-messenger' not 'angel', throughout;
2. I use the literal, much more poetic and indeed totally accurate 'for the ages unto the ages' instead of the RSV's 'for ever and ever'.

There are no more notes of interpretation needed in these last five chapters of the Bible and the book of Revelation, except that 'Gog and Magog' in Revelation 20:8 correspond to the anciently named Gog Magog Hills just outside Cambridge, England, the only nearby hills. Also, the city of New Jerusalem as described in Revelation 21:12-21 is sketched after the text that follows.

REVELATION CHAPTER EIGHTEEN

1. After this I saw another angel-messenger coming down out of heaven, having great authority, and the earth was enlightened from his glory.
2. And he cried in a strong voice, saying, "Fallen, fallen is Babylon the great, and become a dwelling-place of demons, and a prison of every unclean spirit, and a prison of every unclean and hated bird,
3. because all the nations have drunk of the wine of the anger of her fornication, and the kings of the earth practiced fornication with her, and the merchants of the earth became rich from the power of her luxury".
4. Then I heard another voice out of heaven saying, "Come you out of her, my people, lest you share in her sins, and lest you receive of her plagues;
5. Because her sins were heaped up to heaven, and God remembered her misdeeds.
6. Give you back to her as indeed she gave back, and double you her double-deeds; mix her a double draught in the cup she mixed.
7. How she glorified herself and luxuriated, so give her a like measure of torment and sorrow. Because in her heart she says, 'A queen I sit, I am no widow, and sorrow by no means do I see'.
8. Therefore in one day will her plagues come, death and sorrow and famine, and she will be consumed with fire; because mighty is the Lord God judging her".
9. And the kings of the earth, who practised fornication and luxuriated with her, will weep and wail over her, when they see the smoke of her burning,
10. standing afar because of the fear of her torment, saying, "Woe, woe, the great city, Babylon the mighty city, in one hour your judgement came."
11. And the merchants of the earth weep and sorrow over her, because no one buys their cargo any more,
12. cargo of gold, silver, jewels and pearls, fine linen, purple, silk and scarlet, all kinds of scented wood, all ivory vessels, all vessels of valuable wood, bronze, iron and marble,
13. cinnamon, spice, incenses, wine, oil, fine flour and wheat, cattle and sheep, horses and carriages, and bodies and souls of men.

14. Your fruit of the lust of the soul went away from you, and all the sumptuous and bright things perished from you, and nobody shall ever find them again!
15. The merchants of these wares, who got rich through her, will stand afar because of the fear of the torment of her weeping and sorrowing, saying,
16. "Woe, woe, the great city, which was clothed with fine linen and purple and scarlet, and gilded with gold and precious stone and pearl!
17. In one hour such great wealth has been laid waste!" And every steersmen and person sailing on the sea, and sailor, and all who work the sea, stood far off,
18. and cried out as they saw the smoke of her burning, saying, "Who was like the great city?"
19. And they threw dust onto their heads, and cried out weeping and sorrowing, saying, "Woe, woe, the great city, whose worth made rich all those who had ships on the sea, for in one hour she was made desolate!
20. Be glad over her, heaven and the saints, apostles and prophets, because God judged her by your judgement".
21. Then a mighty angel-messenger took up a stone like a great millstone, and threw it into the sea, saying, "Thus Babylon the great city will be thrown, with a rush, and shall be found no longer.
22. And the sound of harpists and musicians and flutists and trumpeters will never be heard in you again, and any craftsman of any craft shall not be found in you any more; and the sound of a factory shall not be heard in you any more;
23. And the light of a lamp shall shine in you no longer, and the voice of bridegroom and of bride shall be heard in you no more; for your merchants were the great ones of the earth, because your sorcery deceived all the nations,
24. and in her was found the blood of prophets and of saints, and of all those slain on the earth".

REVELATION CHAPTER NINETEEN

1. After these things I heard what seemed to be a great voice of a great crowd in heaven, saying, "Hallelujah! The salvation and the glory and the power of our God!

2. For true and righteous are his judgements; because he judged the great harlot who defiled the earth with her fornication, and he avenged the blood of his slaves by her hand".
3. Secondly they cried, "Hallelujah! The smoke of her goes up unto the ages of the ages".
4. The twenty-four elders and the four living creatures fell and worshipped God sitting on the throne, saying, "Amen. Hallelujah!"
5. And a voice came out from the throne, saying, "Praise you our God, all his slaves, you who fear him, the small and the great".
6. Then I heard what seemed to be the sound of a great crowd, like the sound of many waters, and like the sound of loud thunders, saying, "Hallelujah! For the Lord our God the Almighty reigned.
7. Let us rejoice and exult, and give the glory to him, for the marriage of the lamb has come, and his bride prepared herself,
8. and she was granted to be clothed in bright clean fine linen – for the fine linen is the righteous deeds of the saints".
9. And he tells me, "Write you: Blessed are the ones who have been called to the marriage supper of the lamb". And he says to me, "These are true words of God".
10. Then I fell down at his feet to worship him, but he said to me, "You, do not do that! I am a fellow slave with you and your brothers with the witness of Jesus; worship God". For the witness of Jesus is the spirit of prophecy.

11. Then I saw heaven opened, and behold, a white horse! The one sitting on it is called faithful and true, and in righteousness he judges and makes war.
12. His eyes are like flames of fire, and on his head are many diadems, and he has a name inscribed which nobody knows but him.
13. He is clothed in a robe dipped in blood, and the name by which he is called is The Word of God.
14. The armies in heaven followed him on white horses, dressed in white fine linen.
15. From his mouth proceeds a sharp sword, with which to smite the nations, and he will shepherd them with an iron

staff; he treads the winepress of the wine of the anger, of the wrath of God the Almighty.
16. He has on his robe and on his thigh a name inscribed, KING OF KINGS AND LORD OF LORDS.

17. I saw one angel-messenger standing in the sun, and he cried out in a great voice, saying to all the birds flying in mid-heaven, "Come you, assemble you for the great supper of God,
18. to eat the flesh of kings, the flesh of chiliarchs[generals], the flesh of strong men, the flesh of horses and those sitting on them, the flesh of all men, both free and slave, both small and great".
19. And I saw the beast and the kings of the earth and their armies assembled to make war with the one sitting on the horse and with his army.
20. And the beast was seized, and with it the false prophet [pseudo-prophet] which had performed the signs before it, deceiving those who had received the mark of the beast and worshipped its image; these two were cast alive into the lake of fire burning with sulphur.
21. And the rest were slain by the sword of the one sitting on the horse, the sword that proceeds from his mouth, and all the birds were gorged with their flesh.

NOTES ON REVELATION CHAPTER NINETEEN

Verses 17-21 depict an Angel summoning all the birds of the air, which might seem fanciful until one considers the recent and massively growing scientific evidence from fossils in China – that birds suddenly appeared out of the preceding dinosaur species that lorded it over the earth for so many million years. Furthermore they did so in just a few generations or possibly just one generation, completely defying the 'laws of evolution' of Charles Darwin. Birds were created – by God – from dinosaurs, complete with the sudden ability to fly. Birds are highly intelligent, their beautiful song is known to be very structured language, yet often dismissed. Can they indeed understand – even speak – human languages? That is the only way that one can take the last part of this chapter literally – and seriously – for it might not just be parrots and Mynah birds alone that can talk!

REVELATION CHAPTER TWENTY

1. Then I saw an angel-messenger coming down out of heaven, holding in his hand the key of the abyss and a great chain.
2. And he laid hold of the dragon, the old serpent, who is the Devil and Satan, and bound him a thousand years,
3. and cast him into the abyss, and shut and sealed it over him, so that he should no longer deceive the nations, until the thousand years are finished. After that he must be loosed for a little while.
4. Then I saw thrones, and seated on them were those to whom judgement was given. Also I saw the souls of those who had been beheaded because of the witness of Jesus and because of the word of God, and who did not worship the beast nor its image, and did not receive the mark on their forehead or their hand. They lived [again] and reigned with Christ a thousand years.
5. The rest of the dead did not live [again] until the thousand years were finished. This is the first resurrection.
6. Blessed and holy is he who shares in the first resurrection! Over these the second death has no authority, but they will be priests of God and of Christ, and will reign with him the thousand years.

7. And when the thousand years are ended, Satan will be loosed from his prison
8. and will go forth to deceive the nations in the four corners of the earth, Gog and Magog, to assemble them for war; their number is like the sand of the sea.
9. And they went up over the breadth of the land, and encircled the camp of the saints and the beloved city; but fire came down out of heaven and devoured them;
10. and the devil who deceived them was cast into the lake of fire and sulphur, where also the beast and the false prophet were, and they will be tormented day and night unto the ages of the ages.

11. And I saw a great white throne and him who sat upon it, from whose face the earth and the heavens fled, and no place was found for them.
12. And I saw the dead, the great and the small, standing before the throne, and books were opened; and another

book was opened, which is of life; and the dead were judged by the things written in the books, according to their works.
13. And the sea gave up the dead in it, and death and Hades gave up the dead in them, and each one was judged according to their works.
14. Then death and Hades were cast into the lake of fire. This is the second death, the lake of fire.
15. If anyone was not found in the book of life that had been written, he was cast into the lake of fire.

Future
Present
Past

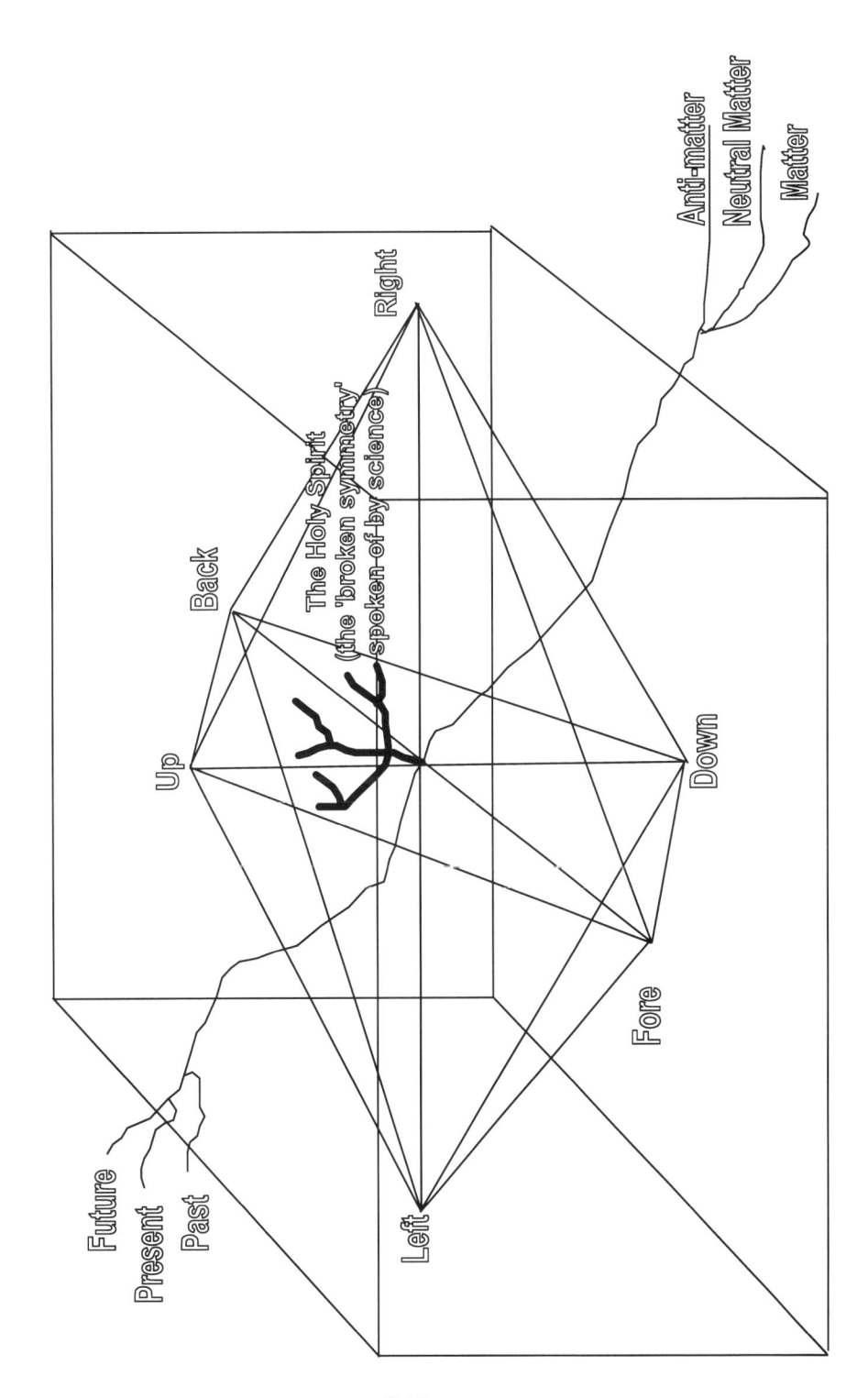

Up
Back

The Holy Spirit
(the 'broken symmetry'
spoken of by science)

Right

Left

Down

Fore

Anti-matter
Neutral Matter
Matter

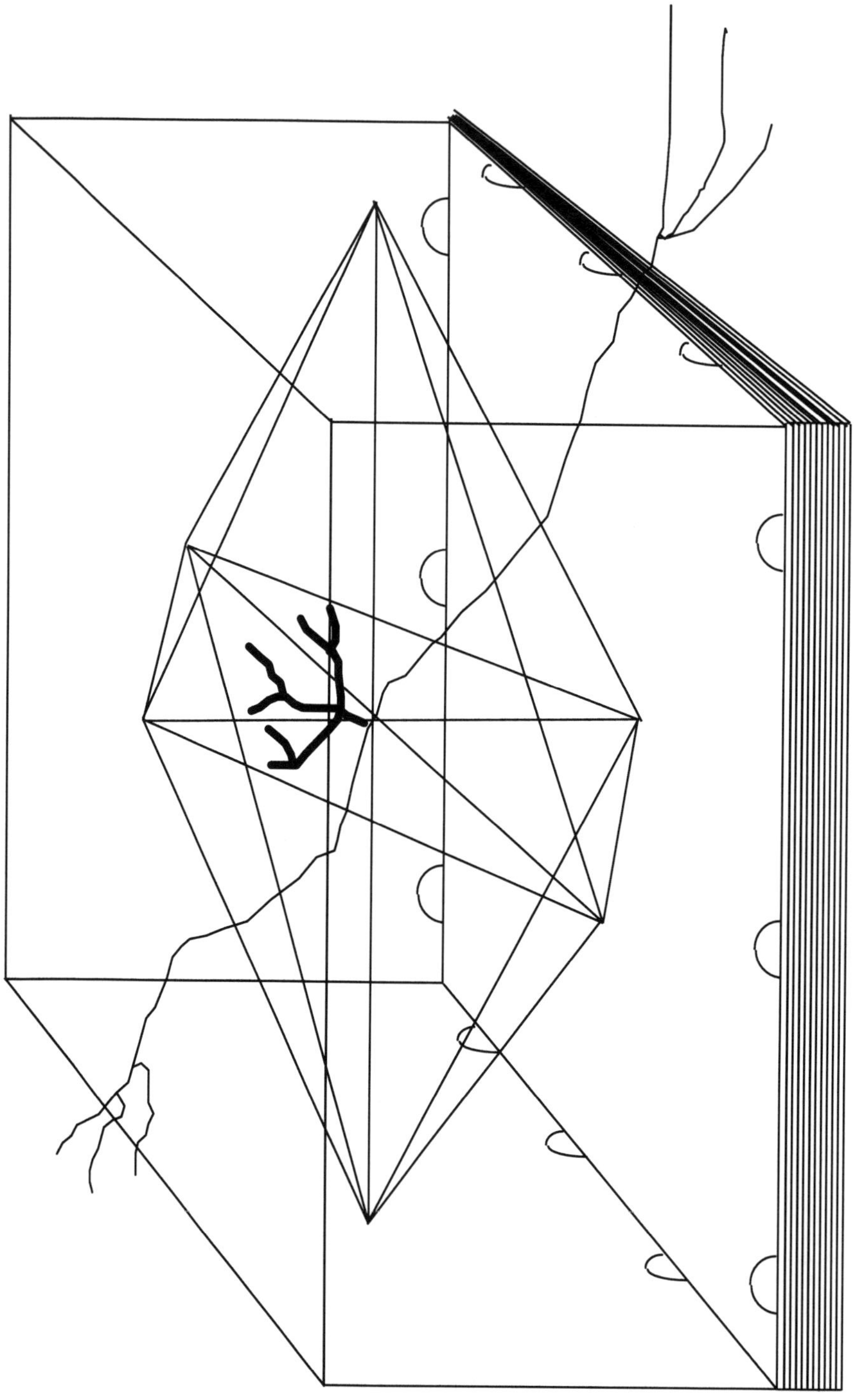

REVELATION CHAPTER TWENTY-ONE

1. Then I saw a new heaven and a new earth; for the first heaven and the first earth passed away, and the sea was no more.
2. And I saw the holy city, new Jerusalem, coming down out of heaven from God, prepared as a bride adorned for her husband.
3. And I heard a great voice out of the throne saying, "Behold, the tabernacle of God is with men, and he will tabernacle with them, and they will be his peoples, and God himself will be with them,
4. and will wipe off every tear out of their eyes, and death will be no longer, nor will sorrow nor clamour nor pain be any longer; for the first things passed away."
5. And the one sitting on the throne said, 'Behold, I make all things new!' And he says, 'Write you, for these words are faithful and true'.
6. And he said to me, "It is done! I am the alpha and the omega, the beginning and the end. To the thirsty I will give freely out of the fountain of the water of life.
7. The one who overcomes shall inherit these things, and I will be God to him and he will be to me a son.
8. But for the cowardly and the unbelieving, the polluted, murderers, fornicators, sorcerers, idolaters and all the false ones, their lot shall be in the lake burning with fire and sulphur, which is the second death"-
9. Then came one of the seven angel-messengers with the seven bowls filled with the seven last plagues, and spoke with me, saying, "Come, I will show you the bride, the wife of the lamb".
10. And he bore me away in Spirit onto a great, high mountain, and showed me the holy city Jerusalem coming down out of heaven from God,
11. having the glory of God; its light was like a very valuable stone, like a jasper stone clear as crystal.
12. It had a great, high wall, with twelve gates, and at the gates twelve angel-messengers, and names inscribed, which are of the twelve tribes of Israel.
13. From the east three gates, from the north three gates, from the south three gates, and from the west three gates.

14. And the wall of the city had twelve foundations, and on them the twelve names of the apostles of the lamb.
15. The one speaking with me had a golden measuring-reed, in order that he might measure the city and its gates and its wall.
16. The city lies square, and its length is equal to its breadth. He measured the city with the reed at twelve thousand furlongs [1,500 miles]; its length and its breadth and its height are equal.
17. He measured its wall of a hundred and forty-four cubits, a man's measure, that is, that of an angel-messenger.
18. The coping of the wall was jasper, and the city was clean gold like clean glass.
19. The foundation of the wall of the city was adorned with every precious stone; the first was jasper, the second sapphire, the third agate, the fourth emerald,
20. the fifth onyx, the sixth carnelian, the seventh chrysolite, the eighth beryl, the ninth topaz, the tenth chrysoprase, the eleventh jacinth, the twelfth amethyst.
21. The twelve gates were twelve pearls, each of the gates was one pearl. And the street of the city was clean gold as transparent as glass.
22. And I saw no shrine in the city, for the Lord God Almighty is its shrine, and the Lamb.
23. And the city has no need of the sun nor of the moon, for the glory of God enlightens it, and its lamp is the Lamb,
24. and through its light shall the nations walk, and the kings of the nations bring their light into it.
25. Its gates shall never be shut by day, for night shall not be there;
26. and they will bring the glory and the honour of the nations into it.
27. By no means may any profane thing or any cause for abomination, or any lie enter it, only those written in the Lamb's book of life.

Notes on Revelation Chapter Twenty-One

The Holy City of New Jerusalem will cover the whole of the original Ancient World, being 1,500 miles square so VAST – but above all it is 1,500 miles HIGH as well – reaching out into outer space. In modern terms – a mother spacecraft of mother spacecraft – that completely destroys 'the sea' as it lands – the Mediterranean was 'the sea' (the only one) in ancient times! One corner will doubtless land in Britain, one in Russia, one in Asia and one in Africa – with its 1,500-mile square geometry.

Appealing to New Age folk, the city is made of crystal, enabling it to safely fly through outer space ('Heaven') and land as described here. The walls of this vast cubic spaceship are a huge seventy metres thick to suitably protect the continent squared held within. The twelve types of crystal in the vast foundations provide GRAVITY to enable the inhabitants of this Heaven to live as they once did on Earth – walking upright, with a sense of direction, not helpless like our weightless terrestrial astronauts.

The Bible says that the crystal walls, roof and foundations of this 'crystal city' are lit by 'enlightenment light' – from God, Jesus and the saints who dwell there!

REVELATION CHAPTER TWENTY-TWO

1. Then he showed me a river of water of life, bright as crystal, proceeding out of the throne of God and of the Lamb.
2. In the midst of its street and from the river there came hence a tree of life producing twelve fruits, yielding its fruits according to each month, and the leaves of the tree are for the healing of the nations. [The twelve constituent fruit of the Fruit of the Spirit (or Wisdom): - Joy and Love, Health and Beauty, Peace and Grace as described in Volume A of this book].
3. There will be no more curses. The throne of God and of the Lamb will be in it, and his slaves will do service to him,
4. and they will see his face, and his name will be upon their foreheads.
5. And night will be no longer, and they will not have any need of light of lamp and light of the sun, because the Lord God will shed light on them, and they will reign unto the ages of the ages.
6. And he said to me, 'These words are faithful and true, and the Lord, the God of the spirits of the prophets, sent his angel-messenger to show to his slaves, things which must occur quickly.
7. And behold, I am coming quickly. Blessed is the one keeping the words of the prophecy of this book.
8. And I, John, am the one hearing and seeing these things. And when I heard and I saw, I fell down to worship before the feet of the angel-messenger showing me these things.
9. He tells me, "See you dost not do that! I am a fellow-slave with you and your brothers the prophets and of the ones keeping the words of this book. You worship God".
10. He tells me, "Do not seal the words of prophecy of this book; for the time is near.
11. Let the unjust one still act unjustly, and the filthy one still act filthily, and the righteous one let him still do righteousness, and let the holy still be hallowed.
12. Behold I am coming quickly, and my reward is with me, to render to each man according to his work.
13. I am the alpha and the omega, the first and the last, the beginning and the end.

14. Blessed are those washing their robes, in order that they may have authority over the tree of life, and may enter the city by the gates.
15. Outside are the dogs and the sorcerers and the fornicators and the murderers and the idolaters and everyone who loves and makes a lie.
16. I, Jesus, sent my angel-messenger to witness to you these things, for the churches. I am the root and the offspring of David, the bright morning star."
17. The Spirit and the bride say, "Come". And let the one who hears say "Come". And the thirsty let him come, anyone who wishes let him take the water of life freely.
18. I witness to everyone hearing the words of the prophecy of this book: if any one adds to them, God will add to him the plagues written in this book,
19. and if any one takes away from the words of the book of this prophecy, God will take away from him his share of the tree of life and the holy city, of the things written in this book.
20. Says the one witnessing these things, "Yes, I am coming quickly". Amen, come Lord Jesus!
21. The grace of the Lord Jesus with all.

The three great Apocalyptic Books of the Bible

2. The Old Testament and its first and only Apocalyptic Book

The Book of Daniel

BACKGROUND AND INTRODUCTION

In the Introduction to Part 1 of this Volume B of the book that we just looked at, I said that I had translated the Book of Revelation from the Ancient Greek, without any knowledge of that ancient tongue, by making use of an *Interlinear RSV Bible* – which gives the original Greek with a literal translation of each word or phrase, with the English translation as well. For these next two Parts of this Volume B of this book my task is even easier. I translate into English similar to that of Part 1, taking out the "ye" and "thou", etc, the Book of Daniel in this Part 2 and the Second Book of Esdras in Part 3 – from the English! For I am merely translating into this book on a *computer scanner* from a standard text, the 1611, 'Authorised' King James Bible, the original printed English Bible; then 'modernising' the language.

There is another, personally very pleasing indeed, way in which this new work of translation and interpretation is a lot easier than doing Part I. My original notes for Part I (naturally much revised in what appears here) were written two and a half years ago, in 2003, in a place of confinement far more intensively stressful than any prison, where I languished ill. Furthermore, I did two thirds of that work overnight, yet stayed up all the next day! For the work on the present book, I am by total contrast working in the cosy comfort of my studio flat, on my own familiar computer (so I know it works, and I can look up anything I need to in books or on the Internet).

So in two ways – the nature of the work – and the much more pleasant environment it is taking place in – I am looking forward to getting my ideas about the next five Parts or aspects of this book down on paper. Inspiration and realisation that I am 'cracking hitherto un-cracked biblical meanings' has been pouring into me for about ten days, ever since I bought the particular 1611 bible I wanted once I saw it in the bookshop.

Daniel at the Court of Babylon (Chaldaea of the Chaldeans)

Daniel was captured as a boy and taken as a Judean exile to Babylon of the Chaldean empire in 605 BC. For after defeating Egypt at Carcemish, Nebuchadnezzar the king of Babylon attacked Jerusalem, and took Daniel hostage with many other Judean children to guarantee the good behaviour from then, of king Jehoiakim of Judah, who had been installed on the throne by the pharaoh of Egypt. Daniel was taken to Chaldaea as an exile a few years earlier than his fellow prophet Ezekiel of the preceding book in the Bible. Like all his colleagues adopted after some years of training by the Babylonian royal court, he was picked out for good looks and intelligence, and for coming from a noble or possibly royal family in Judah (see Daniel 1:3-4).

Chapters one to six of the Book of Daniel describe how, his remarkable faith in God rather than any clairvoyance, astrology or divination, as used by his opponents, leading to a nearly unique ability to solve mysteries, especially dreams and visions, soon led Daniel to increasing positions of authority as a powerful statesman in the core of this foreign imperial power. There are strong parallels to the stories of Joseph in the Court of Pharaoh in Egypt, at the foundation of the identity of the people of Israel, with the stories told around the Book of Exodus much earlier in the Old Testament. The remaining chapters, 7-12, describe a set of visions of the future, and we will be seeing my own views coming out as very different to most conventional interpretations – often relating to the last 100 years or so of world history, as of now; not confined to the Ancient World around the Mediterranean two thousand years or so ago.

Two languages appear in the text of Daniel. Chapter 2:4 to 7:28 is written in Aramaic, the international language of the time; and the rest is in ancient Hebrew. It is extremely clearly written in the original, and intact, so I can be very confident that the English translation I give here, which is essentially a modernisation by myself of the text in the 1611 'Authorised' King James Bible, is very accurate indeed. My commentary follows the commentary in Revelation from Part 1 of this Volume B, and so emphasises strongly the Apocalyptic aspects of the dreams and visions in the Book of Daniel. Hence I do not comment on chapters 1-6 in what follows, apart from giving a commentary on the great Dream of Nebuchadnezzar in Chapter 2. Leaving the very clear text to speak for itself, and for the reader to consult any of the more traditional commentaries on the Bible, such as the popular Lion Handbook, over any points of doubt, including of course to see what the more traditional interpretation, incomplete as it is, has to say. The stories of

Daniel 1-6 are quite famous, including those of Daniel's friends in the fiery furnace I chapter 3 (along with a 'Son of Man' that some say is an angel, others say is Jesus himself) and Daniel in the lions' den, in chapter 6.

For my own views are based on inspiration, a realisation that some of Daniel has only just come true, 2,500 years later in this 21st Century, a pressing need to relay this information on to fellow believers; and so quite radical!

DANIEL CHAPTER ONE

1 In the third year of the reign of Jehoiakim king of Judah, Nebuchadnezzar king of Babylon came to Jerusalem and besieged it.
2 And the Lord gave Jehoiakim king of Judah into his hand, along with some of the vessels and articles of the house of God. These he carried into the land of Shinar to the house of his god in Babylon; and brought into the treasure house of his god.
3 And the king ordered Ashpenaz, the master of his eunuchs, that he should bring certain of the children of Israel, and of the royal family;
4 Children with no physical blemish, attractive, and skilful in all wisdom, and knowledge, and understanding science, and such as had ability in them to serve in the king's palace. To whom they should teach the learning and the language of the Chaldeans.
5 The king appointed them a daily provision of the king's food, and of the wine which he drank. So nourishing them for three years, that at the end they might serve the king.
6 Now among these were some children from Judah: Daniel, Hananiah, Mishael, and Azariah.
7 The prince of the eunuchs gave them Chaldean names, giving to Daniel the name of Belteshazzar; and to Hananiah, of Shadrach; and to Mishael, of Meshach; and to Azariah, of Abednego.
8 But Daniel was determined that he would not defile himself with the portion of the king's food, nor with the wine which he drank. Therefore he requested of the prince of the eunuchs to allow him not to defile himself.
9 Now God had brought Daniel into favour and tender love with the prince of the eunuchs.
10 And the prince of the eunuchs said to Daniel, "I fear my lord the king, who appointed your food and drink. Why should he see your faces looking worse than the children which are of your age? Then you shall put my life in danger with the king."
11 Daniel then said to Melzar, whom the prince of the eunuchs had set over Daniel, Hananiah, Mishael, and Azariah,
12 "Prove your servants, I implore you, ten days; and let them give us pulse to eat, and water to drink.

13 Then let our appearance be looked upon before you, and the appearance of the children that eat of the portion of the king's meat. Then as you see fit, deal with your servants."
14 So he consented to them in this matter, and tested them for ten days.
15 And at the end of ten days their appearance seemed fairer and fatter in flesh than all the children which ate the portion of the king's food.
16 So Melzar took away the portion of their food, and the wine that they should drink; and gave them pulse.
17 As for these four children, God gave them knowledge and skill in all learning and wisdom; and Daniel had understanding in all visions and dreams.
18 Now at the end of the days that the king had said he should bring them in, then the prince of the eunuchs brought them in before Nebuchadnezzar.
19 And the king communed with them; and among them all was found none like Daniel, Hananiah, Mishael, and Azariah. So they entered the king's service.
20 And in all matters of wisdom and understanding, that the king enquired of them, he found them ten times better than all the magicians and astrologers that were in all his realm.
21 And Daniel continued even until the first year of king Cyrus.

DANIEL CHAPTER TWO

1 And in the second year of his reign, Nebuchadnezzar dreamed dreams, his spirit was troubled, and he could not sleep.
2 Then the king summoned the magicians, and the astrologers, and the sorcerers, and the Chaldeans, to show the king his dreams. So they came and stood before the king.
3 And the king said to them, "I have dreamed a dream, and my spirit was troubled to know the dream."

[The text from here to chapter seven is in Aramaic.]

4 The Chaldeans said to the king, "O king, live for ever! Tell your servants the dream, and we will give the interpretation."

5 The king answered and said to the Chaldeans, "The thing is gone from me. If you will not make known to me the dream, with the interpretation of it, you shall be cut in pieces, and your houses shall be made a dunghill.
6 But if you show the dream, and the interpretation, you shall receive gifts and rewards and great honour from me. Therefore show me the dream, and its interpretation."
7 They answered again and said, "Let the king tell his servants the dream, and we will show the interpretation of it."
8 The king answered and said, "I am certain that you would like to gain time, because you see the thing is gone from me.
9 But if you will not make known to me the dream, there is but one decree for you. For you have prepared lying and corrupt words to speak before me, hoping to gain time. Therefore tell me the dream, and I shall know that you can show me the interpretation.

10 The Chaldeans answered the king, "There is not a man upon the earth that can show the king's matter; therefore there is no king, lord, nor ruler, that ever asked such things of any magician, or astrologer, or Chaldean.
11 And it is a rare thing that the king requires, and there is none other that can show it to the king, except the gods, whose dwelling is not with flesh."
12 For this reason the king was angry and very furious, and commanded to destroy all the wise men of Babylon.
13 And the decree went out that the wise men should be slain; and they sought Daniel and his fellows to be slain.

14 Then Daniel answered with counsel and wisdom to Arioch the captain of the king's guard, which had gone out to slay the wise men of Babylon.
15 He answered and said to Arioch the king's captain, "Why is the decree so hasty from the king?" Then Arioch made the thing known to Daniel.
16 Then Daniel went in, and desired of the king that he would give him time, and that he would show the king the interpretation.
17 Then Daniel went to his house, and made the thing known to Hananiah, Mishach, and Azariah, his companions.
18 That they would desire mercies of the God of heaven concerning this secret; that Daniel and his fellows should not perish with the rest of the wise men of Babylon.

19 Then the secret was revealed to Daniel in a night vision. Then Daniel blessed the God of heaven.
20 Daniel answered and said, "Blessed be the name of God for ever and ever, for wisdom and might are his;
21 And he changes the times and the seasons. He removes kings, and sets up kings. He gives wisdom to the wise, and knowledge to them that know understanding.
22 He reveals the deep and secret things. He knows what is in the darkness, and the light dwells with him.
23 I thank you, and praise you, O you God of my fathers, who has given me wisdom and might, and has made known to me now what we desired of you. For you have now made known to us the king's matter.

24 Therefore Daniel went in to see Arioch, whom the king had ordered to destroy the wise men of Babylon, and said, "Do not destroy the wise men of Babylon. Bring me in before the king, and I will show the king the interpretation."
25 Then Arioch brought in Daniel before the king in haste, and said to him, "I have found a man of the captives of Judah, that will make known the interpretation to the king."
26 The king answered and said to Daniel, whose name was Belteshazzar, "Are you able to make known to me the dream which I have seen, and the interpretation of it?"
27 Daniel answered the king, and said, "The secret which the king has demanded; the wise men, the astrologers, the magicians, and the soothsayers, cannot show the king;
28 But there is a God in heaven that reveals secrets, and makes known to the king Nebuchadnezzar what shall be in the latter days. Your dream, and the visions of your head upon your bed, were these;
29 As for you, O king, your thoughts came into your mind upon your bed, what should come to pass. He that reveals secrets made known to you what shall come to pass.
30 But as for me, this secret is not revealed to me for any wisdom that I have more than any living, but for their sakes that shall make known the interpretation to the king, and that you might know the thoughts of your heart.

31 You, O king, saw, and behold a great image. This great image, whose brightness was excellent, stood before you; and its form was terrible.
32 This image's head was of fine gold, his breast and his arms of silver, his belly and his thighs of brass,

33 His legs of iron, his feet part of iron and part of clay.
34 You saw till a stone was cut out without hands, which struck the image upon his feet of iron and day, and broke them to pieces.
35 Then the iron, the clay, the brass, the silver, and the gold, were broken to pieces together, and became like the chaff of the summer threshing-floors; and the wind carried them away, that no place was found for them. The stone that smote the image became a great mountain, and filled the whole earth.
36 That is the dream; and we will tell you the interpretation of it, O king.
37 You, O king, are a king of kings, for the God of heaven has given you a kingdom, power, and strength, and glory.
38 And wherever the children of men dwell, he has given the beasts of the field and the fowls of the heaven into your hand, and has made you ruler over them all. You are this head of gold.
39 And after you shall arise another kingdom inferior to you, and another third kingdom of brass, which shall rule over all the earth.
40 And the fourth kingdom shall be strong as iron. Like iron which breaks in pieces and subdues all things. Like iron that breaks all these, shall it break in pieces and bruise.
41 And whereas you saw the feet and toes, part of potters' clay, and part of iron, the kingdom shall be divided; but there shall be in it of the strength of the iron, just as you saw the iron mixed with miry clay.
42 And as the toes of the feet were part of iron, and part of clay, so the kingdom shall be partly strong, and partly broken.
43 And whereas you saw iron mixed with miry clay, they shall mingle themselves with the seed of men. But they shall not cleave one to another, even as iron is not mixed with day.
44 And in the days of these kings shall the God of heaven set up a kingdom, which shall never be destroyed. The kingdom shall not be left to other people, but it shall break in pieces and consume all these kingdoms, and it shall stand for ever.
45 When you saw that the stone was cut out of the mountain without hands, and that it broke in pieces the iron, the brass, the clay, the silver, and the gold; the great God has made known to the king what shall come to pass. The dream is certain, and the interpretation of it sure."

46 Then the king Nebuchadnezzar fell upon his face, and worshipped Daniel, and commanded that they should make him an offering, and give sweet odours to him.

47 The king answered Daniel, and said, "It is certain, that your God is a God of gods, and a Lord of kings, and a revealer of secrets, seeing you could reveal this secret."

48 Then the king made Daniel a great man, and gave him many great gifts, and made him ruler over the whole province of Babylon, and chief of the governors over all the wise men of Babylon.

49 Then Daniel requested of the king, and he set Shadrach, Meshach, and Abednego, over the affairs of the province of Babylon; but Daniel sat in the gate of the king.

Notes on Daniel Chapter Two

This prophetic dream, which Daniel interprets to the king to his complete satisfaction, can readily be interpreted. It describes domination of the then known world by four successive empires, starting with that of king Nebudanezzar, the Chaldean or Babylonian Empire. After Babylon (the golden head) there was to be in the future, complete domination of the Ancient World by the Empire of the Medes and Persians (the silver breast and arms); the Greek Empire (the brass belly and thighs); and finally, what is normally taken to be the Roman Empire (the iron legs, and feet of iron mixed with clay).

Indeed, all Christians would say that it is quite clear that the 'stone cut out without hands' of verse 2:34 was the equally historically verifiable figure of *Jesus Christ*. After his Mission of roughly 27 – 33AD, as described in the Gospels of the New Testament, and Crucifixion at the first Easter 33AD, followed by his Resurrection, and Ascent into Heaven, he returned briefly and instructed his followers to establish his church. Principally St. Paul was converted from a persecutor and slayer of the early Christians, on the road to Damascus in the story, and became an incredibly hard-working and long-suffering inspiration to all missionaries. Meanwhile Simon Peter, often in dispute with Paul, went to the power centre at Rome of the Roman Empire, and set up the Catholic Church there. Within about two centuries, these two and their colleagues had succeeded in converting nearly the entire Roman Empire as then was, to Christianity. Hence as this then included Medo-Persia, Babylon and Greece – all the four 'kingdoms' or empires did indeed fall to the 'stone' that was Jesus.

Most Christian commentators, especially many of great authority, have said that that is the end of the story, and that the 'Beast 666' of Revelation 13 (see Part 1 of this Volume B) was also Rome, and that the number merely refers to the symbolic number adopted by the 'Society of Odd Fellows' founded by Emperor Nero, Emperor of Rome between 54-68AD, who started the famous persecution and torture of Christians, such as feeding them to the lions. They say that is the only reason why the author of Revelation, writing about 90AD, refers to that number. However once one realises that the origin of the number 666 is 'CIVITA-TEMPLA-CAESAR' ('estate/states –

temple – emperor/leader') and that the Society founded by Nero had a great influence in Roman times on bringing in this Satanic, 'three-headed' system of government *for the first time ever in history*; you can see its derivation in the modern world of 'constitutional democracy'. In Part 1 of Volume C of this book we look at a highly plausible modern conspiracy theory, giving details of the Freemasons and other secret societies acting today, all of which trace their origins to the Society founded by Emperor Nero. This showed, back in 1997, evidence that is given in great detail, of attempts by the Occult in such societies today, to impose their '666' logo globally, needing only a severe excuse of a threat to global security, to achieve this any time soon.

Evidence that the fourth empire may well have started with Rome, but has persisted up to the present day, comes from equally Apocalyptic writings in the Gospels. Many Christians may object to my placing the last book of the New Testament, and so of the whole Bible, as the first of 'the three great Apocalyptic books of the Bible' at the start of this book. "Why", they might rightly point out, "the whole of the Gospels and much of the letters in the New Testament count just as much as 'apocalyptic'. You have completely ignored them!" My answer is simple. One can get a 100% consistent account of much of the Bible, especially the New Testament, from virtually every Bible commentary or minister, or Jewish rabbi. However, when it comes to the predictions of the future in the Bible, it comes down to speculation, and there are as many opinions as people debating the issue.

So, do I think myself 'special' in any way in order to dare to write all that appears in this book? No, in no way, for despite having been through immense suffering in my life, yet at the same time often pondering Biblical predictions, the only reason that I am writing all this is – time – or the passage of time. For as I write, I have realised that I can make an extremely coherent, totally consistent and organised 'guess' – which is not a guess – at the meaning of absolutely every aspect of these three books of Apocalyptic writing in the Bible.

So, although the 'fourth kingdom' of Daniel 2 was started to be eroded by the 'stone being flung' (Jesus) in the first century AD, with His founding the rival 'Kingdom of God' the scene was set for the intervening power struggle. As I write this book, all the great signs that Jesus indicated were necessary before his return, and the final power struggle won with his Second Coming, have been fulfilled, and the Second Coming (or Time of the End) is imminent. A look at key points in the life and ministry of Jesus will help clearly see this, in the following brief summary (I supply this rather than another complete book on the subject!): -

1. It is wrong to imagine that Jesus was born in the 'year zero' – for there was no such year – 1BC ran into 1AD. Most biblical scholars have established the year of Jesus' birthday, traditionally of course 25th December, as 7BC – or possibly 6BC. He started his mission roughly three years before he died and was resurrected in 33AD, which date is known with much more historical certainty. He was born in a stable of humble parents, with his true parents being divine, of course, according to the story in the New Testament.
2. So he was roughly 37 years of age when he was baptised by his cousin John the Baptist by the Jordan, then on leaving the water the Bible says that, 'the Holy Spirit descended on him in the form of a Dove'. So began a ministry of healing, performing miracles and very radical teaching, so radical that early on before his fame had spread, the Jews of his time often tried to stone him! His mission is often said in the Church to have been one of 'Grace (of the Holy Spirit and God) overcoming the law'. Hence the New Testament is also called 'the New Covenant'.
3. Jesus left his home after his baptism by John (and the dove) and started travelling around, performing more and more difficult miracles in front of a motley band of twelve disciples, from varied and lowly jobs, such as fishermen and tax collectors – with the only one with any qualifications or well-paid profession being Luke, a doctor, one of the writers of the four gospels.
4. Women and children were fiercely repressed by the society of that day, and largely ignored, in parallel to much of Islamic society today, but Jesus' attitude to children is summarised by his famous saying, 'suffer the little children to come unto me'. As for women, he was as impartial as with his choice of male disciples, and had many female followers. (Today two thirds of the British Church is said to be female, continuing this tradition). Many of his followers or disciples, while shunned by the society of his day, were women – famously including Mary Magdalene and another Mary, sister of

Martha. People often speculate whether Jesus had a physical relationship or was even married to Mary Magdalene – but Church authorities usually describe such suggestions as 'deluded or even blasphemous'. Notably the New Testament Gospels and letters in the Bible, as for all its books, were written by men. However, Mary Magdalene is supposed widely to be the author of one of the 'Gnostic gospels' found in a cave in Upper Egypt in December 1945.

5. Fulfilling Old Testament prophecy about the Messiah, when he came, Jesus taught publicly only in parables, leaving some interpretation to his disciples in secret – as now available in any Bible. Most of his healing – often quite time-consuming and physically tiring like the raising of Lazarus from the dead – was also done in private.

6. Jesus' principal mission, however, was to attack the conventional Jewish obsession with assiduously following literally thousands of laws at once, only a few from the Torah, the Jewish legal part of the Bible as then was, the rest propounded by the Chief Rabbis, continually adding to them. Much as today with civil law throughout the world! Jesus answer to the overpowering quantity of Jewish Laws, then as now, was to drastically simplify it. Two principal examples of his radically simple approach illustrate this. He showed lawyers a coin, and said, "Render to God that which is God's, and render to Caesar that which is Caesar's". Meaning, firstly that they had to obey both Roman and Jewish law, so pay the appropriate taxes to both, while the Romans still occupied Israel and Palestine. Secondly, that they should give God what God asked, while keeping the state happy. The second example of his simplistic approach to the law was first a negative 'try not to sin i.e. offend God' followed by an extremely positive, indeed uplifting "The two greatest commandments in the Law are these. Firstly "love the Lord your God with all your soul, all your mind, all your heart and all your soul" and secondly "Love your neighbour as yourself"."

7. About a third of each gospel in the Bible deals with the crucifixion, at Passover in the spring of 33AD. A week earlier, again to fulfil Old Testament prophecy, Jesus entered Jerusalem at the peak of his powers, on a colt, to be greeted as a king, with palm leaves of peace being flung before the colt. He would not accept being crowned King and retreated

to the Mount of Olives and the garden of Gethsemane at its foot. Meanwhile the Jewish Priests thought of a way to destroy him, as they thought, as a threat 'to their nation in the face of the might of Rome'. They accused him of blasphemy to Pontius Pilate, the Roman governor, saying he had called himself 'the Son of Man' or 'Son of God' (which was true!) These days he would have been confined to a mental hospital, like so many latter-day 'sons of God' - or even just 'God'. In those days the penalty was death – and famously one of his own disciples, Judas Iscariot, betrayed him to the Roman soldiers in Gethsemane.

8. Jesus was summoned before Pontius Pilate, who questioned him, could find no crime, so scourged him with a flagella (a particularly vicious sort of Roman whip). He then publicly washed his hands of the crucifixion, literally, and offered the crowd a final chance to have Jesus reprieved from death by crucifixion. Typical mob, having cast palm branches before Jesus a week earlier, now they simply cried out "Crucify him! Crucify him!" Jesus was made to carry his own cross up the long Via Dolorosa road in Jerusalem to Golgotha, 'Place of the Skull'. At three o'clock, as he hung on the cross, the sky went black 'and the curtain of the temple was torn in two'. He died half an hour later, not long for a crucifixion, but he would have been half dead anyway from the whipping with the flagella. He lay in a new tomb for three days, and then the Bible records the ultimate miracle – His Resurrection from the Dead.

9. The Crucifixion (and belief in the Resurrection) are at the very heart of Christian belief – a 'sacrifice of God unto God' – that is said to have caused a sea-change in both the world – and God's attitude to it, shattering the power of Evil forever, to be completed of course when Jesus returns – the Second Coming. It is said that the Resurrection and its deep, profound, incredible mystery was enabled because Jesus was completely innocent of any crime throughout his life, so 'completely free of sin' – even when he claimed to be the 'Son of Man' or 'Son of God' it was *true*, so not blasphemy – for which he died as a criminal, a ghastly death on a crucifix.

10. The disciples of Jesus were devastated by his death, and scattered back to their homes, fearful of the Romans. So they were astonished when Jesus reappeared to small groups of them. Even 'doubting Thomas', one of the disciples,

believed it really was Jesus, once he touched his crucifixion scars. Finally, in a way remembered by Ascension Sunday, Jesus flew up into Heaven, or 'ascended', to 'sit at God's right hand', according to the gospels. His last words on earth, according to the gospel of Matthew, were 'all authority in heaven and on earth has come to me'.

11. So we have seen the life and mission of Jesus' First Coming in that above 'potted summary' – so at length to what he said about his Second Coming. Firstly, one should never attempt to predict *when it will be – a date*. "For of that time nobody knows, not the Son, nor the angels in heaven, only the Father". Secondly, he described very accurately what it has been like to live in the world since He came, until the Second Coming finally happens, in a famous parable of 'the weeds and the wheat'. The 'wheat' or Godly people, as has happened in reality totally precisely, would be forced to live with the ungodly, the 'weeds', mingling close by together. Never more so than today, with the good and bad people of many cultures and languages trying to live together in most countries of the world. At the Time of the End, or His Second Coming, Jesus said that the 'weeds' would be at the point of throttling the 'wheat'. However the weeds would be cut down 'and thrown into the flames'. Those who believe that the 'end of the world' as they call it (while the Christians end the Lord's Prayer with the phrase 'world without end') will come about through global warming causing a New Ice Age or alternatively a Second Great Flood are mistaken. They have not read their Old Testament recently, for Noah was made a covenant by God after the biblical Flood, around 10,000 BC, verified by archaeologists, with a rainbow. God told Noah that whenever he saw a rainbow (God's 'covenant') Noah would know that there would never again be another flood. As the Flood was doubtless the result of the last Ice Age, we can doubtless also rule out another Ice Age. No, the Bible consistently warns throughout about the Time of the End, of 'destruction by flames'. Jesus said that the flames were in Gehenna, which is NOT the same as Hell. Gehenna was simply Jerusalem's municipal rubbish-dump, and the Bible itself indicates that 'sinners' do not go to Hell, as so many afterwards have claimed since Dante in the Middle Ages. They are instead incinerated and put out with the rubbish.

12. Jesus gave his disciples a few other pointers as to what to expect before his return in the Second Coming or Time of the End. Civil unrest, wars, rebellions, revolutions, and permissiveness, increasingly followed by natural disasters, earthquakes and famines. Indeed, the last century has seen literally an exponential growth of all these things. In the space of nine months last year, for instance, we witnessed a tsunami in the Far East killing and making homeless, millions of people; followed by a vast earthquake in Pakistan, and two very severe hurricanes of a record number in the USA. The First World War and Second World War have left a terrible legacy of a World War of the Third World, that has waged worldwide ever since the Second World War ended in 1945. Pray that God makes the Second Coming happen before anything even worse happens!
13. The final important sign Jesus gave of when he would return, in secret to his disciples, has also, crucially, just happened. He said that he would return only 'once this Gospel has been preached in all countries of the world'. The Church reported that that had finally happened, in 2005. So, the stage is set for the return of Jesus any time from now.

DANIEL CHAPTER THREE

1 Nebuchadnezzar the king made an image of gold, whose height was sixty cubits, and breadth six cubits. He set it up in the plain of Dura, in the province of Babylon.
2 Then Nebuchadnezzar the king sent to gather together the princes, the governors, and the captains, the judges, the treasurers, the counsellors, the sheriffs, and all the rulers of the provinces, to come to the dedication of the image which Nebuchadnezzar the king had set up.
3 Then the princes, the governors, and captains, the judges, the treasurers, the counsellors, the sheriffs, and all the rulers of the provinces, were gathered together to the dedication of the image that Nebuchadnezzar the king had set up; and they stood before the image that Nebuchadnezzar had set up.
4 Then a herald cried aloud, "To you it is commanded, O people, nations, and languages,
5 That whenever you hear the sound of the cornet, flute, harp, sackbut, psaltery, dulcimer, and all kinds of music, you fall down and worship the golden image that Nebuchadnezzar the king has set up;
6 And anyone who does not fall down and worship, shall the same hour be cast into the midst of a burning fiery furnace."
7 Therefore at that time, when all the people heard the sound of the cornet, flute, harp, sackbut, psaltery, and all kinds of music, all the people, the nations, and the languages, they fell down and worshipped the golden image that Nebuchadnezzar the king had set up.
8 Now at that time certain Chaldeans came near, and accused the Jews.
9 They addressed the king Nebuchadnezzar, "O king, live for ever."
10 "You, O king, have made a decree, that every man that shall hear the sound of the cornet, flute, harp, sackbut, psaltery, and dulcimer, and all kinds of music, shall fall down and worship the golden image;
11 And anyone who does not fall down and worship should be cast into the midst of a burning fiery furnace.
12 There are certain Jews whom you have set over the affairs of the province of Babylon, Shadrach, Meshach, and Abednego;

these men, O king, have not regarded you. They do not serve your gods, nor worship the golden image which you have set up."

13 Then Nebuchadnezzar in his rage and fury commanded to bring Shadrach, Meshach, and Abednego. Then they brought these men before the king.

14 Nebuchadnezzar spoke and said to them, Is it true, O Shadrach, Meshach, and Abednego, you do not serve my gods, nor worship the golden image which I have set up?

15 Now if you be ready that whenever you hear the sound of the cornet, flute, harp, sackbut, psaltery, and dulcimer, and all kinds of music, you fall down and worship the image which I have made; all very well. If however you will not worship it, you shall be cast the same hour into the midst of a burning fiery furnace; and who is that God that shall deliver you out of my hands?

16 Shadrach, Meshach, and Abednego, answered and said to the king, "O Nebuchadnezzar, we are not careful to answer you in this matter.

17 If it be so, our God whom we serve is able to deliver us from the burning fiery furnace, and he will deliver us out of your hand, O king.

18 But if not, understand, O king, that we will not serve your gods, nor worship the golden image which you have set up."

19 Then was Nebuchadnezzar full of fury, and the form of his visage was changed against Shadrach, Meshach, and Abednego. He spoke, and commanded that they should heat the furnace seven times more than it was wont to be heated.

20 And he commanded the mightiest men that were in his army to bind Shadrach, Meshach, and Abednego, and to cast them into the burning fiery furnace.

21 Then these men were bound in their coats, their hats, and their other garments, and were cast into the midst of the burning fiery furnace.

22 Therefore because the king's commandment was urgent, and the furnace exceeding hot, the flame of the fire slew those men that took up Shadrach, Meshach, and Abednego.

23 And these three men, Shadrach, Meshach, and Abednego, fell down bound into the midst of the burning fiery furnace.

24 Then Nebuchadnezzar the king was astonished, and rose up in haste, and said to his counsellors, "Did not we cast three

men bound into the midst of the fire?" They answered and said unto the king, "True, O king."

25 He answered and said, "Lo, I see four men loose, walking in the midst of the fire, and they have no hurt; and the form of the fourth is like a Son of God."

26 Then Nebuchadnezzar came near to the mouth of the burning fiery furnace, and spoke, and said, "Shadrach, Meshach, and Abednego, you servants of the most high God, come forth, and come here." Then Shadrach, Meshach, and Abednego, came forth of the midst of the fire.

27 And the princes, governors, and captains, and the king's counsellors, being gathered together, saw these men, upon whose bodies the fire had no power, nor was a hair of their head singed, neither were their coats changed, nor had the smell of fire passed on them.

28 Then Nebuchadnezzar spoke, and said, "Blessed be the God of Shadrach, Meshach, and Abednego, who have sent his angel, and delivered his servants that trusted in him, and have changed the king's word, and yielded their bodies, that they might not serve nor worship any god, except their own God.

29 Therefore I make a decree, That every people, nation, and language, which speak anything amiss against the God of Shadrach, Meshach, and Abednego, shall be cut in pieces, and their houses shall be made a dunghill, because there is no other God that can deliver like this."

30 Then the king promoted Shadrach, Meshach, and Abednego, in the province of Babylon.

DANIEL CHAPTER FOUR

1 Nebuchadnezzar the king, unto all people, nations, and languages, that dwell in all the earth: "Peace be multiplied unto you."
2 "I thought it good to tell of the signs and wonders that the high God has wrought toward me.
3 How great are his signs! How mighty are his wonders! His kingdom is an everlasting kingdom, and his dominion is from generation to generation.
    4 I Nebuchadnezzar was at rest in my house, and flourishing in my palace.
5 I saw a dream which made me afraid, and the thoughts upon my bed and the visions of my head troubled me.
6 Therefore I made a decree to bring in all the wise men of Babylon before me, that they might make known unto me the interpretation of the dream.
7 Then the magicians, the astrologers, the Chaldeans, and the soothsayers came in, and I told the dream before them; but they did not make known the interpretation to me.
    8 But at the last Daniel came in before me, whose name was Belteshazzar, according to the name of my god, and in whom is the spirit of the holy gods, and before him I told the dream, saying,
9 'O Belteshazzar, master of the magicians, because I know that the spirit of the holy gods is in you, and no secret troubles you, tell me the visions of my dream that I have seen, and their interpretation.
10 These were the visions of mine head in my bed; I saw, and behold a tree in the midst of the earth, and its height was great.
11 The tree grew, and was strong, and its height reached up to heaven, and the sight of it to the end of all the earth.
12 Its leaves were fair, and it had much fruit, and in it was meat for all. The beasts of the field had shadow under it, and the fowls of the heaven dwelt in its boughs, and all flesh was fed of it.
13 I saw in the visions of my head upon my bed, and behold, a watcher, a holy one, came down from heaven;
14 He cried aloud, and said "Hew down the tree, and cut off his branches, shake off his leaves, and scatter his fruit. Let the

beasts get away from under it, and the fowls from his branches.

15 Nevertheless leave the stump of his roots in the earth, even with a band of iron and brass, in the tender grass of the field; and let it be wet with the dew of heaven, and let his portion be with the beasts in the grass of the earth

16 Let his heart be changed from man's, and let a beast's heart be given to him; and let seven times pass over him.

17 This matter is by the decree of the watchers, and the demand by the word of the holy ones, to the intent that the living may know that the most High rules in the kingdom of men, and gives it to whoever he will, and sets up over it the basest of men.

18 This dream I king Nebuchadnezzar have seen. Now you, O Belteshazzar, declare the interpretation, for all the wise men of my kingdom are not able to make known to me the interpretation. But you are able; for the spirit of the holy gods is in you."

    19 Then Daniel, whose name was Belteshazzar, was astonished for one hour, and his thoughts troubled him. The king spoke, and said, "Belteshazzar, do not let the dream, or its interpretation, trouble you." Belteshazzar answered and said, "My lord, the dream is for them that hate you, and its interpretation so as to shine enemies.

20 The tree that you saw, which grew, and was strong, whose height reached unto the heaven, and could be seen anywhere in the world;

21 Whose leaves were fair, and had much fruit, and in it was meat for all; under which the beasts of the field dwelt, and upon whose branches the fowls of the heaven had their habitation.

22 It is you, O king that are grown and become strong. For your greatness is grown, and reaches unto heaven, and your dominion to the end of the earth.

23 And whereas the king saw a watcher and a holy one coming down from heaven, and saying, "Hew the tree down, and destroy it; yet leave the stump of its roots in the earth, even with a band of iron and brass, in the tender grass of the field; and let it be wet with the dew of heaven, and let his portion be with the beasts of the field, till seven times pass over him;

24 This is the interpretation, O king, and this is the decree of the most High, which is come upon my lord the king;

25 That they shall drive you from men, and your dwelling shall be with the beasts of the field, and they shall make you to eat grass as oxen, and they shall wet you with the dew of heaven, and seven times shall pass over you, till you know that the most High rules in the kingdom of men, and gives it to whoever he will.

26 And whereas they commanded to leave the stump of the tree roots; your kingdom shall be returned to you, after you fully know that the heavens do rule.

27 Wherefore, O king, let my counsel be acceptable unto you, and break off your sins by righteousness, and your iniquities by showing mercy to the poor; if it may be a lengthening of your tranquillity.'

    28 All this came upon the king Nebuchadnezzar.

29 At the end of twelve months he walked in the palace of the kingdom of Babylon.

30 The king spoke, and said, "Is not this great Babylon, that I have built for the house of the kingdom by the might of my power, and for the honour of my majesty?"

31 While the word was in the king's mouth, there fell a voice from heaven, saying, "O king Nebuchadnezzar, to you it is spoken, 'The kingdom is departed from you.'

32 And they shall drive you from men, and your dwelling shall be with the beasts of the field. They shall make you to eat grass as oxen, and seven times shall pass over you, until you know that the most High rules in the kingdom of men, and gives it to whoever he will."

33 The same hour was the thing fulfilled upon Nebuchadnezzar. He was driven from men, and did eat grass as oxen, and his body was wet with the dew of heaven, till his hairs were grown like eagles' feathers, and his nails like birds' claws.

34 "And at the end of the days I Nebuchadnezzar lifted up mine eyes unto heaven, and my understanding returned to me, and I blessed the most High, and I praised and honoured him that lives for ever, whose dominion is an everlasting dominion, and his kingdom is from generation to generation.

35 And all the inhabitants of the earth are reputed as nothing, and he does according to his will in the army of heaven, and among the inhabitants of the earth; and none can stay his hand, or say to him, "What are you doing?"

36 At the same time my reason returned to me; and for the glory of my kingdom, mine honour and brightness returned to

me; and my counsellors and my lords sought after me; and I was established in my kingdom, and excellent majesty was added to me.
37 Now I Nebuchadnezzar praise and extol and honour the King of heaven, all whose works are truth, and his ways judgement. Those that walk in pride he is able to abase."

DANIEL CHAPTER FIVE

1 Belshazzar the king made a great feast to a thousand of his lords, and drank wine before the thousand.
2 Belshazzar, while he tasted the wine, commanded they bring the golden and silver vessels which his father Nebuchadnezzar had taken out of the temple which was in Jerusalem; that the king, and his princes, his wives, and his concubines, might drink from them.
3 Then they brought the golden vessels that were taken out of the temple of the house of God which was at Jerusalem; and the king, and his princes, his wives, and his concubines, drank in them.
4 They drank wine, and praised the gods of gold, and of silver, of brass, of iron, of wood, and of stone.
5 In the same hour came forth fingers of a man's hand, and wrote over against the candlestick upon the plaster of the wall of the king's palace. The king saw the part of the hand that wrote.
6 Then the king's countenance was changed, and his thoughts troubled him, so that the joints of his loins were loosed, and his knees smote one against another.
7 The king cried aloud to bring in the astrologers, the Chaldeans, and the soothsayers. And the king spoke, and said to the wise men of Babylon, "Whoever can read this writing, and show me its interpretation, shall be clothed with scarlet, and have a chain of gold about his neck, and shall be the third ruler in the kingdom."
8 Then all the king's wise men came in, but they could not read the writing, nor make known to the king its interpretation.
9 Then king Belshazzar was greatly troubled, and his countenance was changed in him, and his lords were astonished.

10 Now the queen, by reason of the words of the king and his lords, came into the banquet house. The queen spoke and said, "O king, live for ever! Let not your thoughts trouble you, nor let your countenance be changed;
11 There is a man in your kingdom, in whom is the spirit of the holy gods; and in the days of your father light and understanding and wisdom, like the wisdom of the gods, was found in him; whom the king Nebuchadnezzar your father, the king, I say, your father, made master of the magicians, astrologers, Chaldeans, and soothsayers;
12 For an excellent spirit, and knowledge, and understanding, interpreting of dreams, and showing of hard sentences, and dissolving of doubts, were found in the same Daniel, whom the king named Belteshazzar. Now let Daniel be called, and he will show the interpretation."
13 Then Daniel was brought in before the king. And the king spoke and said to Daniel, "Are you that Daniel, which are of the children of the captivity of Judah, whom the king my father brought out of Judah?
14 I have even heard of you, that the spirit of the gods is in you, and that light and understanding and excellent wisdom is found in you.
15 And now the wise men, the astrologers, have been brought in before me, that they should read this writing, and make known to me its interpretation. But they could not show the interpretation of the thing;
16 And I have heard of you that you can make interpretations, and dissolve doubts. Now if you can read the writing, and make known to me its interpretation, you shall be clothed with scarlet, and have a chain of gold about your neck, and shall be the third ruler in the kingdom."
17 Then Daniel answered and said to the king, Let your gifts be to yourself; and give your rewards to another; yet I will read the writing to the king, and make known to him the interpretation.
18 O you king, the most high God gave Nebuchadnezzar your father a kingdom, and majesty, and glory, and honour.
19 And for the majesty that he gave him, all people, nations, and languages, trembled and feared before him: - whom he would he slew; and whom he would he kept alive; and whom he would he set up; and whom he would he put down.

20 But when his heart was lifted up, and his mind hardened in pride, he was deposed from his kingly throne, and they took his glory from him.
21 And he was driven from the sons of men; and his heart was made like the beasts, and his dwelling was with the wild asses. They fed him with grass like oxen, and his body was wet with the dew of heaven; till he knew that the most high God ruled in the kingdom of men, and that he appoints over it whoever he will.
22 You his son, O Belshazzar, have not been humbled, though you knew all this;
23 But have lifted up yourself against the Lord of heaven; and they have brought the vessels of his house before you, and you, and your lords, your wives, and your concubines, have drunk wine in them; and you have praised the gods of silver, and gold, of brass, iron, wood, and stone, which do not see, nor hear, nor know. And the God in whose hand your breath is, and whose are all your ways, have you not glorified.
24 Then was the part of the hand sent from him; and this writing was written.
25 And this is the writing that was written, MENE, MENE, TEKEL, PERES.
26 This is the interpretation of the thing - MENE - God has numbered your kingdom, and finished it.
27 TEKEL - you are weighed in the balances, and are found wanting.
28 PERES - your kingdom is divided, and given to the Medes and Persians."
29 Then Belshazzar commanded, and they clothed Daniel with scarlet, and put a chain of gold about his neck, and made a proclamation concerning him, that he should be the third ruler in the kingdom.
30 In that night was Belshazzar the king of the Chaldeans slain.
31 And Darius the Mede took the kingdom, being about sixty-two years old.

DANIEL CHAPTER SIX

1 It pleased Darius to set over the kingdom a hundred and twenty princes, which should be over the whole kingdom;

2 And over these three presidents; of whom Daniel was first. So that the princes might give accounts to them, and the king should have no damage.
3 Then this Daniel was preferred above the presidents and princes, because an excellent spirit was in him; and the king thought to set him over the whole realm.
4 Then the presidents and princes sought to find occasion against Daniel concerning the kingdom; but they could find neither occasion nor fault; for he was faithful, neither was there any error or fault found in him.
5 Then said these men, "We shall not find any occasion against this Daniel, except we find it against him concerning the law of his God."
6 Then these presidents and princes assembled together to the king, and said to him, King Darius, live for ever.
7 All the presidents of the kingdom, the governors, and the princes, the counsellors, and the captains, have consulted together to establish a royal statute, and to make a firm decree, that anyone who asks a petition of any God or man for thirty days, save of you, O king, he shall be cast into the den of lions.
8 Now, O king, establish the decree, and sign the writing, that it be not changed, according to the law of the Medes and Persians, which never alters.
9 Therefore king Darius signed the writing and the decree.
10 Now when Daniel knew that the writing was signed, he went into his house; and his windows being open in his chamber toward Jerusalem, he kneeled upon his knees three times a day, and prayed, and gave thanks before his God, as he always did before.
11 Then these men assembled, and found Daniel praying and making supplication before his God.
12 Then they came near, and spoke to the king concerning the king's decree, "Have you not signed a decree, that every man that shall ask a petition of any God or man for thirty days, save of you, O king, shall be cast into the den of lions?" The king answered and said, "The thing is true, according to the law of the Medes and Persians, which never alters."
13 Then they answered and said to the king, "That Daniel, which is of the children of the captivity of Judah, does not regard you, O king, nor the decree that you have signed, but makes his petition three times a day."

14 Then the king, when he heard these words, was sore displeased with himself and set his heart on Daniel to deliver him. He laboured till the going down of the sun to deliver him.
15 Then these men assembled unto the king, and said unto the king, "Know, O king, that the law of the Medes and Persians is, 'That neither decree nor statute which the king establishes may be changed'."
16 Then the king commanded, and they brought Daniel, and cast him into the den of lions. Now the king spoke and said to Daniel, "Your God whom you serve continually, he will deliver you."
17 And a stone was brought, and laid upon the mouth of the den; and the king sealed it with his own signet, and with the signet of his lords; that the purpose might not be changed concerning Daniel.
    18 Then the king went to his palace, and passed the night fasting. Neither were instruments of music brought before him; and his sleep went from him.
19 Then the king arose very early in the morning, and hurried to the den of lions.
20 And when he came to the den, he cried with a lamentable voice to Daniel. The king spoke and said to Daniel, "O Daniel, servant of the living God, is your God, whom you serve continually, able to deliver you from the lions?"
21 Then Daniel said to the king, "O king, live for ever."
22 My God have sent his angel, and has shut the lions' mouths, that they have not hurt me. For before him innocence was found in me; and also before you, O king, I have done no hurt."
23 Then was the king exceeding glad for him, and commanded that they should take Daniel up out of the den. So Daniel was taken up out of the den, and no manner of hurt was found upon him, because he believed in his God.
    24 And the king commanded, and they brought those men which had accused Daniel, and they cast them into the den of lions, them, their children, and their wives; and the lions had the mastery of them, and broke all their bones in pieces before ever they came at the bottom of the den.
    25 Then king Darius wrote to all people, nations, and languages, that dwell in all the earth, "Peace be multiplied unto you."
26 I make a decree, "In every dominion of my kingdom men tremble and fear before the God of Daniel. For he is the living

God, and steadfast forever, and his kingdom that which shall not be destroyed, and his dominion shall be to the end."

27 He delivers and rescues, and he works signs and wonders in heaven and in earth; who has delivered Daniel from the power of the lions.

28 So this Daniel prospered in the reign of Darius, and in the reign of Cyrus the Persian.

DANIEL CHAPTERS SEVEN-TWELVE. AN ACCOUNT OF DANIEL'S GREAT VISIONS

DANIEL CHAPTER SEVEN

1 In the first year of Belshazzar king of Babylon Daniel had a dream and visions of his head as he lay upon his bed. Then he wrote down the dream, and told the sum of the matters.
2 Daniel spoke and said, "I saw in my vision by night, and, behold, the four winds of the heaven strove upon the great sea.
3 And four great beasts came up from the sea, diverse one from another.
4 The first was like a lion, and had eagle's wings. I watched till its wings were plucked off, and it was lifted up from the earth, and made to stand upon its feet like a man, and a man's heart was given to it.
5 And behold another beast, a second, like a bear, and it raised up itself on one side, and it had three ribs in the mouth of it between its teeth. And they said to it, 'Arise, devour much flesh'.
6 After this I watched, and lo another, like a leopard, which had upon its back four wings of a bird; the beast had also four heads; and dominion was given to it.
7 After this I saw in the night visions, and behold a fourth beast, dreadful and terrible, and exceedingly strong; and it had great iron teeth. It devoured and broke in pieces, and stamped the residue with its feet. And it was different from all the beasts that were before it; and it had ten horns.
8 I considered the horns, and, behold, there came up among them another little horn, before whom there were three of the first horns plucked up by the roots. Behold, in this horn were eyes like the eyes of man, and a mouth speaking great things.
 9 I watched till the thrones were set down, and the Ancient of days did sit, whose garment was white as snow, and the hair of his head like the pure wool. His throne was like the fiery flame, and his wheels as burning fire.
10 A fiery stream issued and came forth from before him. A thousand thousands ministered unto him, and ten thousand times ten thousand stood before him. The judgement was set, and the books were opened.

11 I watched then because of the voice of the great words which the horn spoke. I watched even till the beast was slain, and his body destroyed, and given to the burning flame.
12 As concerning the rest of the beasts, they had their dominion taken away. Yet their lives were prolonged for a season and time.
13 I saw in the night visions, and, behold, one like the Son of man came with the clouds of heaven, and came to the Ancient of days, and they brought him near before him.
14 And there was given him dominion, and glory, and a kingdom, that all people, nations, and languages, should serve him. His dominion is an everlasting dominion, which shall not pass away, and his kingdom that which shall not be destroyed.
15 I Daniel was grieved in my spirit in the midst of my body, and the visions of my head troubled me.
16 I came near unto one of them that stood by, and asked him the truth of all this. So he told me, and made me know the interpretation of the things.
17 'These great beasts, which are four, are four kings, which shall arise out of the earth.
18 But the saints of the most High shall take the kingdom, and possess the kingdom for ever, even for ever and ever.'
19 Then I would know the truth of the fourth beast, which was diverse from all the others, exceeding dreadful, whose teeth were of iron, and his nails of brass; which devoured, broke in pieces, and stamped the residue with his feet;
20 And of the ten horns that were in his head, and of the other which came up, and before whom three fell; even of that horn that had eyes, and a mouth that spoke very great things, whose look was more stout than his fellows.
21 I watched, and the same horn made war with the saints, and prevailed against them;
22 Until the Ancient of days came, and judgement was given to the saints of the most High; and the time came that the saints possessed the kingdom.
23 Thus he said, 'The fourth beast shall be the fourth kingdom upon earth, which shall be different from all kingdoms, and shall devour the whole earth, and shall tread it down, and break it in pieces.
24 And the ten horns out of this kingdom are ten kings that shall arise; and another shall rise after them; and he shall be different from the first, and he shall put down three kings.

25 And he shall speak great words against the most High, and shall wear out the saints of the most High, and think to change times and laws, and they shall be given into his hand until a time and times and the dividing of time.
26 But the judgement shall sit, and they shall take away his dominion, to consume and to destroy it unto the end.
27 And the kingdom and dominion, and the greatness of the kingdom under the whole heaven, shall be given to the people of the saints of the most High, whose kingdom is an everlasting kingdom, and all dominions shall serve and obey him'.
28 Here is the end of the matter. As for me Daniel, my thoughts much troubled me, and my countenance changed in me. But I kept the matter in my heart.

[The Aramaic portion of the text of Daniel returns to the Hebrew from here].

Notes on Daniel Chapter Seven

Most biblical commentators bend over backwards to exactly compare this first vision in the Book of Daniel to Nebuchadnezzar's dream in chapter two. Many of them warn most strongly against matching up the symbolism of the four beasts with modern empires rather than ancient ones. I agree with them that the fourth beast of Daniel 7 corresponds to that of Daniel 2. However, as we see in a moment I believe that Daniel 7 describes this fourth beast at a much later stage of its development – in the modern era in fact – than at the start in Daniel 2, when the 'fourth beast' clearly begins its life in the ancient Roman Empire.

I have two probable advantages over most other commentators on the prophecy in the bible. Firstly, over 30 years 1977-2007, God gave me a series of 30 visionary experiences, spread out apparently randomly when I saw them, and at long last, to my relief, I can definitely say that they have all finished 'coming true' often years later. They were heavily veiled symbolic visions of the future, only to be said to have been fulfilled once all the meaning had been turned into crystal clear reality – strictly in hindsight, no amount of 'guessing the meaning before it appeared' would ever work for me, especially in the early visions.

Secondly, I am working on this commentary from a far later position in time than previous commentators, and can see that the modern era can be shown to precisely fulfil the symbolism of the visions in the Bible, and even specific dates of certain events, as we will be seeing in subsequent chapters of Daniel in a moment. Indeed, other commentators have said the 'winged lion' was a symbol of Babylonian royal power, so corresponds to the winged lion of Daniel chapter 7. However, they fail to interpret the clearly vital symbolism of the other three beasts to correspond to Medo-Persia, Greece and Rome, which they say is the only way to understand it. As I see it however, history from the time of Daniel can be divided into three segments, from the broad point of view of this book: -
1. The empires of the then Ancient World, roughly 800BC – 100AD as in Daniel 2 – Babylon, Medo-Persia, Greece and Rome – leading up to the First Coming of Jesus Christ

2. Following the fall of Rome to German tribes, centuries later, there were the Dark Ages and Middle Ages till about 1500AD – during which there were no great world empires.
3. After the discovery and settlement of America by Christopher Columbus after 1492, the world was fully explored, by and large, and accurate maps of the globe appeared. Soon a second wave of empires appeared, as in Daniel Chapter 7, seemingly leading up to a much revived version, and much more complex, of the 'fourth beast' started by the Romans in the 21st Century. The Bible says that Jesus' Second Coming will end this beast forever very soon, as we see from the rest of the Book of Daniel, so ending a fierce rivalry lasting two thousand years with the Kingdom of God being established
4. So there are two waves of four great world-dominating empires in history - preceding Jesus' First and Second Coming!

My own (unique?) and literal interpretation of Daniel Chapter Seven

To repeat, I write what follows with two advantages over most biblical commentators on the visions here and in Part 3 of this Volume of this book that follows.

Firstly, God has given me absolutely assiduous preparation for this task, by making me suffer until in hindsight I was very relieved when all of twenty-eight symbolic visions I saw 'came true' strictly in hindsight in my own life. Relieved, because some of them were very terrifying at first and in the 1990's.

Secondly, I find myself as probably the first biblical commentator ever who can claim to have a totally complete interpretation of *all the symbolism* in the Book of Daniel – even the often mysterious time periods, which we come to in the next few chapters

The American Eagle indeed was 'plucked off' the British lion in 1776AD in the American Revolution. This first beast then, similar to the two that follow, contains more than one, in fact two superpowers, both imperial although most Americans would resent that claim.

The Russian bear has three tusks in its mouth – the ivory countries of India/Pakistan, Japan, and the Far East especially China, all of which had great empires centuries ago, and Japan and China are still emerging as superpowers since being that in the 20th Century; India clearly has such aspirations.

The leopards' spots correspond to the many varied dialects, regions and languages of modern *Europe* – with two principal powers having dominated mainland Europe for hundreds of years – the two-winged cockerel of France, and the eagle of Germany – four wings altogether, just as in Daniel's vision!

The fourth beast corresponds to the two descriptions in Revelation 13 and 17 that we saw in Part 1. The fact that this is 'Wanton (Global) Materialism' today largely spent on 'science & technology' is supplied by the symbolism in Revelation of its 'seven heads – vowels – and ten horns – consonants'. The view in Daniel of this 'beast 666' is rather different, and complements the description of the beast in Revelation, and again in 2 Esdras, that we look at in Part 3 shortly.

For the fourth beast is described as having 'ten horns... among them another little horn, before whom three of the first horns were plucked up by the roots'. The little horn, as all biblical commentators are agreed, is 'the adversary' or 'the legalist' – Satan. The three horns are provided by the three geographical empires or land masses of the first three beasts joining and mingling as they have in the 21st century and before: UNITED STATES (6) – BRITON-EUROPE(6) – ASIANS (6). Each of these three 'plucked up horns' – as we see soon, 2 Esdras 11-12 calls them three heads, are confused indeed in 'leadership'. They all want to rule – just as George Orwell described the modern world in his book '1984'!

Yet each of them *in turn* has three heads of their own – 3-in-3-in-1 or 10-in 1, corresponding to the ten horns of this 'beast of the Time of the End'!

A diagram is best to illustrate this – as below: -

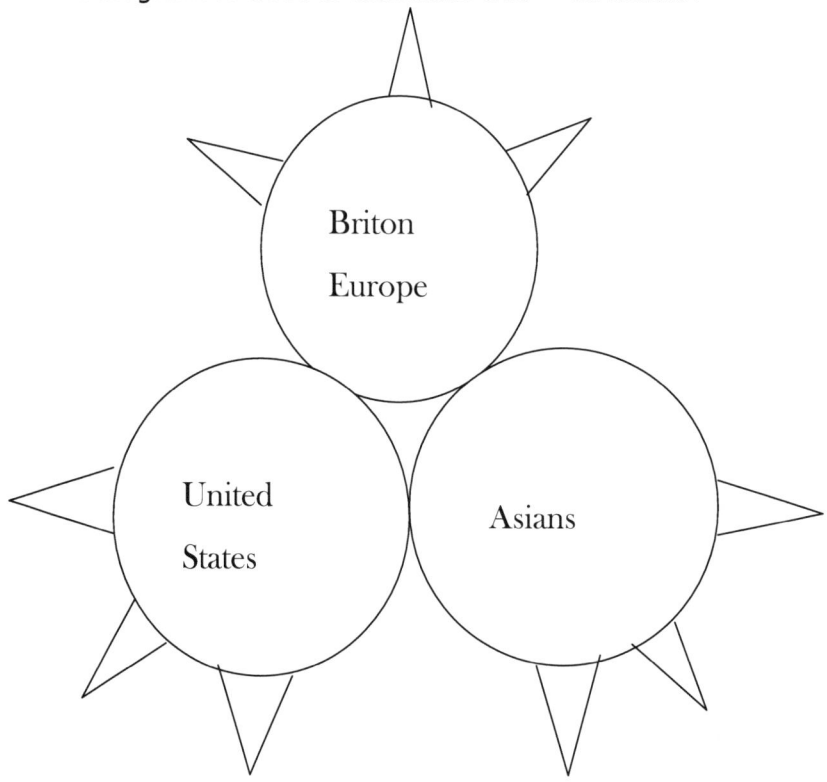

Briton Europe

United States

Asians

The three heads or horns of the Beast of Wanton Global Materialism of: Revelation 13, Daniel 7 and 2 Esdras 11-12

The three little heads/horns on each are: church / states / leader

DANIEL CHAPTER EIGHT

1 In the third year of the reign of king Belshazzar a vision appeared to me, Daniel, after that which appeared to me at the first.
2 And I saw in a vision; and it came to pass, when I saw, that I was at Shushan in the palace, which is in the province of Elam; and I saw in a vision, and I was by the river of Ulai.
3 Then I lifted up my eyes, and saw, and, behold, there stood before the river a ram which had two horns. The two horns were high; but one was higher than the other, and the higher came up last.
4 I saw the ram pushing westward, and northward, and southward; so that no beasts might stand before him, neither was there any that could deliver out of his hand; but he did according to his will, and became great.
5 And as I was considering, behold, a he goat came from the west over the face of the whole earth, and did not touch the ground. The goat had a notable horn between his eyes.
6 And he came to the ram that had two horns, which I had seen standing before the river, and ran at him in the fury of his power.
7 And I saw him come close to the ram, and he was moved with rage against him, and struck the ram, and broke his two horns. There was no power in the ram to stand before him, but he cast him down to the ground, and stamped upon him. And there was none that could deliver the ram out of his hand.
8 Therefore the he goat waxed very great, and when he was strong, the great horn was broken; and instead of it came up four notable ones toward the four winds of heaven.
9 And out of one of them came a little horn, which waxed exceedingly great, toward the south, and toward the east, and toward the pleasant land.
10 And it waxed great, even to the host of heaven; and it cast down some of the host and of the stars to the ground, and stamped upon them.
11 Yea, he magnified himself even to the prince of the host, and by him the daily sacrifice was taken away, and the place of his sanctuary was cast down.

12 And a host was given him against the daily sacrifice by reason of transgression, and it cast down the truth to the ground; and it practised, and prospered.

13 Then I heard one saint speaking, and another saint said unto that certain saint which spoke, "How long shall be the vision concerning the daily sacrifice, and the transgression of desolation, to give both the sanctuary and the host to be trodden under foot?"

14 And he said to me, "Unto two thousand and three hundred days; then shall the sanctuary be cleansed."

15 And it came to pass, when I, Daniel, had seen the vision, and sought for the meaning, then, behold, there stood before me one with the appearance of a man.

16 And I heard a man's voice between the banks of the Ulai, which called, and said, "Gabriel, make this man to understand the vision."

17 So he came near where I stood. When he came, I was afraid, and fell upon my face. But he said to me, "Understand, O son of man. For at the time of the end shall be the vision."

18 Now as he was speaking with me, I was in a deep sleep on my face toward the ground. But he touched me, and set me upright.

19 And he said, "Behold, I will make you know what shall be in the last end of the indignation. For at the appointed time the end shall be.

20 The ram which you saw having two horns are the kings of Media and Persia.

21 And the rough goat is the king of Greece, and the great horn that is between his eyes is the first king.

22 Now that being broken, as four stood up in its place, four kingdoms shall stand up out of the nation, but not in his power.

23 And in the latter time of their kingdom, when the transgressors are come to the full, a king of fierce countenance, and understanding dark sentences, shall stand up.

24 And his power shall be mighty, but not by his own power; and he shall destroy wonderfully, and shall prosper, and practise, and shall destroy the mighty and the holy people.

25 And also through his policy he shall cause craft to prosper in his hand; and he shall magnify himself in his heart, and by peace shall destroy many. He shall also stand up against the Prince of princes; but he shall be broken by no hand.

26 And the vision of the evening and the morning which was told is true. Therefore shut up the vision; for it shall be for many days.

27 And I Daniel fainted, and was sick certain days; afterward I rose up, and did the king's business; and I was astonished at the vision, but none understood it.

Notes on Daniel Chapter Eight

Once again, as for Daniel Chapters 2 and 7, my own interpretation is radical in various aspects. Indeed I take my lead from historical biblical commentators about most aspects of the first phase of this vision, which came true in the conquests of Alexander the Great of the Greek Empire (the Goat's horn or 'first king'). However, such commentaries fail to explain adequately various aspects of Daniel's vision here, or simply fail to even discuss them. Remarkably, I have found yet again completely compelling parallels between events of the 'latter time of their kingdom' of verse 8:23 and the 'last end of the indignation' of verse 8:19; and our 20th and 21st centuries!

First phase – conquest by Alexander the Great.
Daniel chapter two described a dream which accurately described Babylon being destroyed by Medo-Persia, in turn being destroyed by Greece, and finally the ascendancy of the Roman Empire, prior to that eventually turning into the 'Beast 666' today. Most of this present chapter eight concerns the conquest of Medo-Persia as part of a great campaign by Alexander the Great, king of Greece.

However, I differ from most other commentators in not confining my views to that era, as we see below, but seeing incredibly close parallels to the modern age, even down to periods of time as given in the Book of Daniel.

Alexander the Great (356 – 323BC) was the greatest general of ancient history, founding a great ancient Greek Empire. He took the throne at age 20, destroying rivals and consolidating power in Greece. In spring 334BC he began the Persian expedition, conquering West Asia Minor, and storming the Isle of Tyre, his greatest military victory. He subdued Egypt and occupied Babylon in 332BC, marching north in 330BC to occupy Media and then conquering central Asia in 328BC. In 327BC he invaded India. He died at 32 of apparently natural causes after consolidating his gains and his empire. He left his empire to four generals, unrelated to him. Seleucus founded a dynasty in Syria. Ptolemy founded a dynasty in Egypt. The other two kingdoms were Greece and Asia Minor; including the areas of Medo-Persia and Babylon, modern Iran and Iraq.

Phase two – modern Iraq and *Saddam Hussein*

Conventional wisdom has it that the kingdom of verse 9 is Syria, and the 'king of fierce countenance' of verse 23 was one Antiochus IV, who ruled Syria 175-164BC, and that verses 9-14 'vividly depict the atrocities of his reign' as in chapter 11, that we consider later – and to consult Maccabees 1-6 in the Apocrypha about this. This ignores three great facts:

1. It fails to explain the '2,300 days' of verse 14.
2. Verse 19 says this part of the vision is in 'the last end' of the 'appointed time of the end'. So I believe the vision suddenly 'jumps' 2,300 years – from 332BC to recently – 2,300 years later, with no 'year zero', takes us to 1969AD.
3. The only country, to my knowledge, that has *ever* been in a shape 'exceedingly great to the south, towards the east, and towards the pleasant (Holy) land' is Iraq (there is a great buttress of desert in the west of modern Iraq that points directly at Israel, and Iraq has lengthy borders in the east with Iran, and in the south with Saudi Arabia and Kuwait). It cannot possibly be tiny Syria, with the wrong geometry but must be modern Iraq – on the site of ancient Babylon!

So what happened in 1969 to convince me of those things? Well, it is a well-known fact of history that Saddam Hussein came to almost supreme power in Iraq in 1968, and started building his famous lavish and perverted palaces then, finally gaining absolute power as dictator and president in 1979. Since then he has conducted a war lasting 1980-1988 with Iran, and two campaigns of the Gulf Wars against Kuwait and the Western Allies, 1991-1992 and 2003. Verses 9-14 and 23-26 describe him accurately as having a fierce face, and remarkably are totally accurate about him, even though they were written over 2,600 years ago!

However, above all in 1969, man invaded the moon...! (the 'heavens')

DANIEL CHAPTER NINE

1 In the first year of Darius the son of Ahasuerus, of the people of the Medes, who was made king over the realm of the Chaldeans;
2 In the first year of his reign, I, Daniel, understood by the books the number of the years, of which the word of the Lord came to Jeremiah the prophet, that he would accomplish seventy years in the desolations of Jerusalem.

3 And I set my face to the Lord God, to seek by prayer and supplications, with fasting, and sackcloth, and ashes;
4 And I prayed to the Lord my God, and made my confession, and said, "O Lord, the great and dreadful God, keeping the covenant and mercy to them that love him, and to them that keep his commandments;
5 We have sinned, and have committed iniquity, and have done wickedly, and have rebelled, even by departing from your precepts and from your judgements.
6 Neither have we listened to your servants the prophets, who spoke in your name to our kings, our princes, and our fathers, and to all the people of the land.
7 O Lord, righteousness belongs to you, but to us confusion of faces, as at this day; to the men of Judah, and to the inhabitants of Jerusalem, and to all Israel, that are near, and that are far off, through all the countries where you have driven them, because of their trespass that they have trespassed against you.
8 O Lord, to us belongs confusion of face, to our kings, to our princes, and to our fathers, because we have sinned against you.
9 To the Lord our God belong mercies and forgiveness, though we have rebelled against him;
10 Neither have we obeyed the voice of the Lord our God, to walk in his laws, which he set before us by his servants the prophets.
11 Yea, all Israel have transgressed your law, even by departing, that they might not obey your voice; therefore the curse is poured upon us, and the oath that is written in the law of Moses the servant of God, because we have sinned against him.

12 And he has confirmed his words, which he spoke against us, and against our judges that judged us, by bringing upon us a great evil. For under the whole heaven has not been done as has been done upon Jerusalem.

13 As it is written in the law of Moses, all this evil is come upon us. Yet we made not our prayer before the Lord our God, that we might turn from our iniquities, and understand your truth.

14 Therefore the Lord has watched upon the evil, and brought it upon us. For the Lord our God is righteous in all his works which he does. For we obeyed not his voice.

15 And now, O Lord our God, that has brought your people forth out of the land of Egypt with a mighty hand, and has gotten you renown, as at this day; we have sinned, we have done wickedly.

16 O Lord, according to all your righteousness, I beseech you, let your anger and your fury be turned away from your city Jerusalem, your holy mountain. Because for our sins, and for the iniquities of our fathers, Jerusalem and your people have become a reproach to all that are about us.

17 Now therefore, O our God, hear the prayer of your servant, and his supplications, and cause your face to shine upon your sanctuary that is desolate, for the Lord's sake.

18 O my God, incline your ear, and hear; open your eyes, and behold our desolations, and the city which is called by your name. For we do not present our supplications before you for our righteousness, but for your great mercies.

59 O Lord, hear; O Lord, forgive; O Lord, hearken and do; defer not, for your own sake, O my God. For your city and your people are called by your name."

20 And while I was speaking, and praying, and confessing my sin and the sin of my people Israel, and presenting my supplication before the Lord my God for the holy mountain of my God;

25 Yea, while I was speaking in prayer, the man Gabriel, whom I had seen in the vision at the beginning, being caused to fly swiftly, touched me about the time of the evening oblation.

22 And he informed me, and talked with me, and said, "O Daniel, I am now come forth to give you skill and understanding.

23 At the beginning of your supplications the commandment came forth, and I am come to show you; for you are greatly

beloved. Therefore understand the matter and consider the vision.

24 Seventy weeks [*or* 'seventy sevens'] are determined for your people and upon your holy city, to finish the transgression, and to make an end of sins, and to make reconciliation for iniquity, and to bring in everlasting righteousness, and to seal up the vision and prophecy, and to anoint the most Holy.

25 Know therefore and understand, that from the going forth of the commandment to restore and to build Jerusalem, until an Anointed One, a prince [*or* 'the Messiah'] shall be seven weeks and sixty-two weeks [*or* 'seven sevens and sixty-two sevens']. The Street shall be built again, and the wall, even in troubled times.

26 And after sixty-two weeks shall an Anointed One [*or* 'Messiah'] be cut off and will have nothing. The people of the prince that shall come shall destroy the city and the sanctuary; and its end shall be with a flood, and to the end of the war desolations are determined.

27 And he shall confirm the covenant with many for one week. In the midst of the week he shall cause the sacrifice and the oblation to cease, and for the overspreading of abominations he shall make it desolate, even until the consummation, and that determined shall be poured upon the desolate.

Notes on Daniel Chapter Nine

Most people, including myself until last year, and most biblical commentators except the most conservative Christian ones, are baffled by the vision of the last four verses of this chapter! Any attempt to equate the mysterious phrase 'a week or seven of years' to seven years and then try to fit events here to historical timing between the decree to rebuild Jerusalem and the coming or crucifixion of Jesus, simply do not work out in the numbers – unless you are fanatical about it. My own view is radically different. This vision is not about Jesus' First Coming, but about the build-up to his Second Coming! I follow up that claim when I interpret Daniel Chapter 12 soon.

Firstly, what is this mysterious 'seven or week of years'? Seven is a holy number, and often in the bible is associated with a period of great joy or alternatively sorrow and hardship. So, I believe that a 'seven year' for Israel is a tough year indeed in this case, perhaps seeming to last seven years or 'a week of years'.

Secondly, there has indeed been an order in recent times sent out to rebuild and restore Jerusalem – indeed the entire state of Israel was under a British Mandate from the League of Nations until the order came in 1937 to give Israel Independence and establish a State of Israel. Everybody knows the absolute horror of what happened next. Nazi Germany started building concentration camps, to exterminate all Jews in particular, as well as other targeted and ethnic groups. The Second World War lasted until 1945, and a horrifying 6,000,000 or so Jews died in the Holocaust. After that there was a huge rush by Jews to re-occupy their ancient homeland in Israel, which finally and at last, became a state in 1948. Israel has been in a state of war with her Arab neighbours, by and large ever since. The recent success of Hamas in the elections of Palestine just this month, spells nothing but trouble for the region.

So, there is good reason to think that the "seventy week years" started in 1937, so will end in 2007. Meanwhile the Bible talks of an Anointed One 'being cut off and have nothing' after 62 weeks, i.e. 1999. I believe myself, this has a double meaning. The Anointed One is firstly, the *year of 2000* – it cut off two millennia and was full of nothing (three zeroes in it). After that, this century and millennium to date has been like Hell for most people, who with all the problems of looking over their shoulder for terrorists, as well as the global anti-terrorist measures, simply do not smile any more – or give out expressions of Love.

Secondly, since 2,000 started, after the fireworks died away, *the Holy Spirit* got ill. Where are wisdom, joy, love, health, beauty, peace – and Grace – now?

I don't know any more than anybody else what the end of this year, and next year will bring, although things must improve globally soon. Nevertheless this year end is the end of the second period of this vision of 'seven weeks' and as we see soon the end of this year is promised to be very exciting, in Daniel 12.

DANIEL CHAPTER TEN

1 In the third year of Cyrus king of Persia a thing was revealed to Daniel, whose name was called Belteshazzar; and the thing was true, but the time appointed was long. He understood the thing, and had understanding of the vision.
2 In those days I Daniel was mourning for three full weeks.
3 I ate no pleasant bread, neither flesh nor wine came in my mouth, neither did I anoint myself at all, till three whole weeks were fulfilled.
4 And in the twenty-fourth day of the first month, as I was by the side of the great river, which is Hiddekel;
5 Then I lifted up mine eyes, and looked, and behold a certain man clothed in linen, whose loins were girded with fine gold of Uphaz.
6 His body also was like beryl, and his face as the appearance of lightning, and his eyes as lamps of fire, and his arms and his feet like in colour to polished brass, and the voice of his words like the voice of a multitude.
7 And I Daniel alone saw the vision. For the men that were with me saw not the vision; but a great quaking fell upon them, so that they fled to hide themselves.
8 Therefore I was left alone, and saw this great vision, and there remained no strength in me. For my appearance was turned haggard, and I retained no strength.
9 Yet I heard the voice of his words. When I heard the voice of his words, then was I in a deep sleep on my face, and my face toward the ground.
10 And, behold, a hand touched me, which set me upon my knees and upon the palms of my hands.
11 And he said to me, "O Daniel, a man greatly beloved, understand the words that I speak to you, and stand upright. For I am now sent to you." And when he had spoken this word to me, I stood trembling.
12 Then said he to me, "Fear not, Daniel. For, from the first day that you did set your heart to understand, and to chasten yourself before your God, your words were heard, and I am come for your words.
53 But the prince of the kingdom of Persia withstood me twenty-one days. But, lo, Michael, one of the chief princes,

came to help me; and I remained there with the kings of Persia.
14 Now I am come to make you understand what shall befall your people in the latter days. For yet the vision is for many days."
15 And when he had spoken such words to me, I set my face toward the ground, and I became dumb.
16 And, behold, one with the appearance of the sons of men touched my lips. Then I opened my mouth, and spoke, and said to him that stood before me, "O my lord, by the vision my sorrows are turned upon me, and I have retained no strength.
17 For how can the servant of this my lord talk with this my lord? For as for me, straightaway there remained no strength in me, neither is there breath left in me."
18 Then there came again and touched me one like the appearance of a man, and he strengthened me,
19 And said, "O man greatly beloved, fear not. Peace be unto you, be strong, yea, be strong." And when he had spoken to me, I was strengthened, and said, "Let my lord speak, for you have strengthened me."
20 Then said he, "Do you know why I come to you? Now will I return to fight with the prince of Persia. When I am gone forth, lo, the prince of Greece shall come.
21 But I will show you that which is noted in the scripture of truth. For there is none that stands with me in these things, but Michael your prince.

DANIEL CHAPTER ELEVEN

1 Also in the first year of Darius the Mede, I stood to confirm and to strengthen him.
2 And now will I show you the truth. Behold, there shall stand up yet three kings in Persia; and the fourth shall be far richer than they all. By his strength through his riches he shall stir up all against the realm of Greece.
3 And a mighty king shall stand up, that shall rule with great dominion, and do according to his will.
4 And when he shall stand up, his kingdom shall be broken, and shall be divided toward the four winds of heaven; and not to his

posterity, nor according to his dominion which he ruled. For his kingdom shall be plucked up, even for others beside those.

5 And the king of the south shall be strong, and one of his princes; and he shall be strong above him, and have dominion; his dominion shall be a great dominion.

6 And in the end of years they shall join themselves together; for the daughter of the king of the south shall come to the king of the north to make an agreement. But she shall not retain the power of the arm; neither shall he stand, nor his arm. But she shall be given up, and they that brought her, and he that begat her, and he that strengthened her in these times.

7 But out of a branch of her roots shall one stand up in his place, which shall come with an army, and shall enter into the fortress of the king of the north, and shall deal against them, and shall prevail.

8 And shall also carry captives into Egypt their gods, with their princes, and with their precious vessels of silver and of gold; and he shall continue more years than the king of the north.

9 So the king of the south shall come into his kingdom, and shall return into his own land.

10 But his sons shall be stirred up, and shall assemble a multitude of great forces. One shall certainly come, and overflow, and pass through; then shall he return, and be stirred up, even to his fortress.

11 And the king of the south shall be moved with rage, and shall come forth and fight with him, even with the king of the north. He shall set forth a great multitude; but the multitude shall be given into his hand.

12 And when he has taken away the multitude, his heart shall be lifted up; and he shall cast down many ten thousands, but he shall not be strengthened by it.

13 For the king of the north shall return, and shall set forth a multitude greater than the former, and shall certainly come after certain years with a great army and with many riches.

14 And in those times many shall stand up against the king of the south. Also the robbers of your people shall exalt themselves to establish the vision; but they shall fall.

15 So the king of the north shall come, and cast up a mount, and take the most fenced cities. And the arms of the south shall not withstand, neither his chosen people, neither shall there be any strength to withstand.

16 But he that comes against him shall do according to his own will, and none shall stand before him. He shall stand in the glorious land, which by his hand shall be consumed.
17 He shall also set his face to enter with the strength of his whole kingdom, and upright ones with him; thus shall he do, and he shall give him the daughter of women, corrupting her. But she shall not stand on his side, neither be for him.
18 After this shall he turn his face to the isles, and shall take many; but a prince for his own behalf shall cause the reproach offered by him to cease; without his own reproach he shall cause it to turn upon him.
19 Then he shall turn his face toward the fort of his own land, but he shall stumble and fall, and not be found.
20 Then shall stand up in his place a raiser of taxes in the glory of the kingdom; but within a few days he shall be destroyed, neither in anger, nor in battle.
21 And in his place shall stand up a vile person, to whom they shall not give the honour of the kingdom, but he shall come in peaceably, and obtain the kingdom by flatteries.
22 And with the arms of a flood shall they be over-flown from before him, and shall be broken; yea, also the prince of the covenant.
23 And after the league made with him he shall work deceitfully; for he shall come up, and shall become strong with a small people.
24 He shall enter peaceably even upon the fattest places of the province; and he shall do that which his fathers have not done, nor his fathers' fathers; he shall scatter among them the prey, and spoil, and riches; yea, and he shall forecast his devices against the strongholds, even for a time.
25 And he shall stir up his power and his courage against the king of the south with a great army; and the king of the south shall be stirred up to battle with a very great and mighty army; but he shall not stand. For they shall forecast devices against him.
26 Yea, they that feed of the portion of his meat shall destroy him, and his army shall overflow, and many shall fall down slain.
27 And both these kings' hearts shall be to do mischief, and they shall speak lies at one table; but it shall not prosper. For yet the end shall be at the time appointed.

28 Then shall he return into his land with great riches; and his heart shall be against the holy covenant; and he shall do exploits, and return to his own land.
29 At the time appointed he shall return, and come toward the south; but it shall not be as the former, or as the latter.
30 For the ships of Chittim shall come against him. Therefore he shall be grieved, and return, and have indignation against the holy covenant. So shall he do; he shall even return, and have intelligence with them that forsake the holy covenant.
31 And arms shall stand on his part, and they shall pollute the sanctuary of strength, and shall take away the daily sacrifice, and they shall place the abomination that makes desolate.
32 And such as do wickedly against the covenant shall he corrupt by flatteries, but the people that do know their God shall be strong, and do exploits.
33 And they that understand among the people shall instruct many. Yet they shall fall by the sword, and by flame, by captivity, and by spoil, many days.
34 Now when they shall fall, they shall be helped with a little help but many shall cleave to them with flatteries.
35 Some of them of understanding shall fall, to try them, and to purge, and to make them white, even to the time of the end. Because it is yet for a time appointed.
36 And the king shall do according to his will; and he shall exalt himself and magnify himself above every god, and shall speak marvellous things against the God of gods, and shall prosper till the indignation be accomplished. For that which is determined shall be done.
37 Neither shall he regard the God of his fathers, nor the desire of women, nor regard any god. For he shall magnify himself above all.
38 But in his place he shall honour the God of forces. A god whom his fathers did not know he shall honour with gold, and silver, and with precious stones, and pleasant things.
39 Thus shall he do in the most strong fortresses with a strange god, whom he shall acknowledge and increase with glory; and he shall cause them to rule over many, and shall divide the land for gain.
40 And at the time of the end shall the king of the south push at him; and the king of the north shall come against him like a whirlwind, with chariots, and with horsemen, and with many

ships; and he shall enter into the countries, and shall overflow and pass over.
41 He shall enter also into the glorious land, and many countries shall be over thrown; but these shall escape out of his hand, even Edom, and Moab, and the chief of the children of Ammon.
42 He shall stretch forth his hand also upon the countries; and the land of Egypt shall not escape.
43 But he shall have power over the treasures of gold and of silver, and over all the precious things of Egypt; and the Libyans and the Ethiopians shall be at his steps.
44 But tidings out of the east and out of the north shall trouble him. Therefore he shall go forth with great fury to destroy, and utterly to make away many.
45 And he shall plant the tabernacles of his palace between the seas in the glorious holy mountain; yet he shall come to his end, and none shall help him.

DANIEL CHAPTER TWELVE

1 And at that time Michael shall stand up, the great prince who stands for the children of your people, and there shall be a time of trouble, such as never was since there was a nation even to that same time. At that time your people shall be delivered, every one that shall be found written in the book.
2 And many of them that sleep in the dust of the earth shall awake, some to everlasting life, and some to shame and everlasting contempt.
3 And they that are wise shall shine as the brightness of the firmament; and they that turn to righteousness as many as the stars for ever and ever.
4 But you, O Daniel, shut up the words, and seal the book, even to the time of the end; many shall run to and fro, and knowledge shall be increased."
    5 Then I Daniel looked, and, behold, there stood other two, the one on this side of the bank of the river, and the other on that side of the bank of the river.
6 And one said to the man clothed in linen, which was upon the waters of the river, "How long shall it be to the end of these wonders?"

7 And I heard the man clothed in linen, which was upon the waters of the river, when he held up his right hand and his left hand to heaven, and swore by him that lives for ever, that "it shall be for a time, times, and an half; and when he shall have accomplished to scatter the power of the holy people, all these things shall be finished."

8 And I heard, but I did not understand. Then I said, "O my Lord, what shall be the end of these things?"

9 And he said, "Go your way, Daniel. For the words are closed up and sealed till the time of the end."

10 Many shall be purified, and made white, and tried; but the wicked shall do wickedly, and none of the wicked shall understand; but the wise shall understand.

11 And from the time that the daily sacrifice shall be taken away, and the abomination that makes desolate set up, there shall be 1290 days.

12 Blessed is he that waits, and comes to the 1335 days.

13 But you, go your way till the end, for you shall rest, and stand in your lot at the end of the days.

Notes on Daniel Chapters ten through twelve

This set of visions is long and detailed, more so than any that have come before, so we can stand in amazement at the way that they can be seen to have come true. As usual, I take my interpretation in line with those of conventional biblical commentators, then where they give out at verses 11:36-45, I myself see the narrative of the vision jump forward about 2,300 years to modern times, once more.

Chapter ten gives a vision of a figure we can take to be an Archangel, for he says he is in the middle of a spiritual, celestial battle with only Michael, the special guardian angel of the Jewish people, to help him.

Chapter 11 claims to set out the course of human history in detail. Indeed, it does supply an amazing fulfilment in the history of the Greek Empire. There were to be three more Persian kings (verse 2 – Cambyses, Gaumata and Darius I), followed by a fourth (Xerxes). Xerxes invaded Greece but was defeated at Salamis in 480BC. The power then passed onto Greece (verses 3-4; see comments earlier on chapter 7). Verse five refers to Egypt ('the king of the south') and to Ptolemy's one-time general, Seleucus, who became 'king of the north' – the powerful kingdom of Syria and the east. Fifty years later (verse 6) the daughter of Ptolemy II married Antiochus II of Syria. But she was divorced and murdered, and her brother avenged her by attacking Syria (verse 7). Verses 9-13 reflect the struggles between the two powers at the end of the 3rd century BC. The Jews then joined forces with Antiochus III of Syria to defeat Egypt (verses 14-15). They gained their freedom from Egypt (verse 16), and Antiochus made a marriage alliance with Ptolemy V (verse 17). Antiochus invaded Asia Minor and Greece but was defeated by the Romans at Magnesia in 190BC (verses 18-19).

The 'exactor of tribute' (verse 20) was his son Seleuchus IV, who was shortly succeeded by his brother Antiochus IV, the persecutor of the Jews. Verses 21-24 aptly portray his character and policies. Through the treachery of Ptolemy's own men, Antiochus briefly gained control of Egypt in 173BC. On his return he attacked Jerusalem and slaughtered 80,000 Jews (verses 25-28). The next time he attacked Egypt he was thwarted by the Roman fleet (verses 29-30). He turned on Jerusalem again and desecrated the temple (verse 31). He was aided and abetted by some Jews, but others refused to compromise their faith, though they died for it (verses 32-33). Judas Maccabaeus instigated a successful revolt, so helping the faithful (verse 34).

The conventional commentaries like those above now give up!

Is Daniel chapter 11 verses 36-45 at the Time of the End about Saddam Hussein? NO. It is about some other potentate yet to appear at the Time of the End, say verses 35 and 40. With the speed of modern warfare, it could be any time soon, and be any major country. I would rather think that it really means the long-dead Nazi Germany and Adolf Hitler, then move on swiftly to chapter 12, that says that after that Michael, the chief guardian angel of Israel will come, and even gives some dates – the first bad – the second a time soon to look forward to!

First '1290 days' – taken as 'the twelfth day of the ninth month, after ground zero' it is a simple code, only breakable now, well after the event, for 'the day after 9/11' i.e. **12th September 2001**, the very day that the 'war on terrorism' was declared by George Bush, President of the United States!

It is so highly curious that George Bush retaliated so quickly to '9/11' – the very next day – that he must have been waiting for something like it to launch the new insidious 'war on terrorism' the very next day, even, without any chance to consult with his colleagues in the USA or certainly abroad. See Part 1 of Volume C of this book, which gives the text of a very interesting, mostly convincing 'conspiracy theory' dating back to 1997 that claims that the world '666' system that we have seen in Revelation and Daniel has been waiting for just such an excuse to bring in massive security measures worldwide that are massively eroding the good spirits of the people of the world. To 'brand us all 666' in other words. Certainly, in my own country of Great Britain, the recent introduction of measures to introduce a universal ID or identity card for everybody was unthinkable before the start of the 'war on terrorism'.

The second Gulf War was certainly totally contrived, even if you do not think that the 'war on terrorism' still going strong, was contrived by Bush. At the time of the first Gulf War in

1991, Saddam Hussein had been known to use chemical weapons on his Kurdish minority in the mountainous north of Iraq, and to be trying to develop a nuclear weapon capability. However, from 1992 Saddam Hussein appears to have bowed to a long series of United Nations resolutions, and had destroyed by his own people, all his treasured weapons factories for mass destruction.

Having established they had got the United Nations to clear their path of such obviously threatening opposition, in March 2003, the two governments of the USA and Britain claimed emphatically that they had 100% evidence that Saddam in fact had large stocks of such weapons, and as a much less important second factor, was harbouring Islamic militant terrorists. The ensuing onslaught by USA and UK ground, sea and above all air forces was swift and devastating – perhaps the most fierce use of weapons since the atomic bomb in Japan in 1945.

By June the campaign was down to a mopping-up operation, and that December 2003 Saddam Hussein was captured in a most humiliating situation, in a dug out hole in the ground. He has since been put on trial and hanged with rather over the top theatricality involved by both him and his executioners.

So, if there were in fact no weapons of mass destruction left because the Allies had got them destroyed through United Nations resolutions, the reasons of the USA and UK for invading Iraq must be purely ulterior motives. Certainly the possession of Iraq has enabled the USA to achieve a far more potent base to build several of its vast new military bases there – a huge military advantage in the unruly Middle East. There are rumours from the USA, that next the USA intends to turn on Iran, Iraq's eastern neighbour, and the regime of the Muslim clerics or Ayatollahs. However, Iran is nearly all mountainous, unlike the plains of Iraq, so the tanks would not be able to roll up to Tehran, capital of Iran, in any future war there, launched from their bases in Iraq, as American and British tanks found with overwhelming air cover, that they could to Baghdad in 2003 (just as the could in fact easily have done, apart from political and military blunders, back in the first Gulf War of 1991-2).

The overriding reason behind the Second Gulf War of 2003, however, seems to be that the oil-guzzling US economy was desperate for fresh supplies of OIL and other mineral reserves in which Iraq is rich. Despite all appearances of strength, Britain, the US principal ally in the war, was desperate for a piece of that action too.

For in the 1980's and 1990's, under the Tories, the British had replaced our manufacturing base with service industries – banking, law, education, medicine and computing. Now, since 1997 under New Labour, despite all the proud claims we have sunk to the basest pits in order to keep up our standard of living. We are now the most expensive country in the world to live in – much of it huge taxation. Above all 'vice taxes' – tax on things people need in order just to feel comfortable, survive even.

Tax from increasing three times the price of tobacco in five years is called a 'health measure', as is the similar threefold increase in the price of alcohol. Most people call these vices. However, despite the vast reserves of oil in our North Sea fields, the worst example of a 'vice tax' which again hits the poor hardest, is on fuel. Again, petrol is three times more expensive than three years ago under this same government!

So the Bible seems to warn of the fallout of '9/11' – the suspiciously hastily declared 'war on terrorism' declared by George Bush the next day, obviously taking little or no advice, none from foreign powers. Certainly I have never known such a long five years since – the paranoia is so intense that nobody smiles any more! However, wait! Immediately the Bible seems to give another 'date of hope' here in Daniel 12, as follows!

Second '1335 days' – in my strongly held view, '45 days' later than 12th September 2001 - but encoded in some other way. Verse 12:12 says 'blessed is he that waits, and comes to the 1335 days'. I hope you will wait – and indeed hope! Whatever happens in between does not sound very promising!

The three great Apocalyptic Books of the Bible

3. The Central Books of the Bible or 'the Apocrypha'

*The Second Book of Esdras
Chapters 11 – 13*

Background and Introduction

The 'Apocrypha' (as Protestants call these books) or 'deuterocanonical books' (as Roman Catholics call them), do not appear in all bibles, certainly not most Protestant bibles, and when they do appear it is in the middle, between the Old and New Testaments. Deuterocanonical means 'Jewish scripture of less status than the 39 books of the Old Testament'. Of these the Second Book of Esdras that I give the whole of chapters 11-13 here, is the only Apocalyptic book in the Apocrypha.

We have already looked at the Book of Revelation at the end of the New Testament at the end of the Bible, as its only 100% Apocalyptic Book, and likewise at the Book of Daniel, the only 100% Apocalyptic Book in the Old Testament. Hence we now look at the third and middle part of the Bible and the only book in it containing Apocalyptic sections, 2 Esdras Chapters 3-14, of which I have picked out three chapters, 11, 12 and 13, as most relevant to my own book, and extremely interesting.

Esdras is the Greek/Latin equivalent of the Hebrew, Ezra. There are two books by Ezra in the Old Testament, Ezra and Nehemiah, and four more in the Pseudepigrapha, which have never been included in Scripture but which are similar to the Apocrypha: - Greek Apocalypse of Ezra, Vision of Ezra, Questions of Ezra and Revelation of Ezra. The Book of 2 Esdras was probably written in the first Century AD, and claims considerable authority in Chapter 14 with Esdras making himself out to be a prolific prophet, a 'New Moses' who claims to have supplied the Jewish people with 24 books of a ready made set of laws!

We now start with Chapters 11-12, which give yet a third view of the 'Great Beast (666)' of Revelation and Daniel that we saw earlier, and which claim that they supply much more information about it than the Book of Daniel.

Certainly it gave me the most headaches, as scripture, of all three accounts of 'the beast'!

2 ESDRAS CHAPTER ELEVEN

1 Then I saw a dream, and, behold, there came up from the sea an eagle, which had twelve feathered wings, and three heads.
2 And I saw, and, behold, she spread her wings over all the earth, and all the winds of the air blew on her, and were gathered together.
3 And I watched, and out of her wings there grew other contrary wings; and they became little wings and small.
4 But her heads were at rest. The head in the middle was greater than the others, yet rested it with the other two.
5 Moreover I watched, and, lo, the eagle flew with her wings, and reigned upon earth, and over them that dwelt therein.
6 And I saw that all things under heaven were subject to her, and no man spoke against her, no, not one creature upon earth.
7 And I watched, and, lo, the eagle rose upon her talons, and spoke to her wings, saying,
8 "Watch not all at once. Sleep, each one in his own place, and watch what happens.
9 But let the heads be preserved for the last."
10 And I watched, and, lo, the voice went not out of her heads, but from the midst of her body.
11 And I numbered her contrary wings, and, behold, there were eight of them.
12 And I looked, and, behold, on the right side there arose one wing, and reigned over all the earth;
13 And so it was, that when it reigned, the end of it came, and its place appeared no more; so the next following stood up, and reigned, and had a great time;
14 And it happened, that when it reigned, the end of it came also, like as the first, so that it appeared no more.
15 Then a voice came, and said,
16 "Hear, you that have ruled over the earth so long. This I say to you, before you begin to appear no more,
17 None after you shall attain the same time as you, nor even half of it."
18 Then arose the third, and reigned as the other before, and appeared no more.
19 So it went with all the rest one after another, so that each one reigned, and then appeared no more.

20 Then I saw, and, lo, in process of time the wings that followed stood up on the right side, that they might rule also; and some of them ruled, but within a while they appeared no more.
21 For some of them were set up, but did not rule.
22 After this I looked, and, behold, the twelve wings appeared no more, nor the two little wings.
23 And there was no more upon the eagle's body, but three heads that rested, and six little wings.
24 Then I saw also that two little wings divided themselves from the six, and remained under the head that was upon the right side; for the four continued in their place.
25 And I watched, and, lo, the wings that were under the wing thought to set up themselves, and to have the rule.
26 And I saw, and, lo, there was one set up, but shortly it appeared no more.
27 And the second was sooner away than the first.
28 And I saw, and, lo, the two that remained thought also in themselves to reign.
29 And when they thought so, behold, there awaked one of the heads that were at rest, namely, it that was in the midst; for that was greater than the two other heads.
30 And then I saw that the two other heads were joined with it.
31 And, behold, the head was turned with them that were with it, and did eat up the two wings under the wing that would have reigned.
32 But this head put the whole earth in fear, and ruled over all those that dwelt upon the earth with much oppression; and it had the governance of the world more than all the wings that had been.
33 And after this I saw, and, lo, the head that was in the midst suddenly appeared no more, like as the wings.
34 But there remained the two heads, which also in like sort ruled upon the earth, and over those that dwelt therein.
35 And I saw, and, lo, the head upon the right side devoured the one upon the left side.
36 Then I heard a voice, which said to me, "Look before you, and consider the thing that you see".
37 And I saw, and, lo, as it were a roaring lion chased out of the wood. I saw that he spoke with a man's voice to the eagle, and said,

38 "Hear you, I will talk with you, and the Highest shall say to you,

39 'Are you all that remain of the four beasts, whom I made to reign in my world, that the end of their times might come through them?'

40 And the fourth came, and overcame all the beasts that were past, and had power over the world with great fearfulness, and over the whole compass of the earth with much wicked oppression; and for such a long time he dwelt upon the earth with deceit.

41 For the earth you have not judged with truth.

42 For you have afflicted the meek, you have hurt the peaceable, you have loved liars, and destroyed the dwellings of them that produced fruit. You have cast down the walls of such as did you no harm.

43 Therefore your wrongful dealing has come up to the Highest, and your pride to the Mighty.

44 The Highest has also looked upon the proud times, and, behold, they are ended, and his abominations are fulfilled.

45 And therefore appear no more, you eagle, nor your horrible wings, nor your wicked wings, nor your malicious heads, nor your hurtful claws, nor all your vain body.

46 So the earth may be refreshed, and may return, delivered from your violence, and so she may hope for the judgement and mercy of him that made her.

2 ESDRAS CHAPTER TWELVE

1 And it came to pass, while the lion spoke these words to the eagle, I saw,

2 And, behold, the head that remained and the four wings appeared no more, and the two approached it, and set themselves up to reign, and their kingdom was small, and full of uproar.

3 And I saw, and, behold, they appeared no more, and the whole body of the eagle was burnt, so that the earth was in great fear. Then I awoke out of the trouble and trance of my mind, and from great fear, and said to my spirit,

4 "Lo, this you have done to me, in that you search out the ways of the Highest.

5 Lo, yet I am weary in my mind, and very weak in my spirit; and little strength is there in me, for the great fear with which I was affrighted this night.

6 Therefore I will now beseech the Highest, that he will comfort me until the end."

7 And I said, "Lord that bears rule, if I have found grace before your sight, and if I am justified with you before many others, and if my prayer has indeed come before you;

8 Comfort me then, and show me, your servant, the interpretation and plain meaning of this fearful vision, so that you may perfectly comfort my soul.

9 For you have judged me worthy to show me the last times."

10 And he said to me, "This is the interpretation of the vision:

11 The eagle, whom you saw come up from the sea, is the kingdom which was seen in the vision of your brother Daniel.

12 But it was not expounded to him, therefore now I declare it to you.

13 Behold, the days will come, that there shall rise up a kingdom upon earth, and it shall be feared above all the kingdoms that were before it.

14 In this kingdom shall twelve kings reign, one after another.

15 Of these the second shall begin to reign, and shall have more time than any of the twelve.

16 And the twelve wings signify this, which you saw.

17 As for the voice which you heard speak, and that you saw not to go out from the heads, but from the midst of the body of it, this is the interpretation:

18 That after the time of that kingdom there shall arise great strivings, and it shall stand in peril of falling. Nevertheless it shall not then fall, but shall be restored again to its beginning.

19 And as for you seeing eight small under wings sticking to her wings, this is the interpretation:

20 That in her there shall arise eight kings, whose times shall be but small, and their years swift.

21 And two of them shall perish, the middle time approaching. Four shall be kept until their end begins to approach. But two shall be kept until the end.

22 And as for you seeing three heads resting, this is the interpretation:

23 In his last days shall the most High raise up three kingdoms, and renew many things in them, and they shall have the dominion of the earth,

24 And of those that dwell on the earth, with much oppression, above all those that were before them. Therefore they are called the heads of the eagle.
25 For these are they that shall accomplish his wickedness, and that shall finish his last end.
26 And as for you seeing that the head appeared no more, it signifies that one of them shall die upon his bed yet with pain.
27 For the two that remain shall be slain with the sword.
28 For the sword of the one shall devour the other, but at the last he shall fall through the sword himself.
29 And as for you seeing two wings under the wings passing over to the head that is on the right side;
30 It signifies that these are they, whom the Highest has kept till the end. This is the small kingdom and full of trouble, as you saw.
31 And the lion, whom you saw rising up out of the wood, and roaring, and speaking to the eagle, and rebuking her for her unrighteousness with all the words which you have heard;
32 This is the anointed, which the Highest has kept for them and for their wickedness until the end. He shall reprove them, and shall upbraid them with their cruelty.
33 For he shall set them before him alive in judgement, and shall rebuke them, and correct them.
34 For the rest of my people shall he deliver with mercy, those that have been preserved upon my borders, and he shall make them joyful until the coming of the day of judgement, about which I have spoken to you from the beginning.
35 This is the dream that you saw, and these are the interpretations.
36 Only you have been seen fit to know this secret of the Highest.
37 Therefore write all these things that you have seen in a book, and hide them.
38 Teach them to the wise of the people, whose hearts you know may comprehend and keep these secrets.
39 But wait here yourself yet seven days more, that it may be shown to you, whatever it pleases the Highest to declare to you." And with that he went his way.
40 And it came to pass, when all the people saw that the seven days were past, and I did not come again into the city, they gathered them all together, from the least to the greatest, and came to me, and said,

41 "What have we done to offend you? And what evil have we done against you that you forsake us, and sit here in this place?

42 For of all the prophets only you are left us, as a cluster of the vintage, and as a candle in a dark place, and as a haven or ship preserved from the tempest.

43 Are not the evils which are come to us sufficient?

44 If you will forsake us, how much better had it been for us, if we also had been burned in the midst of Sion?

45 For we are not better than they that died there." And they wept with a loud voice. Then I answered them, and said,

46 "Be of good comfort, O Israel; and be not heavy, O house of Jacob.

47 For the Highest has you in remembrance, and the Mighty has not forgotten you in temptation.

48 As for me, I have not forsaken you, neither am I departed from you; but am come into this place, to pray for the desolation of Sion, and that I might seek mercy for the low estate of your sanctuary.

49 And now go your way home every man, and after these days I will return to you."

50 So the people went their way into the city, like as I commanded them.

51 But I remained still in the field seven days, as the angel commanded me; and did eat only in those days of the flowers of the field, and had my meat of the herbs.

Notes on 2 Esdras chapters eleven and twelve

We have already looked at two views of this 'great beast (666 or fourth beast)' in Revelation then Daniel. We see yet again in this vision of the modern world as known since the discovery of America in the 16th century (if not earlier by the Vikings) and Australia, that it has three great heads, joined in cultural and social systems, all in the Northern Hemisphere, but all with worldwide influence: America, Europe and Asia, just as in George Orwell's '1984'. A very muddled up and tyrannical world system, is the world today! The three heads of the eagle/beast are all in turn three-in-one: the 666 system of 'Civita-Templa-Caesar' or 'states / (real) estate – church / temple – leader / crowns'.

The three heads of the Eagle – copy of diagram on Daniel 7 in previous Part 2 of this Volume B of this book

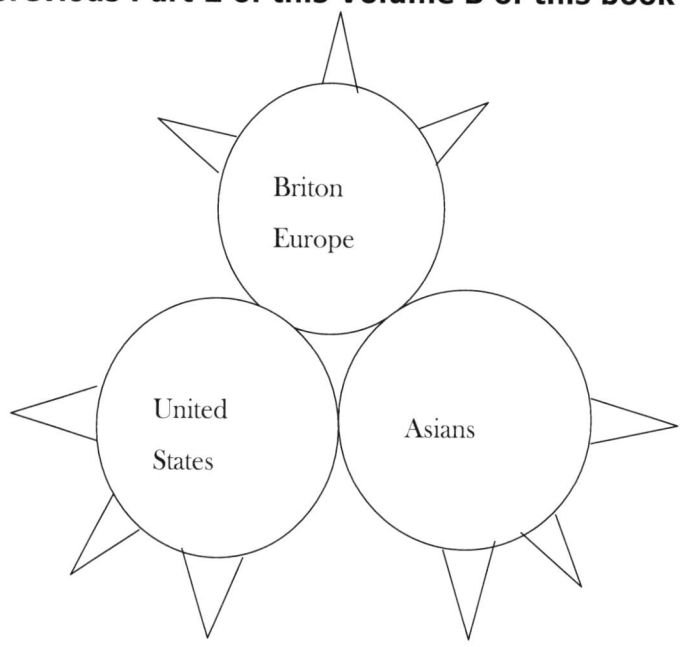

The three heads or horns of the Beast of Wanton Global Materialism of: Revelation 13, Daniel 7 and 2 Esdras 11-12

The three little heads/horns on each are: church / states / leader

2 Esdras Chapter 11-12 states that this vision tells Esdras more than 'his brother Daniel' was told, about the (fourth) beast as discussed earlier in Part 2 of this Volume B.

Indeed, the vision shows twelve wings developing in turn around the eagle, six on the right (eastern) then six on the left (western) 'with contrary wings attached to them', only some ruling the whole earth. The second to appear lasts the longest of the twelve, which as we see below tells me the twelve are not actually people as kings, but priests as leaders – these twelve are twelve great religions!

The 'contrary wings' attached to the twelve wings or religions, then, symbolise the great divisions, discussions and internal conflicts common to them all. For instance, Protestant versus Catholic, with Mormons and Jehovah's witnesses only adding to the confused state of modern Christianity. Likewise in the world of Islam, there are many political viewpoints about their book, the Koran or Qu'uran – such as violence between Sunni and Shi'ite Muslims, all round the world.

Not least the violence between different religions of course, Muslims against Hindus in the Far East, and Christians against Religious Fanatics of terrorists claiming to be Muslims, even though the Qu'uran or Koran denounces violence. Having established that the twelve wings correspond to the twelve most famous religions of East, then West, six in each, from my own analysis as in Volume A, I could sketch the two lists of six from East then West, in indeed a strictly historical sequence: -

The six wings at the right of the Eagle – six important ancient Eastern religions: -
1. Aboriginal religions of the nomadic hunter-gatherer people – 'pagans' / the 'Old Way'. Symbolised, like its 'brother faith', the next one, by **earth.**
2. Priest-kings and priest-emperors of societies such as China, Egypt under the Pharaohs, and the Aztecs. Agriculture by a peasant under-class; often pyramids; and human and other animal sacrifice. Philosophy of the Chinese version mostly supplied by Confucius (Kung fu-tzu) i.e. Confucianism. Historically you can soon verify this 'had the longest rule of the twelve wings'.
3. These two started, according to Archaeologists, before the flood after the last Ice Age, around 10,000 BC. According to

the Bible, Cain and Abel had corresponding occupations, and as the second generation of humans after the original two, Adam and Eve, can be seen from that viewpoint to have been the very founders of those two cultures, the second and first respectively. Only seven couples survived the Great Flood, according to the Bible, but presumably re-founded the above two cultures, evidence of which exists around the world today. However, the third great set of religious principles in the Far East to emerge and still be strong and powerful today, are Taoism (yin and yang, etc) in China and Shinto in Japan. Both symbolised by *water*.
4. Hinduism in India (symbolised by *fire*).
5. Buddhism (symbolised by *air*). This is really not a religion, rather a philosophy or 'ideal way of life' and officially does not recognise any God.
6. Sikh and Jain faiths. Again, evolved in India and the Far East following Hinduism and Buddhism in time.

The six wings at the left of the Eagle – six important Western religions, in time: -

1. Zoroastrianism, the religion of the Pharsees around Iran (Persia), who believed and still believe – like Christians, Jews and Muslims – in good and evil. However Pharsees see them in eternal fine balance, with no final victory for 'Good' over 'Evil'.
2. Judaism – the Jewish culture and faith.
3. Christianity.
4. Islam, the faith of the Muslims.
5. Rastafarianism and other Caribbean and African faiths.
6. New Age, 'spiritualist'; and revived Paganism, now the Church has lost most of its power to stamp this out in the West and we have a very permissive society!

The 'six little wings' of 11:23-31; 12:2-3 and 12:19-30 – can we see modern parallels to these in the world today? Or, rather, 'four pairs of little wings'.

I am sticking my neck out, based on all that has gone before, to give a possible list below identifying the four pairs of 'little wings' as kings or powers in our modern world, which as I see it, as we have seen, is fast approaching Jesus' coming, so there is not a problem with speculating about their identity. So just before I close this commentary on 2 Esdras 11-12, here is my own 'hit list'!: -

1. Verse 11:26-27. Nazis/Fascists in Europe 1939-1945 in the Second World War; with the second wing being the other member of their 'Axis' – Japan?
2. Verse 11:28-31. Iraq – and now this year Iran?
3. Strangely, the fifth and sixth little wings are not mentioned in chapter 11 as trying to come to power. Are they the modern 'industrial phoenix miracle' powers of India and China (with Japan included)?
4. The last two wings have a 'short and turbulent reign'. Is this some kind of utterly unholy alliance between the Devil as one wing, finally coming out of the shadows and dropping his anonymity and even principal lie that 'he does not exist'? The only likely candidate for a partner in crime is artificial intelligence emerging at last from IT – a robotic wing, of some kind! For referring back to my discussion of Daniel 9, it is indeed 70 years since my long-dead predecessor at King's College, Cambridge, Alan Turing, in 1937 built the first real computer. He is widely regarded as the father of modern computer science. The British Government got him to help build the first computer (the 'Bombe') in 1937-1938 – which promptly cracked the German 'Enigma' code – so being a major factor in the winning of the Second World War 1939-45. It is 70 years since the computer was invented – and 70 years since the British Government issued the paper relinquishing control of Israel at long last, back to Jewish control.

2 ESDRAS CHAPTER THIRTEEN

1 And it came to pass after seven days, I dreamed a dream by night.
2 And, lo, there arose such a wind from the sea, that it moved all the waves.
3 And I saw, and, lo, a man flew up from the depths of the sea, that waxed strong with the thousands of heaven. And wherever he turned to look, all the things trembled that were seen under him.
4 And whenever he spoke, they all burned that heard his voice, as the earth fails when it feels the fire.
5 And after this I saw, and, lo, there was gathered together a multitude of men, out of number, from the four winds of the heaven, to subdue the man that came out of the sea.
6 But I watched, and, lo, he had carved himself a great mountain, and flew up upon it.
7 But I would have seen the region or place from where the hill was carved, and I could not.
8 And after this I saw, and, lo, all they which were gathered together to subdue him were sore afraid, and yet dared to fight.
9 And, lo, as he saw the violence of the multitude that came, he neither lifted up his hand, nor held sword, nor any instrument of war.
10 But only I saw that he sent out of his mouth as it had been a blast of fire, and out of his lips a flaming breath, and out of his tongue he cast out sparks and tempests.
11 And they were all mixed together; the blast of fire, the flaming breath, and the great tempest; and fell with violence upon the multitude which was prepared to fight, and burned them up every one. So that suddenly, of an innumerable multitude, nothing was to be seen but only dust and smell of smoke. When I saw this I was afraid.
12 Afterwards I saw the same man come down from the mountain, and call to him another peaceable multitude.
13 And many people came to him, of whom some were glad, some were sorry, some of them were bound, and others, some brought of them that were offered. Then I was sick through great fear, and I awaked, and said,

14 "You have shown your servant these wonders from the beginning, and have counted me worthy that you should receive my prayer.
15 Show me now the interpretation of this dream.
16 For as I conceive in my understanding, woe to them that shall be left in those days! And much more woe to them that are not left behind!
17 For they that were not left were in heaviness.
18 Now I understand the things that are laid up in the latter days, which shall happen to them, and to those that are left behind.
19 Therefore they will come into great perils and many necessities, just as these dreams declare.
20 Yet is it easier for him that is in danger to come into these things, than to pass away as a cloud out of the world, and not to see the things that happen in the last days". And he answered me, and said,
21 "The interpretation of the vision I shall show you, and I will open up to you the thing that you required.
22 As for those that are left behind, this is the interpretation:
23 He that shall endure the peril in that time has kept selfish. They that have fallen into danger are such as have works, and faith toward the Almighty.
24 Know this, therefore, that they which are left behind are more blessed than they that be dead.
25 This is the meaning of the vision. You saw a man coming up from the midst of the sea.
26 The same is he whom God the Highest has kept a great long time, who by his own self shall deliver his creature, and he shall order them that are left behind.
27 And where you saw, that out of his mouth there came a blast of wind, and fire, and storm;
28 And that he held neither sword, nor any instrument of war, but that the rushing in of him destroyed the whole multitude that came to subdue him; this is the interpretation:
29 Behold, the days come, when the most High will begin to deliver them that are upon the earth.
30 And he shall come to the astonishment of them that dwell on the earth.
31 And one shall undertake to fight against another, one city against another, one place against another, one people against another, and one realm against another.

32 And the time shall be when these things shall come to pass, and the signs shall happen which I showed you before, and then shall my Son be declared, whom you saw as a man flying out of the sea.
33 And when all the people hear his voice, every man shall in their own land leave the battle they have one against another.
34 And an innumerable multitude shall be gathered together, as you saw them, willing to come, and to overcome him by fighting.
35 But he shall stand upon the top of the mount Sion.
36 And Sion shall come, and shall be shown to all men, being prepared and built, like you saw the hill graven without hands.
37 And my Son shall rebuke the wicked inventions of those nations, which for their wicked life are fallen into the tempest;
38 And shall lay before them their evil thoughts, and the torments with which they shall begin to be tormented, which are like flames; and he shall destroy them without effort by the law which is like fire.
39 And whereas you saw that he gathered another peaceable multitude to him;
40 Those are the ten tribes, which were carried away prisoners out of their own land in the time of Osea the king, whom Salmanasar the king of Assyria led away captive, and he carried them over the waters, and so they came into another land.
41 But they took this counsel among themselves, that they would leave the multitude of the heathen, and go forth into a further country, where never mankind dwelt,
42 That they might there keep their statutes, which they never kept in their
own land.
43 And they entered into the Euphrates by the narrow passages of the river.
44 For the most High then showed signs for them, and held still the flood, till they were passed over.
45 For through that country there was a great way to go, namely, of a year and
a half; and the same region is called Arsareth.
46 Then dwelt they there until the latter time; and now when they shall begin to come,
47 The Highest shall stay the springs of the stream again, that they may go through. Therefore you saw the multitude with peace.

48 But those that be left behind of your people are they that are found within my borders.

49 Now when he destroys the multitude of the nations that are gathered together, he shall defend his people that remain.

50 And then shall he show them great wonders."

51 Then said I, "O Lord that bears rule, show me this. Why have I seen the man coming up from the midst of the sea?"

52 And he said to me, "Just as you can neither seek out nor know the things that are in the deep of the sea. Even so no man upon earth can see my Son, or those that be with him, except in the light of day.

53 This is the interpretation of the dream which you saw, and which only you only are enlightened by here.

54 For you have forsaken your own way, and applied your diligence to my law, and sought it.

55 You have ordered your life in wisdom, and has called understanding your mother.

56 And therefore I have shown you the treasures of the Highest. After another three days I will speak of other things, and declare to you mighty and wondrous things.

57 Then I went forth into the field, giving great praise and thanks to the most High because of his wonders, which he did in time.

58 And because he governs the same, and such things as fall in their seasons, and there I sat three days.

The Messiah flies out of the sea on top of the long-awaited Mount Sion. This *must* be the Second Coming!

We first saw my sketch of the New Jerusalem, i.e. Mount Sion or Zion, when discussing Revelation chapter 21 in Volume B Part 1. There I may have either surprised or disgusted or delighted you by claiming that any 'city' 1,500 miles wide, long *and indeed high* and with walls seventy metres thick, made of fused crystal, must be, indeed can only be called 'the mother of all spacecraft' – presumably with other spacecraft in its wake. It can only have been made by Jesus and/or God – in Heaven – presumably with the help of the entire population of heaven – angels or the spirits of the Dead. It would need to be built on and come from another planet, presumably nearby! So the Second Coming will feature Jesus at long last turning up – in an enormous spacecraft called Zion or New Jerusalem?!

Footnotes. The 'ten tribes' of 13:39-47.

Firstly, I am pretty certain that the Rastafarians believe that they are these ten tribes! Certainly I heard one of them say so on the radio last year.

Secondly, the drying up of the river Euphrates in 13:44-47 amplifies what is said tersely in the Book of Revelation 16:12.

Volume C.

(The Holy) Spirit overcoming Their Enemies?

1. The "NumeraLogical Calendar"

A "seventy 'sevens' (or 'weeks') of years calendar"

See on Daniel chapter 9 in Volume B...

A new universal peace-making initiative (that initially only, would cause more problems than it eventually solves!)

The
New
Universal
Millennium
Eclectic
Rational
And
Logical
Calendar!

The '**Numera-Logical** Calendar' – or 'TICTOC'

I supply overleaf the complete text of a particularly convincing 'conspiracy theory' that is convincing because it is so detailed, that was posted on the Internet nearly ten years ago, in 1997. It warns of great dangers from a real, deadly and sinister threat from the Occult, poised to take advantage of any serious global crisis like '9/11' or nuclear weapons in Iran. According to the American observer who wrote the theory, one Chris Beard, as highlighted here, many of the world's banks now plot to 'mark us all Chi Xi Sigma' – with a 'Beast 666' silicon implant without which nobody will be able to buy or sell anything – as it will replace cash!

My answer is the TICTOC ('Totally Inoffensive Calendar That's Offered to Christ') described here! This is the NUMERA-Logical Calendar – a Calendar designed to revolutionise time-keeping for the New Millennium and beyond. It is based on principles explained here that I unearthed in the Bible, and is a vast simplification over present world calendars.

Its introduction would force a Cool Calm Collected Complete Computer Census (CCCCCC or 'C6') and far simpler reprogramming of time of every computer in the world. It would thwart the Occult from 'branding us all 666' – by disabling billions of chip implants made since 1997 and fully ready to be imposed globally by banks! It is a potent potential antidote to any similar threat from IT...

1. Introduction

Back in 1999, a relatively new friend, as we shall see appropriately called 'Mark', as a fellow 'Man of Faith', presented me with a terrifying vision of *next year, 2000!* An article he had downloaded from the Internet apparently proves the existence of a conspiracy by very powerful Occult forces in IT to 'impose a Satanic empire through IT' and 'Mark us all 666 – or Chi Xi Sigma'.

So – my own researches are complemented at last by this article, reproduced below, showing the extent that Occult Forces in IT could launch a bid for global domination through Information Technology and the microchip just given a 'convincing' excuse! To put their 'God', Satan, in charge of the planet!

As we shall see in the last section, my view is that to prevent the threat of such a terrifying menace, we could introduce as soon as any similar threat emerges in the world in the near future, a *new, much simpler calendar.*

DISCLAIMER

I merely quote in full, from an obscure website back in 1997, where the article appeared for several months then vanished, in Times New Roman font overleaf to distinguish the views there from my own in the rest of this book, the strongly held views of one Chris Beard (false name? American?) I do not know what he looks like, have never spoken to or written to or been written to by him, and have never read anything else by him. I must most strongly point out that I regard his views overleaf as probably wild and fanciful, as I have seen no evidence of such 'Occult IT' activity in any world bank, especially UK bank, as he suggests, in the 10 years or so since I was first shown his short piece of rather histrionic writing. The sole purpose of reproducing it here is to indicate how very strongly my own antidote to any such threat as this Chris Beard fears, could avert such a threat by the introduction of a LOGICAL CALENDAR as proposed in the course of this section.

Possible occult symbolism by British High Street Banks.

That being said, and the whole of this article disclaimed as by a slightly hysterical author, not myself, some 11 years ago as I write in 2008, it has led me to be on the lookout for possible 'boasting of occult beliefs' by UK Institutions – especially the High Street banks! – like the article claims.

I have actually possibly detected such 'allegiance to occult beliefs - and boasting about it in the company logo – in the Middle Ages the heraldic symbol' – in three UK High Street banks. Why is the ugly NatWest Bank symbol a hex circle of three six pointed, six sided, chevrons – almost certainly symbolising the number 666? Likewise, why is the symbol of HSBC Bank, SIX triangles – again symbolising the same Occult number, 666? Why is the symbol of Barclays Bank, of 'the Beast 666', a three headed eagle that we just looked at as in 2 Esdras 11-12? Why does the bank giro credit symbol, used when money goes between banks, hold strong 666 symbolism?

As you read Chris Beard's article overleaf you will soon see where such thinking comes from – and I hope that once this book is published – either the British Authorities – or should it be the *Spanish Inquisition?!* – may think to investigate all these alerts to possible *witchcraft in the British High Street Banks!* For *the love of money is the ROOT OF ALL EVIL!*

2. THE CASHLESS SOCIETY IS HERE

An article by **Chris Beard** (put on the Internet by him back in 1997)

After years of planning, research, and development, the world's financial institutions are announcing the much-anticipated GLOBAL CASHLESS SOCIETY. The ability to conduct all manner of monetary exchange is now being replaced by microchip technology and electronic currency.

MONDEX is the company providing this cashless system and has already franchised over 20 major nations. This system was created in 1993 by London bankers Tim Jones and Graham Higgins of NATWEST/COUTTS, the personal bank of Britain's Royal Family.

The system is based on SMARTCARD technology which employs microchips concealed in a plastic card, which stores electronic cash, identification, and other information. All transaction systems are being made secure by adopting SET protocols (Secure Electronic Transaction) and will display the SET MARK.

MON-DEX - A compound of the words MONETARY & DEXTER. Webster's Dictionary, Encyclopaedia Edition, defines these words as: -

monetary	pertaining to money
dexter	belonging to or located on the right hand.
SET	Egyptian god of evil – or Satan…

Along with the cards, you may use a PET (Personal Electronic Transfer) device. This wallet-sized calculator-like device allows you to conduct personal currency exchanges with other cardholders. The cards also work with the NORTEL/BELL VISTA 360 phone, MILLENNIUM pay phones, ATMs, your PC, the INTERNET, and online businesses and institutions.

This cashless system has been tested extensively in the city of Guelph, in Ontario, Canada, and in the UK and US. All Canadian banks have signed up to MONDEX and will be promoting it soon. Plans are to have it in widespread use by 1998. The CIBC (Canadian International Bank of Commerce) has even set up a model cashless branch inside NORTEL in Brampton, Ontario.

Over 250 corporations in 20 countries are involved in bringing MONDEX to the world, and many nations have already been franchised to use it. These include the UK, Canada, USA, Australia, New Zealand, Israel, Hong Kong, China, Indonesia, Macao, Malaysia, Philippines, Singapore, Thailand, India, Taiwan, Sri Lanka, Costa Rica, Guatemala, Nicaragua, Panama, Honduras, El Salvador and Belize. The European Union is expected to adopt the MONDEX system as their unified currency solution.

Other SMARTCARD systems are quickly being put aside in favour of MONDEX, especially since MASTERCARD bought a 51% stake in the company. NATWEST will still maintain directorship in its development and implementation. "This is the final stage in becoming a global reality," said Robin O'Kelly of MONDEX International. "With Mastercard's backing, there's nothing to stop MONDEX now from becoming the global standard".

Eventually the idea of carrying a card will become obsolete as people soon discover that it has its security limitations. Namely, being susceptible to damage, loss and theft. The 'final solution' will be to have the microchip simply placed inside the human body as they do now with the microchip pet identification systems.

INFOPET is one of several companies that provide a syringe gun implantable bio-chip that is injected under the skin of an animal. A scanner can read the chip and the code identifying the owner and pet will bring up a file on a computer. The system boasts that it can track over one billion pets by satellites and cellular towers.

MOTOROLA, who produce the microchips for the MONDEX SMARTCARD, has developed several human-implantable bio-chips. The BT952000 chip was engineered by Dr. Carl Sanders who was directed in 17 NEW WORLD ORDER meetings to develop the device for global use in humans for economic and identification purposes.

The biochip measures 7mm long and .75mm in width, about the size of a grain of rice. It contains a transponder and a rechargeable lithium battery.

The battery is charged by a thermo-couple circuit that produces voltage from fluctuations in body temperature. They spent over 1.5 million dollars studying where to place the chip in the human body. They found only two suitable and efficient places - the FOREHEAD, just under the hairline, and the back of the hand, specifically the RIGHT HAND.

"And he causes all, small and great, rich and poor, free men and slaves, to be given a mark in their right hand, or in their forehead. He provides that no one should be able to buy or sell, except one who has the mark, either the name of the beast, or the number of its name".
Revelation 13:16

Dr. Sanders was against the use of the lithium battery because it was known that if it were to break the lithium would cause a BOIL or SORE and cause much agony to the host.

"And the first went and poured out his vial upon the earth, and there fell a loathsome and grievous sore upon the men which had the mark of the beast, and upon them who worshipped his image."
Revelation 16:2

After Dr. Sanders left the project, he was introduced to the prophetic scriptures in the Bible concerning "the mark of the beast 666". He then converted to the Christian faith and now conducts seminars on this topic.

He developed patented medical, surveillance, and security equipment for the FBI, CIA, IRS, IBM, GE, Honeywell, and Teledyne. He has also received the President's and Governor's award for design and excellence.

Mark is in Greek 'charagma'. This means a scratch, or etching, stamp, insignia, or mark of servitude. The number 666 is the Greek phrase 'Chi Xi Sigma', meaning to stick or prick, a mark incised or punched for the recognition of ownership.

The industry name for the advanced smart card developed by GEMPLUS and the US DOD (Department of Defense) is the MARC (Multi-technology Automated Reader Card).

The code name for its development was 'TESSERA'. A 'tessera' was the Roman insignia of ownership placed on their slaves, which if removed would result in the slave being branded with a mark. In November 1996 an agreement was made by which GEMPLUS will supply smartcards for the global implementation of MONDEX.

AT&T/Lucent Technologies purchased the franchise for MONDEX USA. Their logo is the symbol of the Solar Serpent or RED DRAGON - who is Satan.

LUCENT is compounded from LUCIFER-ENTERPRISES. They seem to be quite flagrant in naming their products STYX (a river in Hades), JANUS (2 faced god) and INFERNO – promoted with a quote from "The Inferno", a story about LUCIFER in the bowels of hell. The "Ring of Fire" is the ancient Pantheon. This company deliberately chose to move their new offices into 666 Fifth Avenue in Manhattan.

"Day was departing, and the darkening air called all Earth's creatures to their evening quiet while I alone was preparing as though for war."
The Inferno, Dante, Canto II.

One of their proudest achievements is TTS (text to speech) in which they give the human-like quality of speech to lifeless technology. This only tends to remind one of the apocalyptic scriptures.

"And it was given to him to give breath to the image of the beast, that the image of the beast might even speak."
Revelation 13:15.

Since it is not practical to place a microchip in every product that is to ever be bought and sold an UPC BARCODE does the job nicely.

What most people don't realise is that this is the "mark of the beast 666" for the products we buy, use, and dispose of every day. Every UPC BARCODE contains the numbers 666.

You will find one of two versions of the mark. The most common has 10 numbers divided into two parts. The other has 6 numbers. In both versions there are 3 unidentified bars. Those bars are 6, 6, and 6. These are called guard bars, they tell the scanner when to start, divide, and stop the reading.

"Let the one who has understanding reckon the number of the beast, for the number is a human number, and the number is 666."

Revelation 13:18

PROJECT LUCID

This global police state apparatus was designed to monitor every man, woman, and child once issued a UNIVERSAL BIOMETRICS CARD just like the MARC or MONDEX. Jean Paul Creusat, M.D. and UN-INEOA representative (United Nations International Narcotic Enforcement Officers Association) designed the system. An article appeared in NARC OFFICER magazine, that describes the system. It appears to be closely related to the UN GLOBAL SECURITY PROGRAMME.

Author Texe Marrs has written an entire book on PROJECT LUCID. In it he tells of the refusal to disclose the project's acronym – leading him to believe LUCID may stand for LUCIFER's IDENTIFICATION.

Many proponents of the NEW GLOBAL ORDER are occult, Masonic, or anti-Christian and they seem to take delight with their veiled expressions. With LUCID the global law enforcement authority will be able to track your every move, transaction, and acquaintance. It's that intrusive.

Simon Davies of PRIVACY INTERNATIONAL investigated MONDEX's anonymity claims and found that they were monitoring all transactions in the trials breaking specific trade laws.

Many if not most of MONDEX's original 17 or so financial backers are from the London banking district belonging to the CLUB OF THE ISLES, a HOUSE OF WINDSOR banking cartel that has a major choke hold on GLOBAL economics. Through secretive meetings and strategic alliances these powerful MASONIC institutions influence world politics, finances, resources, and even the policies and structure of the UNITED NATIONS.

Their goal is a NEW WORLD ORDER based on one global government, one global religion, and one global electronic economy.

There is a MAN who is THE BEAST as spoken of by the prophets and the number of his name is 666. He is the LORD OF THE ISLES, a world figure whom many adore but he is also a man of intrigue and his power and influence have been grossly underestimated. He and his family were the first to publicly receive the microchip implant/mark, which was broadcast around the world on CNN in March of 1996.

Because the whole world is asleep, deluded, too busy, and unaware – the god of this world (Satan) continues to work in secrecy.

There are hundreds more companies and people involved with the implementation of the GLOBAL CASHLESS ECONOMY but presented here are a few of the main players. This should give you a brief introduction to what the mark of the beast is and how it is being implemented. I have also included a few explanations of MONDEX symbolism.

MONDEX's logo contains 3 inter-linked rings, a symbol only found in occultic MASONIC orders. Its general meaning regards three gods or the Egyptian/Pagan trinity especially in the Enochian Temple Magick Rituals of the Hermetic Order of the Golden Dawn. Namely Isis, Osiris, and Horus, but originally in the Bible Ashtoreth, Nimrod, and Tammuz/Baal.

The Pagan trinity are three gods manifested in one way whereas the Christian trinity is one god manifested in three ways.

This symbol was also used by the Grand Lodge of England and the Order of Odd Fellows founded by NERO in 55 AD and was originally a symbol of imprisonment and slavery, defeat. The 'golden chain' (in Latin 'catena aurea') was thought of in antiquity as linking heaven and earth (like the tower of Babel in Babylon). This is Homer's 'golden chain', which God, according to the poet, ordered suspended from heaven to earth.

In the symbolism of Freemasonry, the "fraternal chain" is the bond between brother Masons understood as extending across international borders and encircling the globe. The new initiate, when he "sees the light", sees the brothers "standing in the chain". In this connection, the symbolic chain often appears in the names of lodges. The linked rings of the chain signify a powerful and lasting unity. Or that in war – a stronghold has been broken through. See the Dictionary of Symbolism – Hans Biedermann – pp. 63-64.

"Masonry, like all the religions, all the mysteries, conceals its secrets from all except the adepts and sages, or the elect, and uses false explanations and misinterpretations of its symbols to mislead those who deserve only to be misled."

Dictionary of Symbolism, pp. 104,105

"The Blue Degrees are but the outer court or portico of the Temple. Part of the symbols are displayed there to the Initiate, but he is intentionally misled by false interpretations. It is not intended that he shall understand them, but it is intended he shall imagine he understands them."

Albert Pike, "Mason, Morals and Dogma", pp. 819

Another symbol utilized by MONDEX is the butterfly. This symbol has numerous mystical meanings but the most prominent is that of capturing the soul. The Greek word for butterfly and soul is "psyche". Can receiving the "mark of the beast 666", a deal with the Devil, cause you to lose your soul?

"If anyone worships the beast and his image, and receives a mark in his forehead or in his hand, he also will drink of the wine of the wrath of God, which is mixed in full strength in the cup of His anger. He will be tormented with fire and brimstone in the presence of the holy angels and in the presence of the Lamb. And the smoke of their torment goes up for ever and ever, and they have no rest day and night, those who worship the beast and his image, and whoever receives the mark of his name."

Revelation 14:9-11

SO YOU DON'T WANT TO GO CASHLESS. THEN WHAT?
First off, you will find yourself quickly becoming financially handicapped in your payment options. You will also pay heavy fees for using cheques, until cheques are eliminated. You will be pressured and even coerced to have all your bill payments and pay-checks conducted automatically and electronically.

Home banking on your PC or phone will become necessary as tellers and bank branches are replaced by ATM's. Large sums of cash will be next to impossible to obtain. Cash will be recalled and the smartcard will become mandatory. You will then find that you cannot pay your bills or buy groceries. Exchanging gold or silver coins will be illegal without a dealer license.

The Messiah told us to have hope and not despair because He would soon be coming. He told us not to be weighed down with anxieties just to wake up one day and be trapped by circumstances. He told us to occupy ourselves until He comes. He gave us a special end times commission: -

"Who then is the faithful, thoughtful, and wise servant, whom his master has put in charge of his household to give to others their food and supplies at the proper time? Blessed is that servant whom his master finds doing these things when he comes".

Matthew 24:45-46

MAKE THE COMMITMENT TODAY
Please make the commitment today that you will never go under a cashless, debt-based system, and that you will never submit to the mark of the beast. Already natural disasters are increasing in various

places catching people unprepared. There may be man made crises to accelerate the need to unite and surrender our rights, privacy, freedoms, properties for so-called "peace and security". Flee, not for the sake of saving flesh alone, but to fulfil our lives to the fullest taking every opportunity to live and add to the Kingdom of Heaven.

HELPLESS OR HOPEFUL

You will be either helpless or hopeful. Draw the line here, do not go down the easy broad way that MONDEX is opening wide. Our Saviour wants us to overcome what oppression and persecution lies ahead, so that you may receive a crown of great glory. The 'elite' have planned for these events well in advance and they are carrying out their agenda now to create a NEW WORLD ORDER by AD 2000.

They are currently producing one billion MONDEX chips per year and they already have been in production for at least one year. Chances are that if you are reading this, your bank has already signed on to MONDEX and will be promoting it shortly, no matter where in the world you live.

They have discovered that as long as the chip is in the card, there are some serious problems. The chip can be hacked and information changed or counterfeited. The values can be altered. The card contacts wear out within a year. It can be broken, stolen or lost. The electronic cash is not insured for the customer.

There is only one solution to these problems and that is to follow Motorola and Infopet's lead and implant the chip into the flesh where it cannot be successfully circumvented. In either form, it is to the same ends.

Card or flesh, whatever we end up with is the mark of the beast. It is still MONDEX and means "money in the right hand".

3. **The only logically feasible solution to this threat?**
   The only diary you will need for at least 1,000 years!

- Chris Beard was completely wrong. **Do not run away or 'flee' (where?) but confront the Occult and/or Freemasons** - secretive and furtive or not!

- The TICTOC or Numera-Logical Calendar cannot escape the fact that one solar year takes 365.25 days to complete. As now there would be three 'normal' years of 365 days, with every fourth year as now a leap year of 366 days. The leap day will no longer be February 29th but December 36th in a New December ('Amethyst') – normally 35 days long! 2008 would stay as planned in the present calendar, the next leap year of the New Millennium – the first year with 36 not 35 days in December.

- However, months apart from December would all be 30 days long, with six weeks of five days - two alternate five day periods of half and half work and rest! The long-envisaged Age of Leisure arrives!

- There would be 12 months, as now with gemstones associated with them, but the twelve gemstones in Revelation 21, not as now the Occult ones. Every month apart from December (to be renamed 'Amethyst') would have 30 days... December would normally have 35 days but with 36 days instead of this normal 35, every leap year. An extra 'Judas Iscariot Day' on Amethyst 36th every leap year or fourth year. As a result the end of Amethyst (old December) would be able to hold the long-prophesied Twelve Days of Christmas between the 24th (Christmas Eve just as now), Simon Peter Day – the 25th - onto the 35th (Simon of Canaan Day) as 12 'Feast'/'Apostle' Days (13 in leap years).

- Seasons would be named differently in northern and southern hemispheres, as 'Vegetables and Nuts' ('Vegan' of course!), Blossom, Grain, and Fruit, and as now in each hemisphere these harmlessly renamed seasons would lag six months behind the other hemisphere in the cycle of the

313

seasons.

- All the most important commemoration or feast days of all the great world faiths would be inserted into the first year onwards that the TICTOC is introduced, as they were in 1999, and preserve the same dates for 1,000 years at least. A much simpler system to administer and very easy to remember – especially in advance. No more moving days of important events in any religion or tradition – or even their weekdays!

- The days of the week would be renamed completely, with the weekdays named after the Five Archangels of the Five Points of the Cross. There would be no less than a very, very restful *five* 'Sabbath days' in each new weekend.
- I have actually heard of many attempts to completely revise the calendar, to have one global calendar that actually logically works. None of them, without exception, have been properly thought out. Likewise many people have tried to replace the twenty-four hour clock. I see absolutely no logical reason for this, whereas there are pressing reasons, as we have seen, for a New Calendar.

- The trick of mine that makes it fully work is to retain the five-day working week but create a five-day long weekend accommodating all the world's religions. So abolishing the present illogical seven-day week to fit in with the Earth's actual 365.25-day (73 New 5-day Week) rotation around the Sun.

- Incidentally, it should have the lovely side-effect of abolishing unemployment for ever – and making work a real pleasure, with a five day holiday each week! Obviously everybody will work in two five-day on/off 'shifts'.

- The world would soon slow down to a far less increasingly frenetic pace!

4. VERY TIREDLY, I ASK 'WHY DO THEY WANT ALL THIS?'

Why should these cowardly, furtive control freaks want to computerise money?

The answer lies in the **true** nature of **cash** and a brief, dismal analysis of the limit of the things which money can buy: -

MONEY CAN ONLY BUY YOU: -

Material things **i.e.** *matter*, in the terms of physics;

Labour, **i.e.** *work,* **or** *energy*, again in the terms of physics;

Power, i.e. equating matter to energy after Einstein: - rate of consuming matter and energy – or degree of consumerism; or ability to make people do work for **you;** and finally, rate of spending cash! ('degree of Materialism')

If they can computerise all cash, 'they' will control all our money and *what we spend it on*, by faceless computer control from 'nerve centres' of banking where the computers controlling it all will be.

To quote the Beatles from the 1960's, however, "Money can't buy me love!" (or indeed anything else Spiritual!)

End of 'anti-spiritual equations'. Now for a workable antidote: -

Jasper
Vegan Season (North)

January
Fruit Season (South)

1 Michael	2 Gabriel	3 Raphael	4 Uriel	5 Ariel
6 SHABAT	7 SHAVA	8 SUNDAY	9 MAGDALENA	10 MARIA
11 Michael	12 Gabriel	13 Raphael	14 Uriel	15 Ariel
16 SHABAT	17 SHAVA	18 SUNDAY	19 MAGDALENA	20 MARIA
21 Michael	22 Gabriel	23 Raphael	24 Uriel	25 Ariel
26 SHABAT	27 SHAVA	28 SUNDAY	29 MAGDALENA	30 MARIA

Sapphire
Blossom Season (North)

February
Grain Season (South)

1 Michael	2 Gabriel	3 Raphael	4 Uriel	5 Ariel
6 SHABAT	7 SHAVA	8 SUNDAY	9 MAGDALENA	10 MARIA
11 Michael	12 Gabriel	13 Raphael	14 Uriel	15 Ariel
16 SHABAT	17 SHAVA	18 SUNDAY	19 MAGDALENA	20 MARIA
21 Michael	22 Gabriel	23 Raphael	24 Uriel	25 Ariel
26 SHABAT	27 SHAVA	28 SUNDAY	29 MAGDALENA	30 MARIA

Agate *March*
Blossom Season (North) *Grain Season (South)*

1 Michael	2 Gabriel	3 Raphael	4 Uriel	5 Ariel
6 SHABAT	7 SHAVA	8 SUNDAY	9 MAG-DALENA	10 MARIA
11 Michael	12 Gabriel	13 Raphael	14 Uriel	15 Ariel
16 SHABAT	17 SHAVA	18 SUNDAY	19 MAG-DALENA	20 MARIA
21 Michael	22 Gabriel	23 Raphael	24 Uriel	25 Ariel
26 SHABAT	27 SHAVA	28 SUNDAY	29 MAG-DALENA	30 MARIA

← Four days of Easter, permanently enshrined →

Emerald *April*
Blossom Season (North) *Grain Season (South)*

1 Michael	2 Gabriel	3 Raphael	4 Uriel	5 Ariel
6 SHABAT	7 SHAVA	8 SUNDAY	9 MAG-DALENA	10 MARIA
11 Michael	12 Gabriel	13 Raphael	14 Uriel	15 Ariel
16 SHABAT	17 SHAVA	18 SUNDAY	19 MAG-DALENA	20 MARIA
21 Michael	22 Gabriel	23 Raphael	24 Uriel	25 Ariel
26 SHABAT	27 SHAVA	28 SUNDAY	29 MAG-DALENA	30 MARIA

Onyx
Fruit Season (North)

May
Vegan Season (South)

1 Michael	2 Gabriel	3 Raphael	4 Uriel	5 Ariel
6 SHABAT	7 SHAVA	8 SUNDAY	9 MAG-DALENA	10 MARIA
11 Michael	12 Gabriel	13 Raphael	14 Uriel	15 Ariel
16 SHABAT	17 SHAVA	18 SUNDAY	19 MAG-DALENA	20 MARIA
21 Michael	22 Gabriel	23 Raphael	24 Uriel	25 Ariel
26 SHABAT	27 SHAVA	28 SUNDAY	29 MAG-DALENA	30 MARIA

Cornelian
Fruit Season (North)

June
Vegan Season (South)

1 Michael	2 Gabriel	3 Raphael	4 Uriel	5 Ariel
6 SHABAT	7 SHAVA	8 SUNDAY	9 MAG-DALENA	10 MARIA
11 Michael	12 Gabriel	13 Raphael	14 Uriel	15 Ariel
16 SHABAT	17 SHAVA	18 SUNDAY	19 MAG-DALENA	20 MARIA
21 Michael	22 Gabriel	23 Raphael	24 Uriel	25 Ariel
26 SHABAT	27 SHAVA	28 SUNDAY	29 MAG-DALENA	30 MARIA

Chrysolite
Fruit Season (North)

July
Vegan Season (South)

1 Michael	2 Gabriel	3 Raphael	4 Uriel	5 Ariel
6 SHABAT	7 SHAVA	8 SUNDAY	9 MAG-DALENA	10 MARIA
11 Michael	12 Gabriel	13 Raphael	14 Uriel	15 Ariel
16 SHABAT	17 SHAVA	18 SUNDAY	19 MAG-DALENA	20 MARIA
21 Michael	22 Gabriel	23 Raphael	24 Uriel	25 Ariel
26 SHABAT	27 SHAVA	28 SUNDAY	29 MAG-DALENA	30 MARIA

Beryl
Grain Season (North)

August
Blossom Season (South)

1 Michael	2 Gabriel	3 Raphael	4 Uriel	5 Ariel
6 SHABAT	7 SHAVA	8 SUNDAY	9 MAG-DALENA	10 MARIA
11 Michael	12 Gabriel	13 Raphael	14 Uriel	15 Ariel
16 SHABAT	17 SHAVA	18 SUNDAY	19 MAG-DALENA	20 MARIA
21 Michael	22 Gabriel	23 Raphael	24 Uriel	25 Ariel
26 SHABAT	27 SHAVA	28 SUNDAY	29 MAG-DALENA	30 MARIA

Topaz   September
Grain Season (North)   Blossom Season (South)

1 Michael	2 Gabriel	3 Raphael	4 Uriel	5 Ariel
6 SHABAT	7 SHAVA	8 SUNDAY	9 MAG-DALENA	10 MARIA
11 Michael	12 Gabriel	13 Raphael	14 Uriel	15 Ariel
16 SHABAT	17 SHAVA	18 SUNDAY	19 MAG-DALENA	20 MARIA
21 Michael	22 Gabriel	23 Raphael	24 Uriel	25 Ariel
26 SHABAT	27 SHAVA	28 SUNDAY	29 MAG-DALENA	30 MARIA

Chrysophase   October
Grain Season (North)   Blossom Season (South)

1 Michael	2 Gabriel	3 Raphael	4 Uriel	5 Ariel
6 SHABAT	7 SHAVA	8 SUNDAY	9 MAG-DALENA	10 MARIA
11 Michael	12 Gabriel	13 Raphael	14 Uriel	15 Ariel
16 SHABAT	17 SHAVA	18 SUNDAY	19 MAG-DALENA	20 MARIA
21 Michael	22 Gabriel	23 Raphael	24 Uriel	25 Ariel
26 SHABAT	27 SHAVA	28 SUNDAY	29 MAG-DALENA	30 MARIA

Jacinth   *November*
Vegan Season (North)   *Fruit Season (South)*

1 Michael	2 Gabriel	3 Raphael	4 Uriel	5 Ariel
6 SHABAT	7 SHAVA	8 SUNDAY	9 MAG-DALENA	10 MARIA
11 Michael	12 Gabriel	13 Raphael	14 Uriel	15 Ariel
16 SHABAT	17 SHAVA	18 SUNDAY	19 MAG-DALENA	20 MARIA
21 Michael	22 Gabriel	23 Raphael	24 Uriel	25 Ariel
26 SHABAT	27 SHAVA	28 SUNDAY	29 MAG-DALENA	30 MARIA

Amethyst   *December*
Vegan Season (North)   *Fruit Season (South)*

1 Michael	2 Gabriel	3 Raphael	4 Uriel	5 Ariel
6 SHABAT	7 SHAVA	8 SUNDAY	9 MAG-DALENA	10 MARIA
11 Michael	12 Gabriel	13 Raphael	14 Uriel	15 Ariel
16 SHABAT	17 SHAVA	18 SUNDAY	19 MAG-DALENA	20 MARIA
21 Michael	22 Gabriel	23 Raphael	24 Christmas Eve	25 Simon Peter
26 James brother of John	27 John	28 Andrew	29 Philip	30 Bartholomew
31 Matthew	32 Thomas	33 James son of Alphaeus	34 Thaddaeus	35 Simon of Canaan
36 {Judas Iscariot}				

←ONLY in 2008AD, 2012AD, 2016AD, …

322

2. A new theory of – and cures for – all *mental illnesses*

I present here a new theory that the CAUSE of most mental illness is far from biochemical, it is instead a maladjusted perception of Time and/or various aspects of the Holy Spirit.

In other words, this goes close to the Biblical description of a mentally ill person as 'having an "evil" spirit' i.e. a human spirit out of pace or kilter with the great Body of the Holy Spirit.

Is it possibly to actually CURE mental illness (by 'time/spirit therapy') rather than just suppress the symptoms of illness with anti-psychotic drugs as psychiatry still relies on as its only answer to madness? As soon as the drugs are stopped patients relapse back into illness!

1. Introduction. Neuroscience and especially Psychiatry are still completely 'Black Arts' – pseudo-sciences in their infancy...

'Mental illness' and other 'problems of the mind' have been with us, usually formerly called 'madness' or 'insanity', since the dawn of mankind. At any one time, it is estimated that between 40% and as high as 60% of the population will have had a mental health problem at some stage or stages of their life. Figures indicate that those figures have risen sharply and steadily in the last, ever more stressful century.

The phrase 'mental illness' increasingly rapidly started to take over from the older very insulting descriptions, nearly as soon as psychiatrists were given access in the late 1940's to the earliest, very primitive anti-psychotic drugs following neuroscientific and biochemical research, of which chlorpromazine, still commonly used today, was one of the first. The range of drugs available, and progress in eliminating as many side-effects as possible, has grown enormously, until today the psychiatrists have a whole large small-print manual to choose from.

It is vitally important to realise, however, that these drugs only ever extremely rarely and unusually, actually 'cure' mild cases of mental illness. Instead they usually have to be taken for long periods, if not for life – because *these anti-psychotic drugs only suppress symptoms and 'abnormal' thoughts.*

Also, treatment by most psychiatrists is still a 'black art'. Their use of drugs to suppress symptoms, rather than cure, is very 'hit and miss' and 'trial and error'. In addition, no two patients are ever precisely the same in terms of treatment, many psychiatrists have told me, so redoubling the experimental nature of treatment, often causing a lot of stress to patients.

Their notorious 'hospitals' don't help either. Most patients get ten times more ill shortly after admission. The environment is sterile, boring, bleak and very un-homely, and above all very stressful indeed – as all the patients crammed in there have their own unique problems so symptoms. Most patients only stand a chance of getting out of the terrible environment, once they have somehow roused themselves to get well enough, or the 'hit and miss' experiments with drugs have worked, to get some increasing time in their home – 'away from the madness'.

Above all, the staff behave in these places in an ever-increasingly 'politically correct' rather than 'caring' way – seemingly for fear that a simple reassuring hug might be interpreted as 'assault' - such is the atmosphere of today!

It appears to me strongly that psychiatrists and the related (pseudo-) sciences have missed out an awful lot by restricting themselves to a purely biochemical, and neurological, model of the mind – as if made of matter, with no actual mind, to speak of! In section 2 overleaf, I first give a new suggestion – a 'spiritually rather than materially oriented model of the human mind'. Then I follow that with even more radical views in section 3 that follows. I have found ways in which I can divide mental illness as a whole into two categories, provoking the question 'can actual cures, not just suppression of symptoms, be developed using this spiritual model of the mind?' These two categories are 'time perception related' and 'general spiritual perception related'.

2. All language, thoughts, emotions and feelings, are encapsulated in microscopic 'transcendental building blocks'

'Nice thoughts' – 'male and female', in both men and women – occupy very elegant 'hyper-cubes within hyper-cubes'; which is reflected in Far Eastern traditions, especially Buddhism. All of our sublime or spiritual thoughts occupy dodecahedrons.

'Sick' thoughts, by contrast, fill jarring, nasty, triangular pyramids.

Our brain and nervous system are designed, naturally enough, to operate far better with cubic, 'nice', or 'normal', and also dodecahedral or 'sublime' or 'spiritual' thoughts – than with their opposite – 'nasty triangular pyramids'...

What I have said in this book will almost certainly be anathema to most neuro-scientists and their cousin 'scientists', the Psychiatrists. Yet it could revolutionise both grey areas, both claiming to be pre-eminent about 'mind' yet not really believing at all in 'mind' as such, in any way. Most of them are such devout Atheists that they have convinced themselves that 'thought is made of chemicals'. Most Psychiatrists are given such outrageously massive personal legal powers that: -

"Nearly all Psychiatrists don't believe in God, because...

They believe that they personally are 'God'! "

Compared to the elegance and comparative simplicity of my 'spiritual model' of Mind and Spirit, culminating in the present Paper, the devoutly Atheist, materialistic and extremely blinkered view of such people that 'it is all chemical – we hope to prove it some day...' is poles apart. I have even taken the trouble to correlate my own ideas with those of my own native science, physics – and found a compelling whole set of matches with physical 'Theories of Everything'. To the extent that those Theories, thanks to this book, might even be completed. So long as these scientists sacrifice their complete disdain for The Arts, and above all 'Things Spiritual'.

So, how do the chemical structures of brain and nerves fit into my own spiritual model, which we now complete? We have already started to discuss how brain and nerve cells 'amplify' and 'act as vessels' for thoughts in the form of spiritual energy. We have seen that they readily hold hyper-cubic spiritual energies, singly or in 'cubes of cubes', and the effect of 'spiritual dodecahedral thoughts' is far more radiant. Thus the brain, as you already know, can store thoughts – our memory.

I know nothing about the different parts of the brain and how several areas, the infant science of neuro-science says, seem to be involved in different activities such as thought, music, bodily control and so on. Maybe if they overcome their atheist, materialist prejudices, and actually expand their own minds enough to absorb and act on the essays presented here, particularly this one, enough to 'absorb the very notion of spiritual dimensions', they may find it a useful, fruitful exercise in their researches.

Perhaps my final points in this section, the way that thoughts move around the brain and body, *and even outside it, to and fro,* are the most relevant to my last pointed remarks. Neuro-science fails to acknowledge my earlier statement, instead modelling the brain around that most awkward invention and mockery of the brain, the digital computer, which was that: -

The brain is "a spirit-processing and spirit-memorising machine"

So, they are still clutching at straws by trying to relate the mere chemicals of acetyl-choline, dopamine and other neuro-transmitters, to some kind of unfathomable 'language of chemicals' in the brain. My own model says that these and other such transmitters carry no such bizarrely hard to discern 'chemical message' – but words and sentences and paragraphs – made of Spirit! They are minute 'spiritual transporters, carrying a thought' – cubic, spiritual, or 'nasty'.

However, there are no transmitters required when Spiritual Messages leave – and enter from outside the body. As Taoists and Zen Buddhists put it, as earlier, "there is no real 'self' and no 'other than self'". I gave a whole Paper, the Blue Paper, over to how this happens – resulting in prayers, prayers being answered, and Visions – which the heathen, as above, call 'religious hallucinations', of course.

Likewise, the Bible discusses the 'Gifts of the Holy Spirit'. I am lucky enough to have been given by God, a considerable number of these, seemingly in compensation for immense suffering since 1992. For instance, since as long ago as 1978, I have seen all of twenty Visions, nearly all now having come true, with me left in eager, full anticipation that the rest will too. The outstanding ones, unlike most of those up to this year, are all *positive* – very much so...

As a result of this lengthy suffering, on 16th March 1994 I prayed for, and instantly received, the 'Baptism of the Holy Spirit'. A rapidly fluent Gift of Tongues soon developed, as well as a strong, rapidly growing Faith – both of which I was to really need. Words of Wisdom and Knowledge soon followed (words of *God* forming in my mind!), and finally last year, while I was in great distress, Gifts of Healing by Laying on of Hands – and Interpretation of Tongues.

I explain these Gifts as being latent in absolutely everybody's brain and spirit, activated solely by and through the Holy Spirit as an extension of all the gifts we are born with. We are all born with the capacity to have these in addition to more 'normal' secular gifts like intelligence, but often, as in my case, only 'connect with God' enough to have these fantastic privileges 'opened up', through suffering...

3. A Spiritual Model of the common forms of Mental Illness based on the above 'spiritual' model of the mind.

This section jumps in immediately with a table of 'spiritual categories of all major types of mental illness' – then we go on in the next section to discuss, in much more detail, the relationship between, in both spiritual and mental terms, the spiritual cause I try here to give here for each, so a possible cure if at all possible. The traditional comprehensive list of factors in mental illness developing is as follows. In other words, 'a healthy body means a healthy mind': -
- Genetic factors
- Standard of living
- Other environmental factors such as housing
- Stress especially work and personal relationships, and possibly violence
- Diet (*half* of people with mental illness eat no fruit nor drink any fruit juice)
- Glandular problems such as thyroid or sexual hormones
- Abuse of alcohol and illegal substances
- A basic immaturity!

However, the question of which illness is caused by which of the above set of factors, is a mystery, by and large to psychiatry. To me it is also a mystery – except to say it is the 'luck of the draw' i.e. as the master of mental illness which the Bible calls 'having an evil spirit', the 'lord of that luck' is *Satan!*

These factors, in my view, *damage the human spirit,* which as we saw in Volume A of this book, has a massive effect on *the mind and our thoughts.* One well-known way to 'get well again' – as far as possible after such a nasty onslaught as a nervous breakdown or similar – is so-called 'cognitive recognition' – 'mind over illness' rather than 'mind over matter'. So now to my 'spiritual categories'.

Mental illnesses involving a distorted or 'abnormal' perception of *time*

1. Depression. The person's perception of time is speeded up because their mind is slower than normal in time. Everything seems to whiz past and become confusing and frightening – so ultimately paranoia can set in. The slowing down of the mind flattens the spirits and the mood is lowered – the person is said to have 'low spirits'.

2. Mania. Quite the opposite! The person's perception of time is slowed down because their mind is faster and faster than normal in time. Everything seems to go slowly and seem trivial and commonplace – so ultimately grandiose thoughts and delusions, but sometimes again paranoia can set in. The speeding up of the mind elates the spirits and the mood is drastically unusually high – the person is said to have 'high spirits' to the point of euphoria. They often feel invincible, and spend far too much money they do not have, and similar overconfident unwise actions. A typical physical symptom is 'pressure of speech' – rapid incoherent speech.

3. Hypomania. A form of mania of less intensity – 'hypo' is greek for 'below'.

4. Manic depression (which Psychiatry is trying to replace by the kinder, more neutral phrase 'bipolar disorder' or 'bipolar affective disorder' in full). Either short-term, rapid or more commonly swings between depression and hypomania or even full mania lasting months or years – with long periods of 'highs or lows' between each 'normal' period. My own form of illness is termed bipolar (I) affective disorder – unusually, mostly sometimes lengthy hypomanic periods, with only occasional depressions, that do not last long.

Mental illnesses involving *spiritual damage* on top of an already distorted or 'abnormal' perception of *time*

1. 'Schizophrenia' which does NOT mean 'split personality' as often commonly stated, but rather 'shattered mind' is really 24 or so separate illnesses! All the common important psychiatric manuals such as the US DSM (Diagnostic Systems Manual) and the World Health Organisation equivalent, state that for somebody to be judged to be schizophrenic they have to have at least two of the following five symptoms: -

i. Very confused or 'psychotic' thoughts for a long time
ii. Paranoia i.e. acute irrational fear, e.g. a feeling they are being talked about

iii. Bizarre delusions, e.g. that they are somebody else entirely, or are God, or are made of plastic
iv. Visual / Auditory hallucinations – 'seeing visions' and/or 'hearing voices'
v. 'Negative symptoms' – violence towards others, or on the other hand, self harm (see below).

As all these combinations are possible, 'schizophrenia' is really dozens of illnesses all with the same dreadful label!

2. **Schizo-affective disorder. Schizophrenia combined with mania, hypomania or manic depression.**
3. **Self-harm.** Self abuse with drugs (prescribed or illegal), cutting or burning, is often associated with one of the above two forms of schizophrenia.
4. **Compulsive-obsessive disorder.** Strong cycling in time of the same repetitive behaviour pattern, which is often bizarre to onlookers.

Other medical conditions related but not identical to mental illness, yet that are often treated with the same types of anti-psychotic drugs.

These include dementia, Parkinson's disease and Cronin's disease. These all appear to be strongly caused by the passage of time, but dementia can strike very young indeed – even to people of less than middle age, in their 30's or 40's. Some anti-psychotic drugs are used to help ease these conditions, but there is no known medical cure as such, as for mental illness. I will not be offering any alternative non-chemical 'cure' for these in my discussion on the next page, because I take the conventional view that these are physical conditions with only a biochemical response seeming at present to work.

4. Alternatives to the present overwhelming reliance by psychiatry on *drugs*

A call for an end to the current overwhelming obsession of psychiatry with using anti-psychotic drugs exclusively, merely to suppress the *symptoms* of mental illness. Why is there not a great deal more use of the precursors to such drugs? A call for vaster expenditure on counselling, psycho-therapy – and above all the use of *genuine spiritual healing*; as well as on much better *food* in hospitals.

Up to 50 years age there *were* no anti-psychotic drugs. The authorities, then not all government, for the church has been replaced in this role, used whatever their budget provided, to give the patient: - comfort, good food and drink, peace and quiet for rest, and some light activities or work to do - and lots of *talk.* Such counselling is much less common these days – is it because drugs are much cheaper, and cost no labour? 'Talking therapies' mostly comprise: -
- Counselling, i.e. discussing the problems and searching for solutions
- Psycho-therapy i.e. going further and breaking down the person's weaknesses ('illness' included) in order to rebuild them – even more draining on both patient and therapist
- Teaching patients techniques for self-help e.g. cognitive recognition therapy, which I personally find useful for solving problems, especially when they recur in cycles, so fail to go away.

Often, when in hospital, I would have liked to have access to such 'talk' rather than merely being 'observed' like a laboratory rat in between taking pills. Oh that the London Healing Mission that I went to 12 years ago in 1994 had not shut down then. They could have trained dozens of *genuine* spiritual healers to break down the taboos, and be allowed if not actively encouraged into all mental hospitals to offer help to the many patients with a faith of some sort – I have met many with a strong faith, as mine clearly is. It certainly worked for me then!

Finally I propose two new non chemical therapies – 'PACE' – the patient pacing their own thoughts – and 'SORT' - 'spiritual organisation recognition therapy'. The first is of use for *all* the various illnesses I discussed above, but particularly for the first group – of 'time perception disorders'. It would be focussed on teaching sufferers of depression or any degree of mania, or both, to use their mind to *control the PACE of their thoughts.* Giving them a watch is a start! In addition, for depression, I would recommend what have been called 'random acts of kindness' – getting them out of their misery by often at random moments, surprising them – by spoiling them. This for most dejected depressed people, feeling 'in the pits', works really well when I could afford it, I have found.

I propose SORT as 'spiritual awareness' – teaching patients to recognise any 'abnormal' thoughts or behaviours that they don't like - as a precursor to discussing them with a counsellor or nurse as they see fit. Teaching them what is to be expected as irregular thinking or behaviour is the start to this. The key to both proposed new actual cures for the *causes* of the illness is Time and Spirit – which as for the whole of the book we now finish, requires a whole education!

Manifesto: Abolish All Money!

maam.org.uk

**Census all computer based equipment!
License all computers!**

The Manifesto as presented here is available either as a low cost brochure or a download – along with 'Scientific Proof that (God The Holy) Spirit Exists' and other books at **www.silee.me.uk** – or – **www.lulu.com/authormeuk**

Mister il Professori Simon Richard Lee OA BA MA KCC (St. Albans School 1968-75; King's College, Cambridge 1976-83) CEng MIEE MIET MInstMC

Easter 2009. It is the height of the **Second Great Depression** (**'credit crunch'** in silly common parlance! It is much more serious than that trashy phrase!)

Money has been literally 'the root of all evil' in the whole world for eighteen months since the credit crunch started; and this situation may persist for some years despite all the joint efforts of world leaders and governments.

This Manifesto argues a solid case that we could all create a far better New World if we all abolished money and lived without it...

In a 'World Union - of Father Christmas States'!

Copyright © Easter 2009 : -
Mister il Professori Simon Richard Lee OA BA MA KCC (Saint Albans School 1968-75 & King's College, Cambridge 1976-83) CEng MIEE MIET MInstMC

{every one of these certified labels are fully genuine and fully paid up to date – at great cost by HM Government}

This book employs advice and a female viewpoint from a close friend, Julie, a professional Care Worker

Dedicated to our families – alive or passed on – especially my Mother RIP...

Keywords: - money, abolish money, abolish all money, money abolition, abolition money, manifesto, recession, depression, great depression, second great depression, cash, credit, credit card, debit, debit card, computer census, census computer, license computer, computer license, no money, no cash, no credit, zero money, zero cash, zero credit, free money, free cash, free credit, money free, cash free, credit free, Father Christmas state, computer money complex, utopia, paradise, world peace

CONTENTS

1. **Introduction.** Imagine a world with 'Money as a thing of the past'! With the clock wound back all of 70 years so there are only a few computers again!

2. **Money and computers are filthy** – they carry most germs! "**Filthy** leukah"! "Filthy rich versus filthy poor"?

3. Money and computers are just filthy dirty middle-men! Money and computers underpin our 'modern 21st Century World' – but it is unbearably awkward, clunky and inhuman! The oil of human relations would run rich in a world freed of both!

4. Resources and possessions. No more force of economics! No more "haves and have not's" – everybody happy!

5. Food, clothing, land, housing and furnishings, comfortable environment (decent lighting, temperatures, air, water and sanitation) – all our essential basic needs would become **free for all** – even in the undeveloped world – the very least that this proposal offers after the abolition of money

6. Work, agriculture, shops and industry. How about a five day week – five days on five days off – in two shifts?

7. Walking, road, rail, sea, air and space transport

8. No more need for banks, taxes, gambling, casinos or Stock Markets – or charities or state benefits on the other hand...

9. The Law – very little crime; so punishment; left possible!

10. Local, national and international Governments

11. Multinational cultural and language differences and Travel

12. Trade; the fair distribution of wealth once money were abolished; the end of the Great International Rich-Poor Divide

13. Children and families

14. Poverty and debt obsolete – personal and national

15. Teaching and Education

16. Science and Technology, especially regarding information

17. The Arts

18. Entertainment and communications: - post offices and services, radio, TV, (mobile) telephones, papers, magazines, books; information and computer technology, and the Internet

19. Sport, Recreation Activities and Holidays

20. Health, Beauty, Hygiene, Safety, Medicine, Hospitals, Legal and Illegal Drugs, Social Services, Welfare, and The Elderly

21. The Environment; Natural Resources; Environmental Health. Global Warming, 'carbon footprints', pollution, climate change all made too a 'thing of the past'

22. Nature and Wildlife

23. Politics replaced by true leadership

24. World Peace and Security replacing Permanent War

25. Sexism, sexuality, homophobia, ageism, racism, etc, etc

26. Stresses and Strains, the Pace of Life and Mental Health

27. Human or spiritual values and freedom of choice. Religion – is it affected at all?

28. The biblical basis of the census then abolition of most computers – on top of all money! The Book of Revelation chapters 15 through 19.

29. Any counter arguments to zero money are few and weak!

30. Overall - a very simple and high Quality of Life for all!

1. **Introduction. Imagine a world with 'Money as a thing of the past'! With the clock wound back all of 70 years so there are only a few computers again!**

The current worldwide recession (I share the increasing views of many commentators that it is a Second Great Depression that may last years if unchecked by a world government initiative) started life as the tritely and glibly misnamed 'credit crunch' back in September 2007. Banks stopped giving out vast amounts of cheap credit – around that time the long term bubble in massive and escalating property prices on both sides of the Atlantic, also burst.

Since then world stock markets have collapsed in a series of drastic falls, notably in September 2008, a year after the start of this 'credit crunch' cum Second Great Depression. Now the world and its leaders are both apportioning blame as ever, often quite wildly, and grasping onto straws to find ways to get the apple cart of the world economy upright and working again. Was it all greedy bankers' fault – or was it greedy homeowners? They ask!

My own answers are extremely radical and totally mind-blowingly far-reaching: -
- A lot of the problem is the vast over-proliferation of a population of nearly totally uncontrolled, unregulated, **computers**, especially in this 21st Century, way beyond in Size and Complexity, the ability of their designers to actually control their design. Above all the Internet! As a computer systems designer who first worked on them using paper tape and cards back in 1971, I find the current generation of systems (a) far too complex and BIG for anybody alive to understand let alone manage (b) since '9/11' and the ensuing war on terrorism, involved in a global system of control and alleged so-called 'security' that serves no human being any more – only the 'Great God of MONEY'! Something described in my own book 'Scientific Proof that (God The Holy) Spirit Exists' as described and sold at www.silee.me.uk is now required to deal with this 'computer-money complex' that is now totally out of control and threatens to destroy all world prosperity – then peace, as a direct result.
- I propose here what I proposed there – a 'CCCCCC' or 'C6' – a 'cool, calm, collected complete computer census'! Computers were invented between 1937 and 1939 as **weapons** – the first

digital electronic computer was based at Bletchley in England throughout the Second World War. This 'Enigma Machine' enabled Britain and so the Allies to break the code of every single German military radio signal during the war – and had Prime Minister Winston Churchill taken this work much more seriously, it has been said that the result could have been a far quicker ending of that terrible conflict. The man who published the original design was one Alan Turing, a predecessor of mine at King's College, Cambridge. He got into a lot of trouble with the homophobism of the then Government about his very precocious early blatancy about his homosexuality – and the resulting persecution eventually drove him to suicide. I am very glad even in this day and age, that I do not suffer from either his homosexual or suicidal tendencies!
- I claim in a future world where we 'put the genie of these computers' back in the bottle the only computers we would need are these limited forms: -
- (a) Calculation, measurement and control devices – but ONLY where humans cannot match the performance, accuracy, complexity or need for health and safety of these   (b) Word processing and graphics   (c) Music   (d) CONTROLLED communications   (e) MORE (much) control over stored information (data)
- The **KEY** to causing such a counter-revolution would seem Luddite and backward were it not for the radical, totally idealistic, crazy to some, nature of my own solution to the ever-worsening Second Great Depression of our 21st Century, totally out of control and unregulated, 'computer-money complex'. That is: -
- **Problem – (the love of) Money is the Root of All Evil**
- **Only Logical Answer – ABOLISH ALL MONEY!**
- The next two sections, (2) and (3), describe the main problems of this 'computer-money complex' as I see them. The first of these should be blindingly obvious from the very description of money by the slang phrase 'filthy leukah' but will shock and terrify most people! In remaining sections, firstly in most I describe the 'Ideal money free world' in all its aspects – and secondly confine my attentions to religion and even a biblical basis for all of this – to just a few sections at the very end.
- To summarise: - the **'Root of all Evil'** was planted by The Devil right at the very start of things. Satan invented money. For the

last 70 years, computer automation has rocketed in importance and fallen correspondingly massively in price to the point of the current Second Great Depression **having been caused by** a 'computer-money complex' that no longer serves people – only the Great Gods. The Original Great God of Money – Satan's Offspring, the Root of All Evil, remember – and The New Second Upstart Great God of IT - Machines or Technology.

- It is time that humanity took this Second Great Depression as a golden opportunity to make a massive step in **growing up** - into a wonderful New World! As we see in this Manifesto, if we Abolish All Money, that is the only catalyst we need to provide, to create a world free of poverty and greed, yet full of opportunity for all on a truly equal basis.
- This Booklet is termed a Manifesto on the cover even though it transcends all political views, which are largely money-based. It is a Manifesto that seeks to Marshal a whole Movement of a Majority of Like-Minded Minds! (an MMMMMM??!!) To do the following. To dig up the ancient, hoary, cobwebbed, part rotting, part fossilized, it is so old, Root of All Evil, Money Itself, dripping with oceans of the blood, sweat and tears of generations of the poverty-stricken, ironically most of them alive today! Do not burn it but **completely** destroy it in a very modern way indeed – **recycle** all the metal and paper of the coins and notes, and re-cycle the plastic of all debit and credit cards! Then computers could easily be re-bottled like the genies or Evil Spirits that they are – only to be let out again under extremely controlled circumstances! The ones that were scrapped would also provide a wealth of recycled materials – especially gold and other precious minerals and metals.

2. Money and computers are filthy – they carry most germs! "Filthy leukah"! "Filthy rich versus filthy poor"?

In the next two sections (2) and (3) I give my two principal, both devastating objections to the worlds of 'cash' and 'the computer-money complex'. The first, in this section, will probably strike you as common sense, but nevertheless something you will almost certainly never have thought of – because society makes money so sacred a Sacred Cow – that is actually **very shocking.** Consider: -

- Whenever you give and take money in a shop, those notes and coins will have been handled by dozens and hundreds of people in their time, many with infectious diseases. The dirt on those notes and coins, built up increasingly with age, carries **toxic, infectious, microbes, bacteria, viruses and other microscopic germs!!!**
- **Money is filthy! Your average wallet, purse, or pocket of money is absolutely riddled with disease and germs!**
- Especially these days, with 'chip and PIN' keyboards replacing signatures, the same is only slightly less true of debit and credit cards – 20 people an hour touch the same keyboard to enter their PIN, passing on infectious germs and so diseases!
- So what about the cash till operators? They typically do a two hour shift, handling not only the toxic infected money – but **all of the goods being sold!!!** Then their shift changes because operating a cash till is only allowed for a certain amount of time because it is intensive i.e. very stressful. **Another** cash till operator uses the very same cash till keyboard – spreading even more germs and disease!
- The same is true of computer keyboards worldwide, for the vast majority of these are shared between company employees and members of families and their friends at home!

I am a 'heavy' smoker so am well aware of the current fierce coercion in my own country England, to initially ban all smoking in public places that started two years ago, obviously with the long term agenda being to outlaw smoking altogether. However I feel that the Government led health warnings on tobacco could be used even more urgently on **money – notes, coins and cards**. This would take place in a 'grass roots way', with at first families, then towns and villages, declaring themselves to be 'money free / cash free / credit free zones' which would be vastly more effective than such communities in the past rather 'pissing in the wind' by declaring themselves rather pointlessly to be 'nuclear free zones'. Finally whole states and counties, then whole countries, would become 'cash free zones', in this New World.

Bank notes, debit and credit cards, and keyboards would initially be marked with the chemical skull and crossbones symbol for 'poison', and be inscribed with the warning,
"Contains toxic, poisonous dirt, microbes, bacteria and viruses"

Coins are too small for such a warning message – but the 'tails' side could have stamped on it in yellow and black the same 'poison' skull and crossbones warning…

In Volume C Part 1 of my book 'Scientific Proof that (God The Holy) Spirit Exists' as featured and sold at www.silee.me.uk I quote in full, for it is frighteningly dangerous and straight out of a '1984' or '666' world where people would become just numbers – a conspiracy theory posted on the Internet in 1997. This detailed an alternative to abolishing money that goes completely the other way – into an open invitation to tyranny and state control. This would involve implanting a computer containing all their financial details under the skin of every man, woman and child!!!

My own approach to dealing with the problems of money being dirty and unhygienic – it gets worse, see the next section – is the human, humane approach compared to the above 'Beast 666' one…

So – maam.org.uk would like to see this sort of desperately over-needed measure introduced **first** in my own country, the UK. So I address Her Majesty The Queen in Person : -

"Ma'am! Message from MAAM! Read on for the rest gets better and better after this! Then get your current government of whatever slant to read this too – and all of you **abolish all money** starting here in the UK!"

3. **Money and computers are just filthy dirty middle-men! Money and computers underpin our 'Modern 21st Century World' – but it is unbearably awkward, clunky and inhuman! The oil of human relations would run rich in a world freed of both!**

We have just seen one frighteningly real problem with both money and computers as they co-exist in their 21st Century 'computer-money complex'. We now turn to look at how these two middle men, the terrible twins in this conspiratorial takeover of the world of the last 70 years, increasingly in the last ten years, seem to have brought it nearly to a diabolically awful conclusion since 11th

September 2001 – '9/11' and George Bush Junior's ensuing immediate launch the very next day of the infamous 'war on terrorism'. So let us compare the world now with ten years or so ago, and see how in the Name of Progress a ruinous state of affairs has nearly finished emerging.

I have not pursued my original career in computer systems automation for twelve years now, through ill health that largely amounted to severe abuse (and five elapsed years in awful hospitals) by a series of totally arrogant yet incompetent Doctors. I have continued as a spectator to the development of computers, now mostly using them at home to write this and a series of books as at www.silee.me.uk and www.lulu.com/authormeuk .

So please do not think I am some kind of 'Victor Meldrew' character when you read the long list of severe gripes below with the 'system' as it has now emerged and seems likely to produce only even more of the same dire sort of world. It is just that I have long since lost any of my initial enthusiasm for computers, but it is they not I that are turncoats, for far from their initial purposes mostly for noble purposes 70 years ago – now they only mostly serve the 'computer-money complex'. My list of severe gripes is as follows: -

- Using the telephone to talk to representatives of more and more organizations, especially commercial ones, has become, and is becoming, increasingly fraught. You usually now get a ludicrously positive, beaming, robot humanoid voice, terribly terribly well-spoken, not a real person. You are asked to push a series of buttons supposed to home you in on the option you want to address when you deal with them. Then all too often one of two things happens: - (a) you discover to your horror that this phone call is being answered in a completely inhuman automated way – there is no possibility of actually talking to a human being not a robot humanoid voice interpretation machine that often mishears you or hangs up unexpectedly! (b) You wait ten or twenty minutes listening to that company's taste in piped muzak 'on hold' – most irritating when they play the same (depressing?) muzak track over and over again! Then when you finally get through to a human voice, and ask a slightly difficult question not on their computer screen, they say 'do you mind if I put you on hold for a moment?' which turns into a further ten or twenty minutes, far from 'a moment'! They are really saying, were they honest about it 'I do not mind putting you on hold for ten minutes when I say 'a moment'! You are footing the phone bill and we ensure it is a premium rate number so we get a large payment from the phone company from your bill – for keeping you on hold!'

- Another form of 'computer-money complex' phone abuse, also just keeps getting more and more common and intrusive. Increasingly when my phone rings, it is no friend, not even a real person on the far end. It is a recording of another robot humanoid, pleasantly inviting you to buy their service or pay for everything apart from the actual fare of the Mediterranean Cruise it claims you have won! I don't like con artist robots ringing me up like that!

- My third and final example of what I regard as phone abuse is the familiar phrase once you actually get through to customer services and real people. How often have you heard this, "Sorry please ring back in a few hours! Our system is down!" Whereas the first two problems above are really just symptoms of a now fully emerged "Culture of the computer-money complex" – the "system down!" problem speaks to me, as a Chartered Computer Systems Engineer with a long history of actually designing fully 100% working computer systems years ago, of a much deeper problem, as follows: -

- Probably even now, still the worst offender in this is the very market leader, Microsoft, whom I will ironically name by my affectionate term for them in this discussion: 'Megabollox'. The above company will have been sold their computer system, either to replace a previous paper based system, or more likely these days, with the march of time and such 'Progress' – an upgrade to an earlier version of such a system. Megabollox have caused an entire sales culture of selling new computer systems by appealing to the buyer with the sheer quantity of 'bells, whistles, gadgets and gizmos' that come with it – generally termed 'features'. The trouble is testing all of these vast quantity of such 'features' on just one system so they all always work together or in unison, not just in isolation from each other. Again Megabollox have started another major notorious trend with their software – they release it to a naïve gullible Joe Bloggs public, barely tested beyond the pre-production 'beta' testing phase – and let that public, already hard sold yet another 'jazzy, exciting Megabollox product' do most of the testing for Megabollox instead. Yet for Megabollox, have they already done everything technically feasible seven years ago in 2002 with their 'Windows XP' product? They were immediately assailed by a dodgy army of hackers, and had to spend the next five years introducing literally thousands of security features to stop Windows XP attracting viruses, worms, and other assaults. That was five years that stopped Megabollox introducing Windows Vista as a 'replacement' for Windows XP – but it backfired. Problems were, as I could see them when I bought a laptop briefly with Vista Home Basic installed on it in 2007 when Vista emerged:-

- Initially and for some months, one could not make Vista run any software that ran on Windows XP – apart of course from Megabollox software. All software manufacturers apart from supreme arrogant Megabollox had to rapidly produce new 'Vista compatible' versions of their packages, at vast expense.
- However hard I tried while I had my Vista machine, I could not for the life of me perceive any real difference **technically in the internals** from its predecessor XP that I knew very well. Megabollox emphasised the 'front end' or '(hu)man-machine interface' and indeed that seemed to be where absolutely the only differences lay. What a let down after waiting all of five years – just to get a cosmetically slightly 'sexier' system!
- Yet the biggest problem with Vista, its downfall it was to turn out, was that some of these 'front end' features required vastly more sheer computing power and resources than were available on most machines then and even now – especially some of the more ludicrously 'snazzier' features like three dimensional graphics.
- Overall then, with Vista Megabollox were 'flogging a dead donkey' by presenting this cosmetic, resource-flogging successor to Windows XP falsely as an advance. The marketing hype certainly led hundreds of thousands of gullible punters to do what Microsoft coerced by dropping all their support of XP once Vista had been launched. They coughed up the large license fee often only to feel stranded by the above three problems and by the usual cynical Megabollox

ploy of using the public as guinea pigs to find most of the deeper and more subtle 'bugs' or faults in the new Vista Operating System.
- Yet Megabollox are planning to flog the dead donkey even further into its grave, as it were, by shortly bringing out yet another new version of Windows beyond XP – called 'Windows 7'! Yet the price/performance ratio for the computers it would run on bottomed out at last to £300 for a complete computer vastly more powerful than one a tiny fraction as fast and powerful and large – just 30 years ago – when home computing was unthinkable due to the cost and sheer size of machines then. Plus many computer pundits have pointed out that computers are very near the limits of their design capabilities – due to the limitations of physics itself – they are rapidly approaching a point where 'quantum effects' prohibit them getting any smaller and more compact. For all of 70 years, all world governments have given computer designers a total free rein solely in the name of 'Progress' and 'economic growth' - whereas computers now actually contain most of the world's wealth! It is surely time for computer people everywhere to admit it: - "Come on lads and ladettes – the game is up – the world governments have at last got wind that they have been taken by surprise by us computer nerds for all of 70 years now – so have let us get away with our blue murder of IT technology! The game seems to be up – we have to admit to them that everything possible that can be done with conventional computers has already been done. No, we have not succeeded by any stretch of the imagination in creating a single conscious i.e. truly intelligent computer in that 70 years and our Star Trek dreams of intelligent robots might be one day achieved if 'quantum computing' ever really ceases to be just a pipedream – but that is remotely unlikely. Our long term vastly expensive game seems to be up!'
- My other book 'Scientific Proof that (God The Holy) Spirit Exists' – see www.silee.me.uk - starts off with three papers that demolish any notion of the conventional computer design first originated by Alan Turing in 1937-38 producing consciousness. It has a 'yes', a 'no' and a "don't care" state – where is the fourth and vital missing 'care' "state" of any emotional sentient creature? – and I include most animals and

birds and sea creatures in that! No, conventional computer design, so its price to performance ratio, have reached opposite peak and trough respectively for some years now. A great time to reverse as much of the damage as possible – for the Cool, Calm, Collected Complete Computer Census or CCCCCC (C6) I mentioned earlier – at the same time as laws are passed worldwide to outlaw and criminalise **money!**

- Have computer systems really peaked? Or is it not rather the case that they have gone way beyond any reasonable such peak – especially in the vast wastelands of cyberspace that constitute the newly arrived and already nearly world dominant **Internet?** I speak as a medically retired Chartered Computer and Instrument and Measurement and Control Engineer, who from 1975 to 1997 regularly used, where regularly millions of computer 'bytes' are totally wastefully used today, a few hundreds or thousands at most of such bytes of program – to achieve a perfectly working, **hand crafted not machine-butchered result!** In a nutshell, I have to work with the Internet to write and promote my writings, but LOATHE it. I find it glitzy, trashy, grossly inefficient and slow, unreliable – and very often either sleazy (with invasions from pornography sites and / or viruses etc.) or even sinister next to totally respectable (Marks and Spencer are apparently on a par with sites run by Al'Quaeda terrorists!) Above all there is a total lack of central control by any government's laws as the Internet grandiosely transcends all International Law, so totally frustrating the efforts of international governments everywhere to regulate the Beast. My own proposal is the CCCCCC as we have seen. A bottom-up grass roots approach of a global census of all computer equipment would tackle the problem of the Internet for world governments by taking out the lower supporting 'bricks' of dangerous individual computers first. Come on world, do yourself a favour – carry out just such a CCCCCCC!

- As spending literally hours glued to a computer screen and 'surfing the net' has become commonplace in recent years with the Internet, not just as once the domain solely of 'computer nerds', so we see, as this growth of 'cyber space' has taken place, a parallel loss of interest in most of society in 'real' not 'cyber' games, sports, shopping, crafts and other recreation activities. Yet I have a derisive term for much of the Internet as 'tinsel town' – unreliable information, illegal drug sites, likewise extremely dodgy pornographic sites that often attack you with viruses etc. All totally unregulated of course. International laws on the activities on the Internet, as we just said, are desperately required. As I have found, perhaps the most annoying thing that can happen is if your email address enters the public domain. Then expect a torrent of emails for 'guaranteed' get rich quick on the Web schemes, pornographic sites, and now the latest craze, adverts for non-prescribed Viagra and Cialis male sex enhancement drugs – none of which give a way you can stop them being sent to you.

- The Millennium saw a new phenomenon, initially in richer chains of shops, but now nearly everywhere. Where once the only sound at cash desks in shops was the sound of the cash till, now there is a cacophony of new sounds. The multiple electronic 'peeps' as laser armed cash till computers salute all the '666' based UPC barcodes on all the items of merchandise as they 'scan' the codes (with a '6' at either end and a '6' in the middle – '666' which has been The Imperial Number since Emperor Nero of Rome in AD 70 founded his Society of Odd Fellows – since long developed into the Freemasons and now New World Order!) My book 'Scientific Proof that (God The Holy) Spirit Exists' spends all of Volume B and Volume C Part 1 largely investigating this bizarre subject of the number '666' which is mentioned in the final book of the Bible, the Book of Revelation Chapter 13. See www.silee.me.uk for details of my book and how to get hold of a download or printed copy at reasonable price...

- Money could be described as "the world's oldest and most fiendish **weapon** for controlling resources and people and all living creatures"! Since 1939, exactly 70 years ago, with the first computer, it has been joined in what has nearly been perfected as what I term the 'computer-money complex'. I studied computer science at Cambridge University 1978-79 and our then Professor Maurice Wilkes had worked on the first Enigma computer in that terrible war. One day he told us a totally apocryphal tale. He and a senior colleague on the project took a walk together near the computer at Bletchley, then the only one in the world still remember, just after the War ended. "We might need another one of these by the year 2000" was the incredibly lacking in foresight remark they made – just look at the uncontrolled supernova explosion of computers since, now in every walk of life! That first computer led a wave of such computer 'weapons' into a 'computer-money complex' with the ancient ultimate weapon of money, into whole undreamt of ways of controlling resources and people and animals now. Yet like all weapons of war and military methods, both are almost unbearably clunky, awkward and stiff, middle men only – both inanimate servants that would dominate, with absolutely zero inherent intelligence! They threaten to throttle humanity once and for all as they have caused the current Second Great Depression. My own views are radical – we need to Abolish All Money and put its ally the genie of computers firmly back in the bottle – all before it is all too late. The rewards if we do that are huge!

- That is the end of rather a 'diatribe' in some places against money and computers – now with their "computer-money complex" having caused directly the Second Great Depression of 2009. In the next 20 sections or so, I will be necessarily a lot briefer – because I will trying to imagine what the world would be like (dare I say will be like one day?) when money has been abolished – and the genie of computers put back in the bottle. Nobody can fully imagine this, so I will be sensible and confine myself to what the initial changes might be. As a young boy, I thoroughly enjoyed the Narnia Books of C. S. Lewis, and will paraphrase a 'shout of joy' in the final book of the series – The Last Battle. He greatly reassures us that when the world finally ends, a New World will absolutely immediately appear, ready made, and as the heroes of the story enter this New World they cry out for joy. In a world with money gone and computers shrunk back to their own original size in importance, would the shout be, 'Higher and Further!' then become 'Ever Higher and Ever Further!'?

4. Resources and possessions. No more force of economics! No more "haves and have not's" – everybody happy!

In most of the rest of this Manifesto I look at how the world would at least maybe start to be should we as a species, probably initially in small pockets, abolish all money, i.e. abolish all cash and abolish all credit. That is right: - a world with no money, no cash, no credit, I say again, zero money, zero cash and zero credit. A money-free, cash-free, credit-free world!

Would resources and possessions just disappear in this New World? Of course not – but they would simply have no financial or monetary value associated with them or price tag. They would instead revert to their essential 'intrinsic value' which Karl Marx called their 'use value' in his essay 'the fetishism of commodities' in his famous book 'Das Kapital' which I quote in my own book 'Scientific Proof that (God The Holy) Spirit Exists' at www.silee.me.uk .

A money-free world is the **only way** to achieve the great Noble Aspirations of many of mankind to have a fair distribution of wealth i.e. in That World, only resources and possessions, with no financial strings attached any more. Neither Capitalist nor Communist – but Utterly Liberal with capital U and capital L! It would almost automatically apply two principles from the words of Jesus in the New Testament in the Bible: -
- 'Seek and you shall find'
- 'Ask and you shall receive'

In our 21st Century world it is possible to get hold of anything you could possibly want in life – at a price. In a world where 'money was no object' – where indeed money no longer existed! – all you would do was seek your heart's desire till you found it – in papers, magazines, books, TV, radio as now – and whatever rump was left of the Internet after the CCCCCC I keep advocating. With no money involved, nor indeed would there be any primitive barter unless you absolutely wanted to thank the person with whatever was your heart's desire. For you will simply 'ask (for it – **politely!**) and you will receive - it – **totally free of charge!**' in Our Brave New World.

Really it would be that easy. Fascinating is it not?

15

5. Food, clothing, land, housing and furnishings, comfortable environment (decent lighting, temperatures, air, water and sanitation) – all our essential basic needs would become free for all – even in the undeveloped world – the very least that this incredibly simple proposal offers after the abolition of money

Forget "seeking and finding your heart's desire, and receiving it if you ask politely for it" for a moment. In our present 21st Century World there is an ever deeper growing global "Rich – Poor Divide" and the vast majority of the world's burgeoning population is born into a planet where they do not even have the very basics – as in the title of this section, as I see them.

Finding a way, as many leaders and politicians try fruitlessly to do, to find ways round the stranglehold of the 'computer-money complex' today to reach out and actually give the majority of the world, these basics that some take for granted, is **impossible!**

To Abolish All Money is to create a world where there would be an immediate global rescue operation from West to East and North to South – literally - to provide at least the above basics to absolutely all of the world's population. The Western and Northern Hemisphere actually already have all the adequate resources – it is only the money itself that is currently the only obstacle to absolutely a global panacea!

Taking money itself out of the 'equation of the world's current mess' – gives you instantly, literally, a panacea to all of the world's problems. As we see in the sections that follow...

6. Work, agriculture, shops and industry. How about a five day week – five days on five days off – in two shifts?

In a world free of money so of the 'money motive', at first there might appear to be no incentive for any at all of these! However: -

- **Work** would become optional or part time or full time as you wished – the majority actually enjoy the right sort of work! It would be a golden opportunity to abolish not only unethical money but unethical and onerous forms of work. Also wages!

- **Agriculture** would of course remain essential – but would be able to be cleaned up, with global 'slash and burn', 'cash crops', Genetically Modified Food and Factory Farming, etc, abolished. All food would become **free** so far more exotic and varied. Everybody could enjoy a healthy balanced diet – free!
- **Shops** would only lose their cash tills and become 'Ware Houses' – with everything in them again free!
- **Industry** would lose all money, cash, credit, and most computers in this equation. A golden opportunity for it to clean up its act – to become vastly 'greener and cleaner' overnight – as many politicians now are vainly trying to achieve!
- **An opportunity to bring in a <u>logical</u> five day week – a 365 day year of 73 weeks with 30 days in each month apart from 35 in December to allow for the '12 days of Christmas'!** Such a 'Numera-Logical Calendar' (New Universal Millennium Eclectic Rational and Logical Calendar – phew!) is explored in every detail in my book 'Scientific Proof that (God The Holy) Spirit Exists' as at www.silee.me.uk

7. Walking, road, rail, sea, air and space transport

Of these, all not just walking would become totally free! Yippee! Imagine the drive there will have to be to put non-green cars, motorbikes and busses off the road, non-green trains, ships, planes also out of action – and to stop everybody taking off into space!

8. No more need for banks, taxes, gambling, casinos or Stock Markets – or charities or state benefits on the other hand…

In a money-free world this would speak for itself.

9. The Law – very little crime; so punishment; left possible!

About all that would be left of The Law would be the Ten Commandments of the Old Testament plus the Two Great Commandments of the New. These are, to refresh your memory, 'Love your neighbour as yourself' and 'Love the Lord your God with all your soul, all your mind, all your spirit and all your heart'.

There might well be two graded punishments, for people still using money after it was abolished, as follows: -

- 'Insane about money'. Sectioning in a mental hospital.
- 'Violently insane about money'. Detention in the psychiatric wing of a prison.

Both punishments to involve nasty, rough, toxic tablets and injections administered as now By Law until the prisoner were cured completely!

The basic precept of British Law according to legal practitioners themselves, as The Law has been developed largely by the Victorians and spread to most of the rest of the world, is:-

"Possession is nine tenths of The Law"

These days that might be better put as: -

"Possession is 99.9% of the Law".

In a **cash-free** society the **only law related to possession would be the Commandment 'Do not steal'.** The Law would revert Centuries, Millennia, to an original precept of the Ten Commandments of Moses on Mount Sinai:

"Personal crimes are Nine Tenths of The Law"

Finally the Ten (Twelve?) Commandments would be supplemented by new ones – taken straight from Buddhism: -

- "Do not hurt, abuse, or even offend any living creature"
- "Believe only what **you yourself know to be true**".

10. Local, national and international Governments

As I said before, it is inevitable that the way to the first 'Father Christmas State', the first of a World Union of such 'Father Christmas States', would be very grass roots indeed. 'Money free zones' would lead to money free villages and towns – then finally money free states and counties, and ultimately the money free country then countries. I will now take a tongue in cheek look at what would happen to my own country's government here in Britain, when this finally happens. Government, both local and national, would be elected but unpaid and **voluntary**, completely no longer to do with money and as we just saw, as a direct result, with far fewer laws to worry about. It would drastically **shrink** to just deal with the few remaining things that local and national government would be left to do in a money-free world, of a Father Christmas State:-

- The Treasury and the Bank of England, like all banks, would vanish. They would be replaced by a **Ministry of Joy, Humour and Generosity.**

- The Home Office and Scotland Yard and The Police would have far fewer laws and crimes to deal with. They would become the **Ministry of Wisdom, Reason and DEEP THOUGHT!**

- Any Father Christmas State like that, especially eventually in a World Union of Father Christmas States, would as we see soon enjoy **complete world peace**, so the Ministry of Defence would become the **Ministry of Grace, Peace, Love and Creativity (formerly known as hanky-panky!)**

- The NHS would also now offer free hairdressing, chiropody and beauty treatments – a **Ministry of Health and Beauty!**

- I am open to like humorous suggestions to my email address simon@maam.org.uk for what to merge social services and the Department of Work and Pensions into – something along the lines of **The Ministry of Silly Walks (as immortalized by John Cleese of Monty Python's Flying Circus in the 1960's)** but thoroughly up to date and 21st Century, original – and topical! I may well offer an appropriate prize for this!

11. Multinational cultural and language differences and Travel

The first money-free zones, then towns and villages, and finally Father Christmas Regions or Counties, and finally the first Father Christmas State, would obviously be tourist attractions. They would have to turn away travelers who were would-be immigrants – and tell them to travel back to their home town and 'spread the word' and make that into a money free zone too!

12. Trade; the fair distribution of wealth once money were abolished; the end of the Great International Rich-Poor Divide

Money free zones would exchange goods free (**not barter – that would be very backward-looking**) without any trade. The first full Father Christmas State would probably indeed be a very advanced country like my own country of Great Britain, and give goods away and expect like treatment in return – setting a dramatic example until the full World Union of Father Christmas States were established. Once that happened there would naturally, as I said earlier, be a free rescue operation, from North to South Hemispheres, and West to East – fully **global – International Rescue!** The International Rich-Poor Divide would naturally vanish, almost certainly in months or even less!

13. Children and families

In any Father Christmas State, it would be Christmas every day of the year – Without Price. Naturally, all families especially children, would be over the moon!

14. Poverty and debt obsolete – personal and national

As each Father Christmas State got established, two things would naturally happen: -
- A fair distribution of wealth as in resources and possessions would take place – all poverty would be abolished

- All debt would be cancelled out – as there would be no money!

15. Teaching and Education

- With money no longer any object, the children, and as necessary adults of the whole world would for the first time all receive a decent education.

- Money would either be taught about as a history subject only, like computer systems – or best forgotten about totally as a Very Bad Thing?

- Everybody would enjoy their education, teachers and children alike, totally unlike the present regime around the world!

16. Science and Technology, especially regarding information

- With money no longer any object, again, a dream of many scientists and engineers could be achieved very quickly – Science, Engineering and Technology could be **completed and finished off** - everything possible would have been invented and put to good use. My own book 'Scientific Proof that (God The Holy) Spirit Exists' as at www.silee.me.uk is very much a move towards this immediate goal.

- The big exception to this would be the CCCCCC I have mentioned before – this global computer census would 'put the genie of computers back in the bottle' and global laws would be passed limiting the scope and size of computers drastically!

17. The Arts

- With money no longer an object, yet again, works of art would lose all financial value so only retain their intrinsic or 'aesthetic' value as art.

- In the Age of Leisure that would come once work was done in five day on five day off shifts, and even be purely optional and voluntary, The Arts would flourish.   Drawing, painting, photography, cinema, pottery, textiles, graphic design, architecture, etc, etc, would all flourish – a New Renaissance?!!

18. **Entertainment and communications: - post offices and services, radio, TV, (mobile) telephones, papers, magazines, books; information and computer technology, and the Internet**

All of these are **grossly** over developed and would come under the auspices of the same CCCCCC as for computers – to rationalize and simplify them, and change '300 channels of crap' on TV, for instance back to far fewer, far higher quality output channels.

19. **Sport, Recreation Activities and Holidays**

As for the Arts, in the Age of Leisure that would come these would all become accessible to all, and to a large extent would enjoy a Renaissance – especially with computer games and TV drastically 'having their respective genies put back in the bottle' as discussed already several times.

20. **Health, Beauty, Hygiene, Safety, Medicine, Hospitals, Legal and Illegal Drugs, Social Services, Welfare, and Care For The Elderly**

- The one bad thing here, illegal drugs, would simply and naturally go out of business once the drug barons lost their entire money motive!

- All the other things in this list would be free for all – under the umbrella of a 'Ministry of Health and Beauty' as proposed before.

21. **The Environment; Natural Resources; Environmental Health. Global Warming, 'carbon footprints', pollution, climate change all made too a 'thing of the past'**

The money motive, nearly everyone agrees, is the main reason for the wholesale destruction of The Global Environment – for centuries if not millennia. With that Money Motive abolished if and when we abolish money, an Environmental Renaissance would happen too!

22. Nature and Wildlife

With money abolished, and a New Age of Leisure, we would all have much more time, and the motive, to appreciate Nature and Life in General, much more. Would we clean up the whole planet?

23. Politics replaced by true leadership

Politics could be aptly described as 'electing leaders to act mostly by consensus' in the grim art, mostly, of 'raising taxes then working out how "best" (which political view predominates, determines this) how to spend them'. In a world without money everybody would much more 'be their own leader' or 'be their own Jesus' and it would be a much more mature, grown-up society all round.

24. World Peace and Security replacing Permanent War

One major long term objective that nearly all politicians today are agreed on is of course the cause of World Peace. World Peace would indeed come as naturally as Day follows Night were money abolished – money and to an extent religion cause all wars!

25. Sexism, sexuality, homophobia, ageism, racism, etc, etc

Everybody would have enough of everything they needed – initially the basics, worldwide, to be followed by luxuries of course. Everybody would be recognized as 'equal but **unique and different'** – and these isms and phobias would soon vanish!

26. Stresses and Strains, the Pace of Life and Mental Health

Life would be far less full of stress and strain with no money to worry about! If everybody lived comfortably and above all for free, with no longer any 'money motive' to goad us all on, especially with work optional, the Mental Health of The World would drastically improve. Mental Illness might well even vanish entirely!

27. Human or spiritual values and freedom of choice. Religion – is it affected at all?

- There are of course a huge number of religions, faiths, churches, and sects and denominations within them in this World today. They mostly exhibit huge differences between each other to outsiders, and some have most peculiar practices, especially in this supposedly modern 21st Century.

- The Christian Churches, judging from their speeches this Easter 2009 just gone, do at least vaguely agree on one thing – the 'spiritual life' is much to be honoured and sought after than money and material possessions. Yet ask a cross section of faiths and churches what 'spiritual' actually means – and you get an infinite range of answers!

- Anyway, according to the Bible, the Day on which Easter is currently celebrated – Easter Sunday – is **wrong -** a day early! Jesus 'rose on the third day' – Easter Monday – as his mother and Mary Magdalene discovered when they found his tomb empty 'at the start of the week' – Monday, three not two days on!

- My own book 'Scientific Proof that (God The Holy) Spirit Exists' as promoted by www.silee.me.uk seeks to find a religion that is common sense, logical, provable scientifically. In fact it is Buddhist – I seek to 'believe only that which I know to be true'.

- This book proposes that Spirit is a (Set Of) Quality or Qualities. The Holy Spirit, then, is just the 'Ultimate Set of Qualities'. Unlike the leaders of the Christian churches, who deal regularly in money yet affect an utter dislike of it, I feel that people need possessions but not money to go with them. Just because one of Jesus' sayings was 'a person is not measured by the number of his possessions' does not mean that having personal possessions is fundamentally wrong or even evil, as these Church leaders implied at Easter. It is just the middle-man, money that is wrong and evil – in fact, the Root of All Evil!

- Religion freed of money would contract and simplify itself, quite naturally, and find a much simpler consensus between faiths. It would go through a great peaceful revolution, in fact.

28. The biblical basis of the census then abolition of most computers – on top of all money! The Book of Revelation chapters 15 through 19.

Volume B of my book 'Scientific Proof that (God The Holy) Spirit Exists' gives fresh, literal translations, and a near 99% fresh interpretation of the great Apocalyptic Parts of the Bible. Part 1 is about the last book of the Bible, Revelation. Parts 2 and 3 cover the Book of Daniel and the book 2 Esdras 11-12. In all three parts of this coverage I point out how the infamous '666' system mentioned before is common to all three sets of writing.

In this section I reproduce below my own translation, and brief words of interpretation when otherwise I regard the text in Revelation as fully self explanatory, of chapters 15 through 19. If you wish to read all my version of that infamous last book of the Bible, as well as the other two, see www.silee.me.uk and download or purchase a printed copy of my own book as above. In the meantime I summarise my own interpretations from that book of the first 14 chapters of the Book of Revelation, to set the scene for giving the five chapters 15-19 in full after that: -

Chapters 1-3. Set the scene; and an 'angel-messenger sent by Jesus from the Kingdom of the Heavens' dictates seven messages, mostly severe reprimands, to the seven early churches in Asia.

Chapter 4. John is invited actually inside Heaven – through a door, nothing stranger – to witness the very throne-room of God!

Chapters 5-6. the 'slain but risen Lamb of God' (i.e. Jesus) opens the first six of seven seals of a New Covenant. I believe the 'four horsemen' that appear as a result symbolize **the Four Seasons!**

Chapter 7. An elaborate description of 144,000 saintly folk: 'those that have come out of The Great Holocaust' that follows in Revelation.

Chapter 8-9. The seventh seal is opened and six angel-messengers out of seven given them, in turn blow trumpets causing some Apocalyptic Event in the Future as then i.e. the past as now. Firstly an angel-messenger without a trumpet causes a loud explosion, which I believe corresponds to the invention of gunpowder (in China) hundreds of years after St. John saw this vision. Then the seven angel-messengers are I think all scientists of the last few centuries: -
(1) Gregor Mendel of the late 1800's, the monk often called the 'Father of Genetics'
(2) One of the pioneers of splitting the atom in 1916, Michael Rutherford
(3) Albert Einstein, pioneer of relativity, after observing the behaviour of radioactive material
(4) James Clerk Maxwell, principal pioneer of early work on electricity and magnetism
(5) The team of a fallen star and this fifth angel-messenger in 9:1-2 seems to correspond to the discoverers of the structure and importance of the 'molecule of life', DNA – Francis Crick and James Watson
(6) 9:13-19 to me accurately predicts likewise, Computer and TV Screens – the former invented by Alan Turing in 1937, the latter by the Scot John Logie Baird at a similar time.

Chapter 10. The 'mighty angel-messenger' here is not one of the seven with a trumpet – and from the detailed description seems to predict the great leader of Great Britain during the Second World War, **Winston Churchill.** The mystery of the words of the 'seven thunders' here then seems to be that they said 'first world war and second world war'!

Chapter 11. A symbolic but complete and precisely accurate prediction of the events of **'9/11' – 11th September 2001 in the USA especially New York!**

Chapter 12. A woman that I can only take as symbolizing the Holy Spirit as a Mother Figure gives birth to a 'world leader child –

of The Second Coming' which most commentators agree on. As a result She is severely persecuted by the Devil, who is cast down after 'War in Heaven' with Michael and His Angels, in that famous Battle of Evermore. Is this going on right now, given my own view about Revelation 11, and does it involve the 'war on terror'?

Chapter 13. Mentions a Beast with an ominous number – 666. This is impossible to summarise in just a few sentences – see my book as described below which lends the whole of its Volume B and Volume C section 1 to discuss this 'Supreme Imperial Number' as it works in the world even now – stronger than ever?

Chapter 14. The final lead-up to the final chapters of Revelation, of which I give chapters 15-19 in the same literal translation below, as in my book. The 144,000 of chapter seven (ambassadors of the approximately 144,000 **languages** in the world today?) appear again, as do several more powerful angel-messengers, starting off the action in chapters 15-19 that follow.

As for this entire pithy summary above, full details can be found in my book 'Scientific Proof that (God The Holy) Spirit Exists' as at www.silee.me.uk . I now give the text in full of the next five chapters of Revelation 15-19 along with my commentary – which is surprisingly pithy – just as in my book as above.

REVELATION CHAPTER FIFTEEN

9. Then I saw another sign in heaven, great and wonderful, seven angel-messengers with seven last plagues, for with them the wrath of God is ended.
10. I saw something like a glassy sea mingled with fire, and those who had conquered the beast and its image and the number of its name, standing on the glassy sea, with harps of God. [The glassy sea mingled with fire, is a description of all _semiconductor_ as in all computers! They stand _on_ it – i.e. have _defeated_ it!]
11. They sing the song of Moses, the slave of God, and the song of the lamb, saying, "Great and wonderful are your deeds, O Lord God the Almighty; righteous and true are your ways, king of the nations!

12. Who will not fear and glorify your name, O Lord? Because only you are holy, because all the nations will come and worship before you, because your ordinances were made manifest".
13. After these things I saw, and the shrine opened in heaven of the tabernacle of the testimony,
14. and the seven angel-messengers came forth out of the shrine, with the seven plagues out of the shrine, clothed in bright clean linen, with golden girdles round their breasts.
15. One of the four living creatures gave the seven angel-messengers seven golden bowls full of the anger of God, the living unto the ages of the ages.
16. The temple was filled with smoke from the glory of God and from his power, and no one could enter the shrine until the seven plagues of the seven angel-messengers were ended.

REVELATION CHAPTER SIXTEEN

22. Then I heard a great voice out of the shrine saying to the seven angel-messengers, "Go and pour out the seven bowls of God's anger on the earth".
23. The first went away and poured out his bowl on the earth, and a foul and evil sore came on the men with the mark of the beast and worshipping its image.
24. The second poured out his bowl onto the sea [i.e. the glassy sea of semi-conductor!] and it became like the blood of a dead man, and every living soul died, of the things in the sea. [i.e. all programs and 'artificial intelligence'!]
25. The third poured out his bowl onto the rivers and the fountains of the waters; and they became blood [i.e. all *circuitry* in computers!]
26. And I heard the angel-messenger of the waters saying, "Righteous are you, the Being Now and the Having Been, the holy one, over those you judge,
27. because they shed the blood of saints and prophets, and you have given them blood to drink. It is their due!"
28. And I heard the altar saying, "Yes O Lord God the Almighty, true and righteous are your judgements".

29. The fourth poured out his bowl onto the sun, and it was allowed to scorch men with fire. [as the computers melt as above]
30. They were burnt with a great heat, and they blasphemed the name of God, who had the authority of these plagues, and did not repent and give him glory.
31. The fifth poured out his bowl onto the throne of the beast, and its kingdom became darkened, and they gnawed their tongues from the pain,
32. and they blasphemed the God of heaven from their pains and sores, and did not repent of their works.
33. The sixth poured out his bowl onto the great river Euphrates, and its water was dried up to make way for the kings from the rising of the sun.
34. I saw, issuing out of the mouth of the dragon, and the mouth of the beast, and the mouth of the false prophet, three unclean spirits like frogs;
35. for they are demonic spirits performing signs, which go forth to the kings of the whole earth, to assemble for the war of the great day of God the Almighty.
36. Behold, I am coming as a thief! Blessed is he who watches and keeps his garments, lest he walk naked and men see his shame.
37. They assembled in the place called in Hebrew Armageddon.
38. The seventh poured out his bowl on the air; and a great voice came out of the shrine from the throne saying, "It has happened!"
39. There were lightnings and voices and thunders, and a great earthquake occurred, such as has never been since men were on the earth, so great was that earthquake.
40. And the great city was split in three parts and the cities of the nations fell. And God remembered Babylon the Great, and gave her the cup of wine of his anger and wrath.
41. Every island fled, and no mountains were found.
42. A great hail, a talent in size [50 kg!] came out of heaven on men; and men blasphemed God for the plague of the hail, because the plague was exceedingly great.

REVELATION CHAPTER SEVENTEEN

19. Then one of the angel-messengers who had the seven bowls came to me, and said, "Come, I will show you the judgement of the great harlot seated on many waters,
20. with whom the kings of the earth committed fornication, and the dwellers on earth became drunk on the wine of her fornication."
21. He carried me away in Spirit into a desert. I saw a woman sitting on a scarlet beast, filled with names of blasphemy, with seven heads and ten horns.
22. The woman was clothed in purple and scarlet, gilded with gold and precious stone and pearls, with a golden cup in her hand full of abominations and the unclean things of her fornication,
23. And on her forehead was written a name of mystery, BABYLON THE GREAT, THE MOTHER OF THE HARLOTS AND OF THE ABOMINATIONS OF THE EARTH.
24. I saw the woman being drunk from the blood of the saints, and from the blood of the witness of Jesus. When I saw her, I wondered greatly.
25. But the angel-messenger said to me, "Why wonder? I will tell you the mystery of the woman and of the beast carrying her with the seven heads and the ten horns. [the beast is the phrase *wanton materialism (seven vowels – heads – and ten horns – consonants)* with the double meaning of the 'beast and false prophet' of Revelation 13 – the empire of materialism 'witnessed' by its sister empire of IT or television. Overall, mass production has evolved in the last two centuries out of manual labour to produce the modern 'Babylon' materialistic Empire of 'the world' – as opposed to 'Israel' – i.e. the 'true good spirit of humanity' in its most global meaning].
26. The beast which you saw was and is not, and is about to come up out of the abyss and go to destruction.
27. This needs a mind with wisdom. The seven heads are seven mountains, where the woman sits, and seven kings:
28. Five have fallen, one is, the other has not yet come, and whenever he comes he remains only a little while. [The seven mountains are the seven hills of Rome, which as we soon come to see in Parts 2 and 3 of this Volume B of this book, is where the modern "Empire of Babylon of wanton materialism" started.

The seven kings are *prophets*. The first five are the great prophets of the Old Testament: Elijah, Isaiah, Jeremiah, Ezekiel and Daniel. The one 'who is' – Jesus. The seventh is *Father Christmas!*]

29. The beast which was and is not, even he is an eighth, and is of the seven, and goes to destruction. [astrology / alchemy / witchcraft]
30. The ten horns which you saw are ten kings, who have not yet received a kingdom, but are to receive authority as kings for one hour with the beast.
31. These have one mind, and give their power and authority to the beast.
32. They will make war with the lamb, and the lamb will overcome them, because he is lord of lords and king of kings, and those with him are called and chosen and faithful".
33. He said to me, "The waters where the harlot sits, are peoples and crowds and nations and tongues.
34. The ten horns which you saw will hate the harlot and make her desolate and naked, and eat her flesh, and consume her with fire;
35. for God has put it into their hearts to do his will, by having one mind and give their kingdom to the beast, until the words of God are accomplished.
36. The woman which you saw is the great city which has dominion over the kings of the earth". [Babylon is MONEY, THE ROOT OF ALL EVIL]

REVELATION CHAPTER EIGHTEEN

25. After this I saw another angel-messenger coming down out of heaven, having great authority, and the earth was enlightened from his glory.
26. And he cried in a strong voice, saying, "Fallen, fallen is Babylon the great, and become a dwelling-place of demons, and a prison of every unclean spirit, and a prison of every unclean and hated bird,
27. because all the nations have drunk of the wine of the anger of her fornication, and the kings of the earth practiced fornication

with her, and the merchants of the earth became rich from the power of her luxury".
28. Then I heard another voice out of heaven saying, "Come you out of her, my people, lest you share in her sins, and lest you receive of her plagues;
29. Because her sins were heaped up to heaven, and God remembered her misdeeds.
30. Give you back to her as indeed she gave back, and double you her double-deeds; mix her a double draught in the cup she mixed.
31. How she glorified herself and luxuriated, so give her a like measure of torment and sorrow. Because in her heart she says, 'A queen I sit, I am no widow, and sorrow by no means do I see'.
32. Therefore in one day will her plagues come, death and sorrow and famine, and she will be consumed with fire; because mighty is the Lord God judging her".
33. And the kings of the earth, who practised fornication and luxuriated with her, will weep and wail over her, when they see the smoke of her burning,
34. standing afar because of the fear of her torment, saying, "Woe, woe, the great city, Babylon the mighty city, in one hour your judgement came."
35. And the merchants of the earth weep and sorrow over her, because no one buys their cargo any more,
36. cargo of gold, silver, jewels and pearls, fine linen, purple, silk and scarlet, all kinds of scented wood, all ivory vessels, all vessels of valuable wood, bronze, iron and marble,
37. cinnamon, spice, incenses, wine, oil, fine flour and wheat, cattle and sheep, horses and carriages, and bodies and souls of men.
38. Your fruit of the lust of the soul went away from you, and all the sumptuous and bright things perished from you, and nobody shall ever find them again!
39. The merchants of these wares, who got rich through her, will stand afar because of the fear of the torment of her weeping and sorrowing, saying,
40. "Woe, woe, the great city, which was clothed with fine linen and purple and scarlet, and gilded with gold and precious stone and pearl!

41. In one hour such great wealth has been laid waste!" And every steersmen and person sailing on the sea, and sailor, and all who work the sea, stood far off,
42. and cried out as they saw the smoke of her burning, saying, "Who was like the great city?"
43. And they threw dust onto their heads, and cried out weeping and sorrowing, saying, "Woe, woe, the great city, whose worth made rich all those who had ships on the sea, for in one hour she was made desolate!
44. Be glad over her, heaven and the saints, apostles and prophets, because God judged her by your judgement".
45. Then a mighty angel-messenger took up a stone like a great millstone, and threw it into the sea, saying, "Thus Babylon the great city will be thrown, with a rush, and shall be found no longer.
46. And the sound of harpists and musicians and flutists and trumpeters will never be heard in you again, and any craftsman of any craft shall not be found in you any more; and the sound of a factory shall not be heard in you any more;
47. And the light of a lamp shall shine in you no longer, and the voice of bridegroom and of bride shall be heard in you no more; for your merchants were the great ones of the earth, because your sorcery deceived all the nations,
48. and in her was found the blood of prophets and of saints, and of all those slain on the earth".

REVELATION CHAPTER NINETEEN

22. After these things I heard what seemed to be a great voice of a great crowd in heaven, saying, "Hallelujah! The salvation and the glory and the power of our God!
23. For true and righteous are his judgements; because he judged the great harlot who defiled the earth with her fornication, and he avenged the blood of his slaves by her hand".
24. Secondly they cried, "Hallelujah! The smoke of her goes up unto the ages of the ages".
25. The twenty-four elders and the four living creatures fell and worshipped God sitting on the throne, saying, "Amen. Hallelujah!"

26. And a voice came out from the throne, saying, "Praise you our God, all his slaves, you who fear him, the small and the great".
27. Then I heard what seemed to be the sound of a great crowd, like the sound of many waters, and like the sound of loud thunders, saying, "Hallelujah! For the Lord our God the Almighty reigned.
28. Let us rejoice and exult, and give the glory to him, for the marriage of the lamb has come, and his bride prepared herself,
29. and she was granted to be clothed in bright clean fine linen – for the fine linen is the righteous deeds of the saints".
30. And he tells me, "Write you: Blessed are the ones who have been called to the marriage supper of the lamb". And he says to me, "These are true words of God".
31. Then I fell down at his feet to worship him, but he said to me, "You, do not do that! I am a fellow slave with you and your brothers with the witness of Jesus; worship God". For the witness of Jesus is the spirit of prophecy.

32. Then I saw heaven opened, and behold, a white horse! The one sitting on it is called faithful and true, and in righteousness he judges and makes war.
33. His eyes are like flames of fire, and on his head are many diadems, and he has a name inscribed which nobody knows but him.
34. He is clothed in a robe dipped in blood, and the name by which he is called is The Word of God.
35. The armies in heaven followed him on white horses, dressed in white fine linen.
36. From his mouth proceeds a sharp sword, with which to smite the nations, and he will shepherd them with an iron staff; he treads the winepress of the wine of the anger, of the wrath of God the Almighty.
37. He has on his robe and on his thigh a name inscribed, KING OF KINGS AND LORD OF LORDS.

38. I saw one angel-messenger standing in the sun, and he cried out in a great voice, saying to all the birds flying in mid-heaven, "Come you, assemble you for the great supper of God,
39. to eat the flesh of kings, the flesh of chiliarchs[generals], the flesh of strong men, the flesh of horses and those sitting on

them, the flesh of all men, both free and slave, both small and great".
40. And I saw the beast and the kings of the earth and their armies assembled to make war with the one sitting on the horse and with his army.
41. And the beast was seized, and with it the false prophet [pseudo-prophet] which had performed the signs before it, deceiving those who had received the mark of the beast and worshipped its image; these two were cast alive into the lake of fire burning with sulphur.
42. And the rest were slain by the sword of the one sitting on the horse, the sword that proceeds from his mouth, and all the birds were gorged with their flesh.

NOTES ON REVELATION CHAPTER NINETEEN

Verses 17-21 depict an Angel summoning all the birds of the air, which might seem fanciful until one considers the recent and massively growing scientific evidence from fossils in China – that birds suddenly appeared out of the preceding dinosaur species that lorded it over the earth for so many million years. Furthermore they did so in just a few generations or possibly just one generation, completely defying the 'laws of evolution' of Charles Darwin. Birds were created – by God – from dinosaurs, complete with the sudden ability to fly. Birds are highly intelligent, their beautiful song is known to be very structured language, yet often dismissed. Can they indeed understand – even speak – human languages? That is the only way that one can take the last part of this chapter literally – and seriously – for it might not just be parrots and Mynah birds alone that can talk!

As soon as one realizes and accepts that Chapter 11 of The Book of Revelation is a totally accurate prediction, 1911 years earlier in AD 90 of the events of '9/11' in AD 2001, then it is obvious that the End of Semiconductor and the End of Money as predicted in later chapters as above, could happen any time **now – especially during this Second Great Depression!** The Old Testament has a parallel to this Great End of the Computer-Money Complex – in the story of the Tower of Babel, a Tower in Babylon intended to reach Heaven itself! God ended this monstrous project by 'dividing the tongues of the workforce' so they could not understand each other. The above chapters of Revelation reveal a different end of the 'Computer-Money Complex' – seemingly the microscopic components of computers are to be 'turned to blood' by Angels!

Again, in the New Testament, Jesus described a man who "heard and took in Jesus' words, and built his house on rock. When the winds and rain battered that house, it remained intact." However for another man who failed to listen, and built his house on sand, the slightest storm destroyed it – everything he had. It seems to me that the 'computer-money complex' is all built literally of sand, for the very silicon that computers are made of – is the same chemical element that is the basis of sand itself!

29. Any counter arguments to the abolition of money are few and weak!

- I have presented a whole range of very strong arguments in this Manifesto that we actually all act to Abolish All Money. These arguments cover every aspect of world society in the post '9/11' 21st Century World that we currently inhabit, and how these would change for ever for the good once we Abolish All Money.

- Only those rich people who actually enjoy and luxuriate in their advantages over the poor, while doing nothing about that Great Divide, surely, can raise any serious objections to what I am proposing here.

- In every aspect of life that I have described, there are no disadvantages, only vast advantages, to humanity acting as a whole to Abolish All Money!

30. Overall - a very simple and high Quality of Life for all!
The End of Money, then, would bring about a New World, a Utopia, where everybody was respected for being the individual they are, there would be no rich and poor apart from people being as comfortably off as they needed and wanted to be.

At the same time computers and computer-inspired activities would be subject to a CCCCCC Census – and life without this other half of the current 'computer-money complex' being dominant any more, would get a lot simpler – and Higher Quality.

Is it possible, then, that a World without Money would be for all – the Paradise on Earth envisaged if not promised by many religions? The key to **that** great claim is simple really – Abolish All Money!

Manifesto: Abolish All Money!

maam.org.uk

Census all computer based equipment! License all computers!

Can you seriously imagine a world where **all money is abolished?** This author can, and presents his findings here – of a world where computers, currently totally out of control in his view, will be 'tamed' and the 'genie of computers put back in the bottle' – along with all money!

Mister il Professori Simon Richard Lee OA BA MA KCC (St. Albans School 1968-75; King's College, Cambridge 1976-83) CEng MIEE MIET MInstMC

Scientific Proof that (God The Holy) Spirit Exists

This book was conceived all of 30 years ago in 1977 while the author was an Open Scholar in Natural and Computer Sciences at King's College, Cambridge, England – from just one verse in the Bible – in the Book of Revelation, describing the 'sevenfold' Holy Spirit. 'Aha!' I said. 'The Holy Spirit has structure. I am a scientist. Can I elucidate that (invisible!) structure? First I need to do the apparently impossible – give a scientific basis for spirit!' The latter after a great deal of deep thought, turned out to be based on (masculine) 'urges' leading to (feminine) 'flows' in a 'Freudian' way.

Eventually, after years, I identified that there was indeed a sevenfold binary tree of such 'fundamental spirits' – Wisdom. Joy and Love. Health and Beauty, Peace and Grace. As for individual 'fundamental spirits' these are an urge/three-point flow very similar to three-phase electricity, probably not surprisingly; the concepts of both are similar and so fundamental! To take the base three of this 'Tree of Life of (the Holy) Spirit' in order:

1. 'Reason is a desire for Wisdom which is 100% Faith in one's Knowledge'
2. 'Creativity leads to Love which is Desire for Tenderness'
3. 'Generosity (of spirit) leads to Joy which is Humour causing Delight'.
4. – 7. And so on.

The actual work of this took place in total isolation from the Bible (I rarely go to Church). Some 15 years later, when Christians pointed out the virtually identical 'Fruits of the Spirit' in St Paul's writing, I realised that I had carried out a lengthy process of scientific elimination – confirmed by the Bible!

The final crucial step in solving a veritable 'riddle of the sands' of 'what is (the structure of the sevenfold Holy) Spirit' was to identify a 'home' for this invisible structure. I am basically a physicist and computer scientist, so familiar with notions of 'hyperspace' and 'cyberspace'. The 'home' for these seven 'dimensions of spirit' became obvious once I heard of the newly emerged 'string' and 'superstring' theories in 1993 – once they emerged from obscurity having been born in about 1983, 10 years earlier.

Their mathematical basis absolutely hinges on there being precisely – yes, wait for it! – seven extra dimensions of space beyond the physical three we see around us all the time. That was the home of the Holy Spirit – seven 'spiritual dimensions' – supplied by science...

Simon Richard Lee BA, MA (Cantab.) CEng MIET MInstMC
Author Me UK   author.me.uk